Creating Spaces of Wellbeing and Belonging for Refugee and Asylum-Seeker Students

Creating Spaces of Wellbeing and Belonging for Refugee and Asylum-Seeker Students: Skills and Strategies for Classroom Teachers outlines the ways educators can support positive educational and social outcomes for the most vulnerable children in their communities.

Each chapter briefly outlines the relevant theory, expanding on this through vignettes from research and analytical reflection, helping the reader identify and apply the differentiated pedagogical understandings in their own classrooms. Providing insights from educators who are doing this work successfully across the globe, the book highlights the challenges and considerations that teachers face in multilingual, multicultural classroom environments where students' common experience is trauma and loss and guides them towards effective practice.

This book is intended for use in schools by school leaders and classroom teachers and by educational professionals engaged in supporting schools with students with refugee backgrounds.

Maura Sellars, PhD, has three decades of experience as a teacher and member of school executive teams, and almost two decades as an academic, specialising in differentiation strategies. As an inclusivist, her current research, books and articles focus on authentic school inclusion for students with refugee and asylum-seeker experiences.

Scott Imig, PhD, is a former primary and middle school teacher. He has spent much of his university career studying the qualities of effective and engaging classrooms. His current research focuses on understanding and helping school communities support the integration of families with refugee and asylum-seeker backgrounds.

John C. Fischetti started his career in refugee education working with Haitian and Cambodian refugee children in the United States. His current work focuses on school and leadership transformation, advocating for changing the role of the learner, the role of the teacher and assessment simultaneously to promote learning equity.

Creating Spaces of Wellbeing and Belonging for Refugee and Asylum-Seeker Students

Skills and Strategies for Classroom Teachers

Maura Sellars, Scott Imig and John C. Fischetti

LONDON AND NEW YORK

Cover image: © Mohammad Bashir Aldaher / EyeEm / Getty Images

First published 2023
by Routledge
4 Park Square, Milton Park, Abingdon, Oxon OX14 4RN

and by Routledge
605 Third Avenue, New York, NY 10158

Routledge is an imprint of the Taylor & Francis Group, an informa business

© 2023 Maura Sellars, Scott Imig, John C. Fischetti

The right of Maura Sellars, Scott Imig, John C. Fischetti to be identified as authors of this work has been asserted in accordance with sections 77 and 78 of the Copyright, Designs and Patents Act 1988.

All rights reserved. No part of this book may be reprinted or reproduced or utilised in any form or by any electronic, mechanical, or other means, now known or hereafter invented, including photocopying and recording, or in any information storage or retrieval system, without permission in writing from the publishers.

Trademark notice: Product or corporate names may be trademarks or registered trademarks, and are used only for identification and explanation without intent to infringe.

British Library Cataloguing-in-Publication Data
A catalogue record for this book is available from the British Library

ISBN: 978-1-032-07606-5 (hbk)
ISBN: 978-1-032-07608-9 (pbk)
ISBN: 978-1-003-20790-0 (ebk)

DOI: 10.4324/9781003207900

Typeset in Bembo
by SPi Technologies India Pvt Ltd (Straive)

Contents

	Acknowledgements	vi
	Introduction	1
1	The global refugee crisis and educational implications	3
2	Trauma and its impact	17
3	Learning the language and differentiation	32
4	Communicating effectively	47
5	Numeracy	64
6	Personal development	79
7	Exercise and sport	97
8	Science and technology	113
9	Social studies and diverse perspectives	130
	Index	147

Acknowledgements

We would like to thank sincerely all our participants who found time in their busy lives to share their wisdom, stories and commitment with us. We are privileged to have the opportunity to make these available to many more teachers who strive daily to improve the lives of students with refugee and asylum-seeker experiences and those of their families through education. We also thank Dr Tra Do, Azadeh Motevali Zadeh Ardakani and Dr Kate Smithers for their continual assistance, advice and support. Without each one of you, we would not have a manuscript to publish.

Introduction

The global diaspora has created a new challenge worldwide. There are constantly calls not only for the geographical borders of many countries to be opened to refugee and asylum-seeker communities but also for hearts and minds to be opened to the sheer devastation and traumatic losses experienced by so many in the world. For many of these people, all they have left are their optimism and hope for the future, much of which is predicated on the sincere desire for the education of their children. This book brings together the wisdoms, strategies and reflections of teachers working with students who have refugee and asylum-seeker experiences across five English-speaking countries. It includes the voices of primary teachers in addition to their secondary colleagues. In order to share their stories coherently, the writing has been organised to inform, to inspire and to challenge their peers in similarly diverse classrooms and perhaps to encourage the readers to reach out and set up their own networks for sharing their pedagogies and principles, which are so important for the hope and futures of these students and their families. This book celebrates the work of the teacher participants and the work of like-minded colleagues. It reaches out to support good practice with research findings and theories and to critically reflect on the underpinning philosophical perspectives and principles of our participants' stories.

Chapter 1 focuses on the lifeworlds from which these cohorts have been displaced. It concentrates on bringing some of the most critical information about the catalysts of disaster in five geographical areas of world from which the majority of refugee and asylum-seeker populations originate. It attempts to highlight ways in which these students' prior educational experiences (if any) may support or challenge their expectations, fears and difficulties as students in western school systems which differ considerably from those in their homelands, and consequently, challenge those who seek to support them. It also indicates the qualities that have been found in those who succeed in this challenging task most successfully, identifying the personal and professional characteristics that these teachers bring to their professional work, including the seeking of critically pertinent information that may not have been part of the professional preparation programmes.

Chapter 2 addresses much of the non-clinical information about trauma and its impacts on the neurological balances in the brain, most specifically in the areas of higher-order thinking, attentiveness and incidences of hypervigilance. While this

DOI: 10.4324/9781003207900-1

information may not be new for many teachers who are experienced in supporting the social, emotional and academic growth of these students, it may provide opportunities for reflection on aspects of their professional practice with these students, and the implications for themselves as they share students' stories of war, torture, personal suffering and loss whilst building caring, professional relationships with their communities. The remaining chapters are subject based, meaning that they can be usefully utilised by teachers at all levels of schooling with some customising to suit diverse contexts and student cohorts. While there is no explicit chapter that focuses on the potential of the performing and creative arts disciplines, there are many strategies and tasks in other subjects that require the implementation of many skills that are based in this field. In this approach, the importance of the creative and performing arts cannot be overlooked. In fact, the ways in which everyday pedagogical approaches, curriculum content, school schedules and institutional routines are differentiated to include students with refugee and asylum-seeker experiences is a tribute to creativity, design and innovation.

As there is a considerable amount of readily available literature that is exclusively focused on the ways in which creative and performing arts can contribute to the emotional, social and academic growth of these students, a decision was made for this book to focus how these skills and activities can be used effectively to support other areas of learning where innovative strategising is not so commonly recorded. There are internationally acknowledged areas of culture that need no language to explain or extrapolate their meaning. They are commonly interpreted by people of multiple, diverse cultures, including those from backgrounds of oracy, and can be employed as the means by which experiences, tragedies, losses and hope can be communicated. They are integral parts of the culture of all people, including the branches of Islam which exclusively restrict music and dance to the performance of religious activities. It is hoped that the ideas in this writing, investigated in the generous contributions of our research participants, will inspire you, the reader, to contribute your own personal strengths and gifts to the education of students with refugee and asylum-seeking experiences, through your unique, individual approaches to your professional work.

1 The global refugee crisis and educational implications

Introduction

Displacement has sadly become an everyday term. Currently, more than 84 million people worldwide have been forcibly evacuated from their homes. Moreover, 48 million are internally displaced including 35 million children. Almost 27 million are seeking refuge in other countries, and 4.5 million are seeking asylum (The UN Refugee Agency, 2021a). Over 1 million children have been born as refugees. At the time of writing, these statistics are being swelled daily by those fleeing the Russian invasion of Ukraine. It is estimated that 12 million Ukrainian residents, including nearly 5 million children, have been displaced, and almost half are seeking refuge in other countries (Triesman, 2022). Many people are forced to relocate because of natural disasters, environmental upheaval, civil disruption or, as in the Ukraine, war. In the past few years, 68% of those seeking refuge or asylum have come from just five countries: Syria, Venezuela, Afghanistan, South Sudan and Myanmar. Sadly, many of these populations are currently living in refugee camps on the borders of neighbouring countries, many of which lack the infrastructure, the finances and the physical capacity to support them, leaving them living in extremely overcrowded, unsanitary conditions without adequate food and support systems. The five countries that receive the most refugees are Turkey, Colombia, Uganda, Pakistan and Germany. English-speaking countries and other First World countries host a tiny percentage of people in need. Only 13% of all displaced refugees and asylum seekers are resettled in First World countries, which have the resources to support their wellbeing and offer them and their families hope for the future. Much of that hope centres on the prospects that their children and young people will be able to access improved living conditions, safety and security, and, most importantly, the type of education that will enable them to integrate into their homelands and lead better lives.

In order for this integration to have any chance of occurring, educational systems, school institutions and teachers themselves need to develop a deep understanding of the students with refugee and asylum-seeker experiences who are placed in their classrooms. This writing seeks to specifically address classroom practices and strategies that may support teachers in their professional work. It is widely accepted that teachers need to know their subject content and how to teach it (Shulman, 1987) and to have a profound understanding of their students and how they learn. In the case of these particular groups of students, it is difficult to access much of the psychological stress and emotional trauma of their refugee and asylum-seeking experiences and even more complicated to readily provide for their learning preferences and academic support in regular educational contexts. When these students were born, their families would likely never have envisaged that, in the future, they would have to negotiate the unfamiliar characteristics and complexities of western schooling systems, cultures and customs. Likewise, many western teachers would not have been prepared with the knowledge to support students from such diverse cultural and religious backgrounds in addition to addressing their individual learning needs and personal circumstances. While it is not possible to provide individual, in-depth accounts of the many disruptive and destructive circumstances of displacement globally, the next two sections are designed to provide some knowledge of the complex situations in various parts of the world. This is provided so teachers may gain a better understanding of the nature of experiences that have impacted on the social, emotional and cognitive capacities of students displaced from different locations globally and the journeys they may have travelled to reach their classrooms. Understanding this foundational knowledge is perhaps a first step towards creating classrooms that are places of welcoming and belonging for children with refugee or asylum-seeker experiences.

The diaspora

The diaspora has been created by diverse events occurring in different geographical locations around the world, namely the Middle East and North Africa, sub-Saharan Africa, Asia and the Pacific, Europe and the Americas. Armed conflicts in Afghanistan, Syria, Iraq and Yemen have displaced millions of people in recent years, particularly since 2005. The 2021–2022 withdrawal of American and NATO troops, who had occupied Afghanistan since the 9/11 bombings in the US which were coordinated by the Islamic extremist terrorist group, al Qaeda, created unprecedented, volatile situation in the country. As the Taliban moved in to take over the running of the country after 20 years of armed conflict with the US and allied NATO troops, members of the Afghan Defence Forces and their families were hunted down and executed. Suspected sympathisers were also targeted for punishments, as were many US and allied forces interpreters who had facilitated the communications translations during the country's occupation. Under Taliban rule, women's rights were severely restricted, and they appeared to disappear totally from public life. Girls' schools were shut down or destroyed and strict Muslim dress codes for females were reintroduced. Such was the devastation in the country under the Taliban administration, it was estimated to be responsible for at least 40% of civilian deaths in the country (Roth, 2021), many of whom were Hazaras. These are mainly an Islamic Shi'a group traditionally discriminated against by the majority, who practise Sunni Islam. Media and other communication were restricted, as was freedom of speech. For some of those fortunate enough to escape, especially those working for the military, the clashes between Islam and western Christian-based cultures became another source of loss, anxiety and stress, most particularly for families. Islamic law allows men to have more than one wife, and unprotected women (that is, unmarried women) are considerably at risk in these societies; it is considered honourable for widows to be remarried to another male family member and become part of his household. Islamic law also requires that all wives be treated equally, so the husbands may have children with each of his wives. During the process of resettlement to many western countries however, only one wife may legally be nominated to accompany the husbands, resulting in the abandonment of the other. These additional wives are not only left unprotected unless there are other family members able to protect them, but they are invariably left childless as they unselfishly elect to have their children accompany their father to resettlement safety. Afghanistan is not the only Islamic country to experience political instability and the consequent difficulties in recent history.

Syria has a long history of conflict. However, the events of the last five years have resulted in the displacement of 12.5 million people from their homes, an unprecedented percentage of the population in any one country. The civil war in Syria has, over its 11-year duration, created a surge of refugees seeking resettlement in nearby countries and in Europe. The catalyst for this internal conflict was the successful overthrow of the oppressive governments of other Arab countries, namely Egypt and Tunisia, which made Syrians optimistic about the removal of their president, Bashar al Assad, who 'inherited' the presidency on the death of his father. Graffiti in Syria supporting this movement, known as the 'Arab Spring', resulted in the arrest and torture of its teenaged authors, and the resultant death of a 13-year-old member of the group. The public demonstrations that followed resulted in the deaths of many hundreds of participants and imprisonment of many more. Whilst religious beliefs were not at the heart of the insurgence, religion is playing a considerable part in the ongoing conflict. In a very complex series of events, the historically much discriminated minority group of Islamic followers known as the Alawites currently hold a great deal of power in the country. This has been attributed to al Assad's nepotism as he is a member of the group and challenges the equal representation of majority Muslims who follow Sunni Islam and other religious groups in the country, thus creating religious, in addition to, civil unrest (Rosen, 2011). Coupled with a severe drought, the war has taken an unprecedented toll on the population, the vast majority of whom live in severe poverty. Whilst the plight of Syrian refugees seeking safety in Western Europe has received much media attention, the vast majority of these displaced peoples are living in refugee camps on the borders of the neighbouring countries in which they seek security, mirroring the global trends of western resettlement. Many children and young people have not had any experiences of life without war and civil unrest, life with physical and emotional safety or life with formal educational interactions. Again, Syria being a Muslim country, families from there face several difficulties of resettlement in western Christian countries. The aftermath of the 'Arab Spring' events also led to substantial unrest in Libya which eventually resulted in the overthrow and death of the country's leader Gaddafi. Despite this, and the recent ceasefire announcements, like Yemen, Libya remains a country of extreme unrest with terrorist incidents continuing to threaten the lives of its citizens (*Migration Data Portal*, 2020). The situation in Iraq, also created in the aftermath of the 9/11 al Qaeda terrorist attacks on the US, may have abated somewhat with the recent withdrawal of US troops from the country. However, reports of the incidents that resulted in the migration of 4.5 million people remain current, with reports of suicide bombings and missile attacks continuing to create unsafe, dangerous environments for families and entire communities. Iraqi troops are also still active in the ongoing conflict in Yemen, compounding the economic and social impact of the civil war that erupted when Iraqi-based Shiite rebels revolted against the sanctions imposed by the Sunni government. Whilst many people were unable to leave Yemen, currently over 4 million are internally displaced in the world's worst humanitarian disaster (Robinson, 2022).

Whilst Libyan conflict continues in North Africa, the situation in South Sudan remains as one of the world's worst humanitarian disasters. It is estimated that South Sudan is one of the five most vulnerable countries to the impacts of climate change resulting in equally devastating cycles of floods and droughts. The resultant famines and disease caused by the instability of the economy has led to the re-emergence of historical conflicts between various factions of the country which escalated to civil war. Currently, there are 2.3 million South Sudanese refugees seeking safety, 1.7 million internally displaced, and almost half a million women and 1.4 million children suffering from malnutrition (*The South Sudan Crisis Explained: 5 Things you need to know in 2022*, 2021). The plight of women is particularly dire in this country. Gendered differences are acceptable in all aspects of life, determined by social and cultural traditions and male domination. Rape is commonly used as a weapon of war, as is domestic violence and brutality against females. It is estimated to be one of the most dangerous places in the world to be female. The Sudanese government were accused of planning genocide against the Dinka tribe, who constitute the majority of the South Sudanese refugee population. The wars were particularly brutal, and rape of Dinka females and castration of males was commonplace (Countries and Their People). The reality of the thousands of boys who fled in the aftermath of the Second Sudanese War and became known as the Lost Boys of the Sudan also provides a snapshot of the vulnerability of South Sudanese children, both girls and boys, who are continually at risk of kidnapping, abduction and being forced into gangs, not only in South Sudan but also in other African countries. These children are tortured, raped, brutalised and frequently drugged into becoming merciless killers, most frequently by the people they have to fight alongside. Child soldiers participate in conflicts throughout Africa, in countries including Angola, Burundi, Liberia, Rwanda, Sierra Leone Sudan, Uganda and the Democratic Republic of the Congo (Human Rights Watch, 2015). South Sudan is estimated to have 19,000 child soldiers, the highest number in any single country. As in many other African countries, it is extremely difficult and dangerous for women to try and escape and gain refugee status in other countries, even in the camps, most especially as South Sudanese women are estimated to have the lowest literacy rates in the world (US Aid from the American People, 2013).

In Southeast Asia, the Myanmar crisis is dire. It may be identified more accurately as the Rohingya crisis. Rohingya Muslims represent the largest percentage of Muslims in Myanmar, with the majority living in Rakhine state. Described by the UN as the most persecuted minority in the world, they are the world's largest group of stateless people. Myanmar does not recognise them as one of the many ethnic groups living in the country and does not include them in the census. They have no rights, although they have lived there for many generations. Historically, the subject of racism and discrimination in the predominantly Buddhist country, the military attacks on these communities five years ago led to accusations of genocide against the Myanmar government and its forces. These accusations were based on the mass killings and serious civil rights abuses inflicted on the Rohingya people in 2017 which included thousands massacred, tortured, raped and gang-raped in addition to the millions who were displaced as the result of the attacks (British Broadcasting Corporation, 2020). 1.1 million of these people are now seeking asylum elsewhere in the world. In their defence, the government has claimed that no civilians were targeted in their acts of violence; they were simply retaliating to the Rohingya terrorists who had attacked government agencies. Aerial photographs provided evidence that entire Rohingya villages had been razed to the ground, leaving the neighbouring native villages carefully unscathed. As a result, many thousands of Rohingya embarked on the long dangerous journey to Bangladesh, where nearly a million of them are living precariously in the world's largest refugee camp.

After Syria, Venezuela has the second largest refugee group in the world. It is described as the world's most neglected humanitarian crisis (Matheme, 2018). Currently, 6 million people and almost 1 million asylum seekers are seeking places of safety, most around their neighbouring countries. Once a generous host to refugees from other countries, Venezuela itself is in crisis (The UN Refugee Agency, 2021b). Despite having the world's largest oil reservoirs, decades of poor management, widespread corruption and political instability have resulted in this once richest Latin American country heavily in the grip of famine and disease (World Vision, 2021). As the economic situation deteriorated, political opposition and the threats of violence escalated. In this poverty-stricken country, millions of people were left starving, afraid of the constant presence of violence and with no hope of obtaining necessary medical attention and supplies. The flow of people leaving Venezuela continues as the country descends deeper into crisis. They are predominately families, parents and children, along with the elderly and the infirm. They leave hoping to find a better life elsewhere, to work and to feed their starving families away from the disruptions and threats of violence. While Latin America and the Caribbean countries have accepted hundreds of thousands of these refugees, it is estimated that Colombia alone has granted residence to approximately 1.8 million Venezuelan nationals who have been externally displaced by the crisis. The children in particular have suffered as once-extinct childhood diseases have resurfaced due to poor living conditions and their susceptibility to being infected by Covid-19 (Korbokova, 2020), and the incidents of early marriage have increased. Also contributing to the high numbers of refugee and asylum seekers in South America are people from the Northern Triangle.

The Northern Triangle countries, namely El Salvador, Honduras and Guatemala, are amongst the most violent, dangerous countries in the world, with homicides rates much higher than that of the US (Matheme, 2018). Rated amongst the poorest of all countries in the western hemisphere (Cheatham, 2021), they are characterised or stigmatised by chronic violence, challenges to the environment and lack of economic opportunity, all of which combine to produce societies without hope, characterised by 'dog eat dog' and 'survival of the fittest' world views. These countries are especially dangerous for women and girls and members of lesbian, gay, bisexual, transgender and queer communities (LGBTQ). The rate of femicide in Honduras and El Salvador is exceptionally high, and women and children of both sexes are brutalised physically and sexually by gang members and others within the family. Members of the LGBTQ community fleeing the country also report that they are subjected to extreme physical and sexual violence. There is little protection for any of these groups of people as police reports are frequently circumvented due to gang links, threats of increased violence or death, and the cultural norms of many officials and administrators. In 2017, the top five reasons given on asylum-seeking applications from the countries in the Northern Triangle were threats, assassinations, attempted murder, extortion and the recruitment of children and adolescents into youth gangs (Matheme, 2018). It is estimated that more than 2 million people have left the Northern Triangle countries since 2014 (Cheatham, 2021).

Implications for education

Whilst English-speaking schools may enrol many students from different countries other than those mentioned here, the emerging picture is clear. Climate change, environmental factors, famine, exposure to violence and threats of violence, civil and international war, political manoeuvring and preferencing, discrimination and intolerance all contribute to forced migration, displacement and the subsequent swell in numbers of people seeking refugee status or asylum away from their homelands. Whilst contexts and conditions may vary across the globe, the impacts on children and their educational opportunities are remarkably similar, with schooling for females suffering the most. The fourth United Nations Sustainable Development Goal issues a challenge for all educators to 'ensure inclusive and equitable quality education and promote lifelong learning opportunities for all' (*UNHCR The UN Refugee Agency*, 2019, p. 8). This ambition is far from the reach of most refugee and asylum-seeking children, many of whom are not counted as part of the education system in their resettlement contexts. The United Nations Refugee Agency (UNHCR) contends that only 63% of refugee young people are currently enrolled in primary schools as compared to 91% of the entire population of school-aged children. Of these, only 24% of those of secondary school age are enrolled, compared to 84% of global populations of similar ages. Nearly 4 million refugee children are not at school and not counted in rolls and rosters, creating not just inequitable educational circumstances for these children and young people but also a crisis of school attendance and completion by students with refugee and asylum-seeker experiences.

UNESCO estimates that around the world 129 million girls are currently not enrolled in schools. This includes 32 million primary school-aged children and 97 million secondary school-aged young people. While primary and secondary school enrolment rates are becoming increasingly equal across the globe in terms of gender, 89% of females and 90% of males are enrolled in educational contexts, primary school completion rates are lower for girls in low-income countries (63%) compared to their male counterparts (67%). Likewise, in low-income countries, 36% of females complete lower secondary school (middle school or junior high school) in comparison to 44% of males. This trend continues into upper secondary schooling with completion rates only reaching 26% for males and 21% for females (Kattan, 2022). Learning Poverty (LP) is found in both genders who reportedly are unable to proficiently read by ten years of age. This, in turn, is reflected in the large gender gap in employment rates globally, despite enrolment in tertiary education marginally favouring young females. The lowest female rates of employment are from regions such as the Middle East and North Africa (20%) and South Asia (24%), where gendered roles also play a part in female employment. This is considerably less than regions like East Asia (59%) and Latin America (53%). All areas, however, evidence considerably lower rates of female employment than that of males (Kattan, 2022). However, much of this disparity is attributed to gender bias in whole school approaches, societal poverty and widespread violence, which both determines and prevents access to educational opportunities and school completion. Cultural implications include the issue in some societies of child marriage. The economic impacts of child marriage are detailed in the Global Synthesis Report (2017), which records that more than 41,000 girls under 18 years of age are married daily in sub-Saharan African and South Asian contexts (Kattan, 2022; Wodon et al., 2017), while one in five young women in the Middle East and North Africa are married before their 18th birthdays (UNICEF). Many of these early marriages are based on religious traditions; however, the Venezuelan statistics indicate that early marriage may also be a matter of expediency as there is one less person in the family to feed if girls are married young and become the responsibility of their husbands and his family.

While it certainly appears that women and girls are the most severely impacted by the conditions that are the catalysts for displacement, the way in which educational opportunities can be provided in resettlement countries has the potential to create a more equitable gender balance and improve the prospects for these groups in particular, and for all the children and school-aged young people with refugee and asylum-seeker experiences who are enrolled in schools. Understanding the diaspora and diverse catalysts and impacts can facilitate a deeper understanding of the difficulties in that these students may face in formal education. In the many countries that are at war, the possibility of young people of either gender going to school was negligible. While Arab countries value education, for many living in rural and outback areas no schools may exist. The only educational opportunities that students may have had may be the local imam teaching the boys to read and interpret the Koran. This may be the only print material with which these boys would be familiar. There was frequently no education for girls. In the towns and cities with schools, many Afghani students, for example, would have been unable to attend school, play outside and engage in recreational activities with the friends and teammates during the war in Afghanistan. Female students would have had their studies cut short abruptly as the Taliban regained control of the country.

Schools in Muslim countries are predominately segregated, so much of the devastation of institutions of learning was focused on girls' schools and female universities. Syria had one of the most effective and extensive education systems in the Arab world, and scholarship was highly desirable for both genders, again in segregated institutions. However, as the civil war escalated, students were constantly at risk of attack at school, in addition to the dangers of travelling to and from their institutions, and those most at risk were female students. Safety and survival took precedence over education in war-torn countries, irrespective of the degree to which people valued it for their children and young people. This is particularly so for the Rohingya Muslims as they had no status in Myanmar, have their own language and culture and were not provided with teachers for their village schools after 2012.

The refugee students from South Sudan are mainly from the Dinka people. Traditionally nomadic, these students, like many other African students with refugee and asylum-seeker experiences, come from backgrounds of oracy, and have no official, organised education system. Rites of passage and ritual play a significant part in their cultural lives. Their informal education was dominated by the pedagogical strategies of storytelling and participation, recalling and responding, with dance and action forming a considerable part of the learner experience. Experienced storytellers undertook the role of teachers and had a very particular degree of status in the community. Exceptions to this educational background are those who may have been educated away from their traditional homelands in cities such as Khartoum or further afield. Westernised education is particularly difficult for students with backgrounds of oracy as it is very often dominated by teacher talk with little participating responses from the students, print materials and pre-ordained learning groups based on chronological age and not prior knowledge, expertise or experience. Learning is linear and rarely enriched by music and dance as is the traditional wisdoms and knowledge of their homeland culture. The difficulties associated with making meaning, engaging with the cognitive complexity and manual dexterity of written texts are absent from their early years and make becoming literate a long and arduous process for many of these students. Like the students from a number of Islamic families, they also may have experienced additional loss if their mother was unable to be resettled with them due to the Christian legislations that make polygamy against the law in western countries. For Dinka families, it may be especially problematic as, while it is customary for all the wives to share household chores and work collaboratively, each wife was responsible for raising her own children. It may also cause additional difficulties for school enrolments as senior, prominent members of the Dinka tribe may have as many as 200 wives.

For children coming from backgrounds of abject poverty, like the students with refugee experiences from Venezuela, the primary concern has been keeping them alive. These students are experiencing deprivation of the basic of human needs as identified by Maslow (1943). They have survived the lack of the basic physiological needs of food, water, clothing, shelter and sleep in addition to living without any security or sense of safety. In addition to the impacts of trauma that invariably accompanies the lack of safety and security, inadequate provision of nutrition and lack of sleep also have chemical impacts on the brain that are customarily associated with childhood neglect and abuse (Briere et al., 2001; De Bellis, 2005; De Bellis et al., 2009). It is possible that the impact of trauma suffered by children and young people in war-torn contexts of brutality and constant fear is considerably magnified for students who have suffered deprivation of basic human needs in addition to the trauma created by violence and lack of a sense of safety. As much of the damage that results of the chemical imbalances that are created in these contexts is the impact on brain developmental processes, students who have experienced extreme hunger or starvation may have multiple difficulties learning and may need additional time to achieve their developmental milestones. As students in their resettlement countries, they may exhibit psychological and physiological indications of the impacts of their extreme experiences. Whilst education may be an area of priority for these families once their basic needs and sense of safety are established, it may take some considerable time and professional interventions from a variety of specialist practitioners for the children and young people to recover from their deprivation and trauma and to develop healthy brain capacities to learn effectively in their new homelands (Deprince et al., 2009).

How adept students with refugee and asylum-seeker experiences are at adapting to school in resettlement depends on many variables. These include the educational opportunities that they had prior to their forced migration, the professional standards of the teachers in those schools and the learning supports that were available. Whilst many students may have experienced considerable academic success in their homelands prior to circumstances which disrupted their lives, interrupted schooling may impact considerably on their competencies, rendering them less skilful than they would have been had their education continued. The students who have had long journeys to new homelands may have had long periods of confinement in a refugee camp. No education is provided in these camps, and any educational facilities that are there are organised by volunteers. The children in refugee camps frequently cannot attend the schools in the nearby neighbourhoods, because apart from language difficulties, many of the countries with large camps situated just over their borders simply do not have the infrastructure to accommodate large numbers of additional students, nor have they the financial capacities to remedy the situation, even temporarily. In the case of the world's largest refugee camp in which the vast majority of the Rohingya are situated, the exclusion of students from schools is based on a more political decision. They do not want any of the refugees to be integrated into their societies in the future. They want the Rohingya to go 'home' when the disruptions there have ceased, irrespective of the fact that they have no 'home'; they are stateless people and are not only unwelcome in Myanmar, but actively and consistently persecuted as 'Bengali'. Consequently, Bangladeshi authorities have forbidden any schools to be built in the camp, have expelled any refugee students who had managed to get themselves enrolled in local schools and have prohibited any use of the Bangladeshi curriculum document content by volunteers in the camp in their attempts to ensure that these refugees are not educated to integrate into Bangladesh society. Despite this, support agencies have built clusters of small, covered shelters in which volunteers can continue to teach the Rohingya students. These are the only 'schools' in the camp (British Broadcasting Corporation, 2020). Students being resettled into western schools will undoubtedly have some difficultly as their education has been considerably disrupted.

The situation varies considerably with other groups of refugee students. The Venezuelan children who were granted refuge in Colombia, for example, have full access to the education system in that country, although school-aged children appear to be struggling with the acquisition of the basic numeracy and literacy skills (Rescue.org, 2020). The children and young people who are resettled in western, English-speaking contexts do have access to education. The rules and regulations in each country differ considerably. Some countries require students to be enrolled in mandatory schooling within seven days of arrival. Others have longer adjustment periods, but all children and young people of school age with refugee and asylum-seeker experiences must attend school regularly. While this is undoubtedly in the best interest of the students, life at school can be unconscionably difficult. Again, the degree of difficulty experienced by these students in adjusting to western educational systems varies individually, in addition to the previous educational experiences. Even for those students who have experience of school life, the differences may create challenges for the students themselves, their families and communities. Aspects of school that are simply taken for granted in the context of the new homeland may be not just alien but potentially detrimental to their wellbeing and integration. These aspects include matters of hygiene, such as becoming familiar with a flushing toilet, or a toilet at all, the regulatory systems around wearing uniforms and cultural sensitivity, the requirement for students to wear shoes when they have not ever experienced walking in footwear, the lunchtime routines that don't reflect traditional ways of preparing and partaking in meals. The minutiae of everyday life in western schools can be overwhelming, most especially when students do not have the language to ask questions and explain their difficulties.

Ways of doing and being in western schools are frequently precise, non-negotiable and shrouded in legal complexities. Child protection mandates and duty of care responsibilities can be the source of much concern and misunderstanding. Students in their homeland schools are often subjected to quite severe physical punishment for even the smallest misdemeanour or perceived breach of behavioural expectations. Even small children can be beaten on the soles of the feet with wooden rods for failing to learn effectively. In most well-informed, western school systems, physical punishment is illegal. In many countries, this is also the case for parents and caregivers, with only extremely restricted physical punishment by hand permitted. For parents and caregivers with refugee and asylum-seeking experiences, physical punishment may be the only method they know to discipline their children. It is not uncommon for parents to question why schools are not effectively disciplining their children when necessary, instead of asking to meet with parents to find solutions for ongoing problematic behaviours such as lack of cooperation with teachers and peers, inappropriate physical contact with others and destructive actions. The difficulties escalate when teachers and principals fail to recognise that these parents and caregivers have no strategies other than the traditional and culturally acceptable practices from their homelands. It can frequently be the work of school principals and others to demonstrate and explain strategies such as time out, exclusion from activities which the students may enjoy, such as watching television, playing sport, playing with friends in an outside environment, riding a new bicycle, or investigating the wonders of an iPad. Failure to comprehensively understand the need for different disciplinary strategies in a new homeland has led to incidents of parents being compelled to surrender their children into the care of government agencies: incidents as traumatic as their displacement and loss as the result of the circumstances that led them to seek new homelands. Students also need to be encouraged to respect other disciplinary strategies, and the consistency and clarity of the school disciplinary policy and actions can support them to develop an understanding of both the purpose of the sanctions and the consequences of non-compliance.

The diaspora and the need to include students with refugee and asylum-seeking experiences into classrooms of students who have not had these experiences have placed considerable pressure on those who prepare teachers. It appears that the teachers who are most successfully integrating these groups into their regular school contexts have identifiable traits (reference). They are not only well informed about the neurological impact of trauma on the brain and its capacities to learn effectively, but they are also sensitive to behavioural traits that are also results of traumatic experiences and the insidious impacts of intergenerational trauma (Blackwell & Melzak, 2000; Ehntholt et al., 2005; Jasnow & Ressler, 2010). Successful teachers find ways within their environments to support students who find it difficult to concentrate, who are hypervigilant and who express other, deeply rooted signs of stress and anxiety. They regularly engage in reflective and reflexive practices as foundational aspects of their professional work (Sellars, 2017), and are sensitive to the ways in which education systems, school institutions and multiple degrees of difference from the natives of the new homelands can impact negatively on students' sense of belonging and wellbeing (Sellars, 2020; Sellars, 2021; Sellars & Imig, 2020). In fact, it has been found that many of the most successful teachers have been trained in specialist education (Wiseman & Galegher, 2019). This professional choice depends substantially on individual's capacities to identify and work with positive aspects of all individual students, rather than adopting the deficit perspective that can all too frequently be allocated to students who are not initially exhibiting the knowledge, skills and conceptual understanding of academic progress on their arrival. These teachers are also aware of the complexity of compassion (Nussbaum, 2001) and of empathy itself (Davis, 1983; Mirra, 2018), leading them to develop a critical awareness of the nature and role of radical empathy (Ratcliffe, 2012). The characteristics of these teachers may be innate, due to personal values and beliefs or simply due to their understandings of what it is to be human. Irrespective of the depth of commitment of these teachers, the roles of professional learning and information and strategy sharing are invaluable in building networks of confidence and competence in their complex roles of supporting these diverse cohorts of students.

Conclusion

As teachers with the benefits of being educated, having a high degree of safety in everyday life, shelter, food and somewhere to sleep, it is impossible to envisage the experiences of those who have refugee and asylum-seeker backgrounds. It is challenging to reflect on the degrees of hardship and sorrow that has shaped their lives and drawn on extremes of human resilience, courage, optimism and hope for the future. Whilst the circumstances they have survived have undoubtedly left their scars, these students, now in western classrooms, do not need to be pathologised. They have no need of pity or unproductive sympathy. What they need most is respect, opportunity to use their strengths to learn effectively and teachers who are well informed, imaginative and have the creativity to use their personal and professional skills to understand their different ways of being and doing. At the very heart of supporting student learning is a deep understanding of students and their needs, academic, emotional, social and physical. It is only then that teachers can use their content knowledge and pedagogical strategies to make the strictures and structures of institutional systems welcoming, and educational opportunities accessible. It is a substantial error to believe that these students do not bring anything into their classrooms. They bring not only the qualities that parents wish for in their own children: resilience, courage, optimism and hope for the future, but also the richness of diversity, the capacity to allow others to see the world and their own learning through different world views and perspectives. Teachers do not enter and stay in the profession because it is easy, even in the best circumstances, and the pathways to success when supporting and integrating students with substantial differences into classrooms, in terms of both student experiences and mandated levels of skills and academic confidence, are particularly challenging. What can encourage teachers to face this challenge is the knowledge that their students have already struggled and overcome so many difficulties to be present in those classrooms. These students present a stark reminder of the privilege it is to teach.

References

Blackwell, D., & Melzak, S. (2000). *Far from the battle but still at war: Troubled refugee children in school* (1-900870-17-7). Retrieved May 25, 2021, from http://search.ebscohost.com/login.aspx?direct=true&db=eric&AN=ED462489&site=eds-live

Briere, J., Johnson, K., Bissada, A., Damon, L., Crouch, J., Gil, E., Hanson, R., & Ernst, V. (2001). The trauma symptom checklist for young children (TSCYC): Reliability and association with abuse exposure in a multi-site study. *Child Abuse & Neglect, 25*(8), 1001–1014. https://doi.org/10.1016/S0145-2134(01)00253-8

British Broadcasting Corporation. (2020). *Myanmar Rohingya: What You Need to Know About the Crisis*. Retrieved April 27, from https://www.bbc.com/news/world-asia-41566561

Cheatham, A. (2021). *Central America's Turbulent Northern Triangle*. Council on Public Relations. Retrieved April 28, from https://www.cfr.org/backgrounder/central-americas-turbulent-northern-triangle

Countries and Their People. *Dinka*. Retrieved February 1, 2022, from https://www.everyculture.com/wc/Rwanda-to-Syria/Dinka.html

Davis, M. (1983). Measuring individual differences in empathy: Evidence for a multidimensional approach. *Journal of Personality and Social Psychology*, 44(1), 113–126.

De Bellis, M. (2005). The psychobiology of neglect. *Child Maltreatment*, May(2), 150–172.

De Bellis, M. D., Hooper, S. R., Spratt, E. G., & Woolley, D. P. (2009). Neuropsychological findings in childhood neglect and their relationships to pediatric PTSD. *Journal of the International Neuropsychological Society*, 15(6), 868–878. https://doi.org/10.1017/s1355617709990464

Deprince, A. P., Weinzierl, K. M., & Combs, M. D. (2009). Executive function performance and trauma exposure in a community sample of children. *Child Abuse & Neglect*, 33(6), 353–361. https://doi.org/10.1016/j.chiabu.2008.08.002

Ehntholt, K. A., Smith, P. A., & Yule, W. (2005). School-based cognitive-behavioural therapy group intervention for refugee children who have experienced war-related trauma. *Clinical Child Psychology and Psychiatry*, 10(2), 235–250. https://doi.org/10.1177/1359104505051214

Human Rights Watch. (2015). *"We Can Die Too" Recruitment and Use of Child Soldiers in South Sudan*. Retrieved April 27, from https://www.hrw.org/report/2015/12/14/we-can-die-too/recruitment-and-use-child-soldiers-south-sudan

Jasnow, A., & Ressler, K. (2010). Interpersonal violence as a mediator of stress-related disorders in humans. In C. Worthman, P. Plotsky, D. Schechter, & C. Cummings (Eds.), *Formative Experiences: The Interactions of Caregiving, Culture and Developmental Psychobiology* (pp. 451–462). Cambridge.

Kattan, R. (2022). *Girls' Education*.

Korbokova, N. (2020). *A Double Edged Sword: Protection Risks Facing Venezuelan Children During the COVID-19 Pandemic*. World Vision International.

Maslow, A. (1943). A theory of human motivation. *Psychological Review*, 50(4), 370–396.

Matheme, S. (2018). *They Are (Still) Refugees: People Continue to Flee Violence in Latin American Countries*. CAP. Retrieved April 28, from https://www.americanprogress.org/article/still-refugees-people-continue-flee-violence-latin-american-countries/

Migration Data Portal. (2020). *Migration Data in Northern Africa*.

Mirra, N. (2018). *Educating for Empathy*. Teachers College Press.

Nussbaum, M. C. (2001). *Upheavals of Thought: The Intelligence of Emotions*. Cambridge University Press. https://doi.org/10.1017/CBO9780511840715

Ratcliffe, M. (2012). Phenomenology as a form of empathy. *Inquiry*, 55(5), 473–495. https://doi.org/10.1080/0020174x.2012.716196

Rescue.org. (2020). *Colombia's Education Crisis: Results from a Learning Assessment of Host Community and Venezuelan Refugee Children*. Retrieved April 29, from https://reliefweb.int/sites/reliefweb.int/files/resources/colombiabrief111020.pdf

Robinson, K. (2022). *Yemen's Tragedy: War, Stalemate, and Suffering*. Council on Foreign Relations. Retrieved April 27, from https://www.cfr.org/backgrounder/yemen-crisis

Rosen, N. (2011). *Assad's Alawites: The Guardians of the Throne Syria's Alawite Community have a History of Persecution, but Dominate the Ruling Family's Security Forces*. Retrieved April 27, from https://www.aljazeera.com/features/2011/10/10/assads-alawites-the-guardians-of-the-throne/

Roth, K. (2021). *Afghanistan: Events of 2021*. Human Rights Watch. Retrieved April 27, from https://www.hrw.org/world-report/2022/country-chapters/afghanistan

Sellars, M. (2017). *Reflective Practice for Teachers*. Sage.

Sellars, M. (2020). *Educating Students with Refugee and Asylum Seeker Experiences: A Commitment to Humanity*. Verlag Barbara Budrich

Sellars, M. (2021). Belonging and being: Developing inclusive ethos. *International Journal of Leadership in Education*, 1–24. https://doi.org/10.1080/13603124.2021.1942994

Sellars, M., & Imig, S. (2020). The real cost of neoliberalism for educators and students. *International Journal of Leadership in Education*, 1–13. https://doi.org/10.1080/13603124.2020.1823488

Shulman, L. (1987). Knowledge and teaching: foundations of the new reform. *Harvard Educational Review*, 57(1), 1–22.

The South Sudan Crisis Explained: 5 Things You Need to Know in 2022. (2021). Concern Worldwide US. Retrieved April 27, from https://www.concernusa.org/story/south-sudan-crisis-explained/

The UN Refugee Agency. (2021a). *Refugee Data Finder*. Retrieved April 27, from https://www.unhcr.org/refugee-statistics/

The UN Refugee Agency. (2021b). *Venezuela Situation*. Retrieved April 28, from https://www.unhcr.org/en-au/venezuela-emergency.html

Triesman, R. (2022). The number of people fleeing ukraine has surpassed 5 million. *NPR*. Retrieved April 22, 2022, from https://www.npr.org/2022/04/20/1093760280/ukraine-refugees-5-million#:~:text=More%20than%205%20million%20refugees%20have%20fled%20Ukraine%20%3A%20NPR&text=More%20than%205%20million%20refugees%20have%20fled%20Ukraine%20The%20U.N.,been%20displaced%20by%20the%20conflict.

UNHCR The UN Refugee Agency. (2019). *Stepping Up: Refugee Education in Crisis Report*.

UNICEF. *A Profile of Child Marriage in the Middle East and North Africa*. Retrieved April 26, from data.unicef.org

US Aid from the American People. (2013). *Education in South Sudan*. Retrieved April 28, from https://www.usaid.gov/sites/default/files/documents/1865/SouthSudanInfo.pdf

Wiseman, A. W., & Galegher, E. (2019). Impact of teacher preparation and professional development on refugee and Asylum-seeking student outcomes in OECD countries. In A. Wiseman, L. Damaschke-Deitrick, E. Galegher, & M. F. Park (Eds.), *Comparative Perspectives on Refugee Youth* (pp. 50–77). Routledge.

Wodon, Q. T., Male, C., Nayihouba, K. A., Onagoruwa, A. O., Savadogo, A., Yedan, A., Edmeades, J., Kes, A., John, N., Murithi, L., Steinhaus, M., & Petroni, S. (2017). *Economic Impacts of Child Marriage: Global Synthesis Report*. The World Bank and International Center for Research on Women.

World Vision. (2021). *Venezuela Crisis: Facts, FAQs, and How to Help*. Retrieved April 28, from https://www.worldvision.org/disaster-relief-news-stories/venezuela-crisis-facts#:~:text=More%20than%206%20million%20refugees,recent%20years%20of%20political%20turmoil

2 Trauma and its impact

Introduction

Few people are able to live a lifetime without some trauma. For many, it is simple trauma created by the death of a loved one, an accident or illness or another situation that is particularly stressful. Although the details of the chemical reaction in their bodies and brains may not be of interest to those who are stressed at the time of these occurrences, individuals know that there are changes to their feelings, capacities to think clearly and cope effectively on these occasions. Students with refugee and asylum-seeker experiences have experienced traumatic episodes from multiple occurrences, including the experiences of displacement, that is, loss of home, friends and possessions, and perhaps of witnessing torture, pain and death of others including loved ones. Others have experienced trauma as ongoing, facing multiple stresses repeatedly. These are not simple trauma. They are experiences of complex trauma (Gabowitz et al., 2008), which, while if extreme, necessitate clinical interventions (Bartlett et al., 2018; Lawson & Quinn, 2013), invariably impact on the emotional, cognitive and social development of these students, even if they are not exhibiting symptoms of post-trauma stress disorder (McDonald et al., 2014). Ongoing medical research also show that intergenerational trauma may also impact on the physical development, being transferred from one generation to the other. Whilst trauma is certainly a challenge for educators, both in supporting the students in schools and in protecting themselves from the impact of vicarious trauma (Pearlman & Caringi, 2009), this chapter provides evidence of the remarkable impact that teachers can have on these students in their classrooms. Understanding trauma itself, exploring ways in which the students can experience belonging through positive relationship development and sensitive learning environments can provide substantial support for these students and their families.

Trauma

Many of the teacher participants in this research discussed their awareness of and concerns about the trauma that their students had suffered pre-migration and on their journeys to their new homelands (Arar et al., 2019a). For many students and their families, negotiating the procedures and policies that awaited them when they arrived in these new homelands added to the constancy and complexity of their trauma (Sanggaran et al., 2016; Schoultz, 2016). Whilst these concerns were certainly legitimate and deserving of considerations and accommodations that were made for the participants' students with refugee and asylum-seeker backgrounds, it is also critical that these students and their communities are not 'pathologized' as being helpless or without any capacity to recover. It appears there is a fine balance between recognising, understanding and providing therapeutic support for trauma-impacted students (Ehntholt et al., 2005) and diminishing their capacity for resilience and autonomy (Bonanno, 2004).

Seeking this balance amongst the plethora of policies and practices that are in place in education systems requires teachers to be well educated in trauma-informed practices and pedagogical approaches that have the potential to mitigate the impact of these diverse experiences and provide social, emotional and cognitive support for these students (see, for example, Ahmadzadeh et al., 2014; Arar et al., 2019a; Barrett & Berger, 2021; Bond, 1963; Dobson et al., 2021; Easton-Calabria & Omata, 2018; Hek, 2005; Lee, 2019; Madziva & Thondhlana, 2017; Purkey, 2013; Sellars, 2020, 2021a; Van der Dussen Toukan, 2018). Much depends on the individual's pre-migration conditions, and their exposure to violence, fear and loss and to their personal and collective capacities to endure pain and loss as cultural competencies. Teachers are the heart of many school interactions and have the capacities, not simply for compassion and empathy, but for creative strategising and innovating to help students learn despite the multiple impacts of traumatic experiences on the neurological balances of the brain (Beers & De Bellis, 2002; De Bellis, 2005, 2010). These impacts include impairment of the cognitive capacities of executive function (Sellars, 2012), which include regulation of emotion, task completion, concentration and attentiveness in addition to tendencies for hypervigilance, irrational thinking and undefined anxiety.

> Post-traumatic stress disorder (PTSD) is characterized by four symptom clusters as defined by the Diagnostic and Statistical Manual, Fifth Edition (DSM-5) [1]: re-experiencing, avoidance of stimuli associated with the trauma, negative cognitions and affect associated with the trauma, and hyperarousal symptoms and signs. Fifty to 85% of Americans experience at least one traumatic event during their lifetimes, but only 7.8% go on to develop PTSD [2]. Thus, the question that frequently arises is: why do some people develop PTSD after experiencing trauma, while others do not? Possible explanations could be: an underlying genetic or epigenetic risk in those who are more prone to develop PTSD and/or a protective (epi) genetic makeup, or some form of high psychological resiliency in those who do not develop PTSD or who quickly recover from PTSD, i.e., resilient individuals. PTSD has long been established to be due to exposure to trauma, and it has been assumed that only environmental factors would contribute to the development of PTSD. On the other hand, heritability of PTSD has been estimated to be between 30% and 70% in twin studies [3–7]. Genetic studies of both candidate gene and genome-wide association studies (GWAS) have provided many interesting and promising findings, yet (so far)

> no robust genetic variants for PTSD have been identified [8]. This risk is unlikely to be fully explained by only structural genetics [9]. Thus, the field of epigenetics could offer insights into differential susceptibility of risk to develop psychopathology. According to Goldberg et al. [9], epigenetics is the study of functionally stable and ideally/heritable changes in gene expression or cellular phenotype that occurs without changes in base pairing. In other words, epigenetics involves functional changes to the gene without sequence changes. The best studied epigenetic mechanism so far is via DNA methylation. …Transgenerational epigenetic transmission is defined as the transmission of genomic information (in this paper DNA methylation) from one generation to the next without changing the main structure of DNA (i.e., nucleotides sequence). (Youssef et al., 2018, pp. 1–2)

We spoke with an experienced primary teacher in regional Australia who stressed the importance of overtly valuing diversity.

Context: I started here a few years ago and have been supervising stages two and three (grades 3–6). This year I am working in instructional leadership. Prior to coming here, I worked at another primary school for more than ten years as an instructional leader and classroom teacher. Over 70% of enrolled students in our school are from English as an Additional Language or Dialect (EAL/D). We have refugee families, overseas students and children of parents completing postgraduate degrees or working temporarily in Australia are enrolled. Aboriginal students make up 8% of enrolments.

> These students had quite varied experiences with school. Some have had schooling in their home country or in the country that they were in before they came to Australia. Some really have had very limited schooling, so it's not just curriculum that these students need to learn, they're learning what school is, they are learning about routines, they're learning about expectations, they're learning that they're safe here. They need support to learn about life in Australia. But the most critical thing that we really try to do first is built those relationships, so that we can support. We are obviously such a diverse school. We really value that cultural diversity and I think that is probably quite essential to students trusting us to building those relationships, valuing home languages and just them feeling accepted within the school.
>
> I would really encourage a new teacher, to take the time to build relationships with those students and also get to know the families as well. That's absolutely one hundred percent the most important thing that matters, I don't think that you're going to be able to really go deep into the curriculum without having those really strong relationships. First, take the time to establish that safe and supportive learning environment. Be clear about expectations. It's all of those things that I think you would tell any beginning teacher in setting up their classroom in terms of creating that safe space.

In regard to the trauma, I think it is just to be mindful of potential triggers in working with beginning teachers. I had a practicum student; she was teaching a geography unit and it was around the Kokoda Track. My advice to her was around being really mindful and don't go too much into the war aspect there, rather look at some other aspects. Given that so many children in your class have come from war zones, we need to be mindful of what can potentially trigger. And I think especially working with upper primary, the best way to do that sometimes is to talk to the kids. Ask them what they are comfortable with, what they want and give them that option to be able to say, 'I don't feel comfortable with this'. What I found was that the students responded really well to books and quality texts that refer to refugees, I had one girl pick up 'The Little Refugee' and she goes, "oh this is about me! I'm a refugee". Having access to some of those quality texts that they can pick up and say, 'I actually can relate to this, I can make a connection here, this relates to my life story.' I think don't be too afraid to remove all references to being a refugee or anything like that, I think that it is their life, and we need to normalize that.

We have to make sure the classroom is a really safe and supportive space. The other thing is that making sure that children feel comfortable to come to the teacher is super important. Sometimes it's important that children have opportunities to talk [in class] but I also developed the understanding that a quiet conversation with the teacher is probably more appropriate in some instances than a whole class conversation, particularly when we're talking about things that can be potentially quite traumatic. I had a student quite casually tell me quite a traumatic story from back in Afghanistan, and he said that to me kind of quietly. He didn't necessarily share that with the whole class, which is fortunate. Really, not all of our students need to hear about that, but the other thing is to him that's his normal. He's done all of his schooling here in Australia, he is in year six currently, so it's quite a long time ago that this has happened. It's obviously still something that pops into his mind. But I think keeping calm and composed, because these stories, that's his reality, that's his life experience and overreacting to something like that isn't going to be helpful really either.

Unique contexts, global principles

This teacher is keenly aware of the harmful and lasting effects of trauma, and she is mindful of the importance of building trusting relationships to support her students, many of whom are new to the very idea of school. She is measured in her approach and is careful of not triggering students, as evidenced by her concerns regarding teaching the *Kokoda Track (a World War II campaign)*. Yet, she is also clear about the need to not shelter her newly arrived students and have honest dialogue with them about what they think they can handle. By incorporating some instructional materials that reflect her students with refugee backgrounds, she normalises their experiences and helps to make her classroom welcoming and safe. When her male student privately shared a long-ago traumatic occurrence from his life in

Afghanistan, she did not overreact; she remained calm and engaged with him. But she also applies this same sensitivity and understanding to her Australian-born students, realising they may not be able to handle the brutal life experiences of their newly arrived peers. In addressing these complex challenges, this primary teacher is reflective and grounds her decisions in the situation rather than relying on a blanket policy or school mandate.

For children who have been forcibly removed from their home, who may have lost family members or friends and who have come to a new and unfamiliar country, starting in a new school is likely to add to their trauma, and that is where the classroom teacher is so important. The first order of business is developing relationships and creating an environment where newly arrived students see themselves and feel valued. This can be achieved through personal conversations and by incorporating or having available resources that relate to students' home countries or the refugee experience. This is not tokenistic, nor should it be complete immersion in the refugee experience. These students are talented, intelligent and capable, and teachers need to be careful not to pander to or pathologise them. Many students will have had limited schooling or no schooling, and this will foster anxiety. Teachers need to respond to this by being purposeful in introducing routines and expectations, even if the rest of the students are acclimated to the norms of the classroom. Teachers also need to understand that there isn't a 'normal' for coping with trauma and that it can emerge in a student's words and actions at any point, even years after a horrific event has occurred. Teachers can respond by showing empathy and compassion but being mindful of not letting the events minimise their perceptions of a student's abilities. As our primary teacher and dozens of others whom we interviewed asserted, there are no hard rules for dealing with the complexities of trauma, other than being present, being purposeful and being kind.

Belonging

Much of the teachers' work in supporting students with refugee and asylum-seeker experience begins with developing a sense of belonging. The focus on inclusivity was a major theme for the participants of this research who articulated a desire for their students not just to 'fit in' but to authentically belong to their classroom communities despite the many degrees of difference that demonstrate their diversity. Whilst it is not possible to 'make' people belong, it is important to understand that an openness to belonging is an individual capacity, often determined by multiple factors beyond the school and classroom itself. Principals and teachers may, with good intentions, work towards helping their students with refugee and asylum-seeker experiences fit in to the cultural characteristics of their school and wider communities. This is not surprising as historically the research literature has been heavily focused on the unidirectional model of acculturation which proposes that the adaptation process to the new cultural identity is achieved by totally dismissing or 'shedding' the former cultural behaviours and attitudes of the individuals involved.

The other model, a bi-directional model, instead advocates the benefits of retaining many of the heritage cultural characteristics whilst simultaneously adapting to the new culture (McLachlan, 1997; Renzaho, 2009). This type of acculturation comprises a four-part model which identifies the cultural orientations of immigrants into four categories (Berry, 1990). These four categories are the results of measures of the orientation of individuals towards their home and host cultures and include (i) separation where the home culture remains dominant and there is little engagement with the host culture, (ii) assimilation where all reference to home culture ceases and the host culture dominates – this is the practice of 'fitting in' (iii) integration where the host and home cultures are equally important and connection with the home culture is preserved whilst acculturation into the host culture is on progress. This is the critical aspect of belonging, both in schools and on the wider community. Individuals are accepted for who they are, and there is no expectation that the home culture is dismissed in favour of the host culture (McLachlan, 1997) and (iv) marginalisation in which individuals identify with neither home nor host culture having rejected home culture and failed to connect meaningfully with the host culture (Berry, 1997; Berry, 2001; Doná & Berry, 1994; Sam & Berry, 2010; Ward & Kus, 2012). In their research on immigrant youth, Berry et al. (2006) found that the individuals who had integrated their home culture into their new host culture scored the highest on scales of psychological adjustment and healthy social relationships. It appears that integration, the pathway to acceptance and belonging that allows individuals to simultaneously feel connected to both home and host cultures, can foster the emotional and social health of students with refugee and asylum-seeker experiences, and teachers and their principals are frequently the people who facilitate this in their classrooms (Bradley & Sellars, 2020; Imig et al., 2021; Sellars, 2021a, 2021b). Many of the participating teachers indicated in their responses that they realised the importance of the maintenance of the home language and cultural traditions and sought to include these considerations in their classroom communities in a non-tokenistic manner.

> Teachers who have many newcomer students in classes often struggle between meeting newcomer students' individual learning needs and the required curriculum content and outcomes. Not all teachers feel confident and sufficiently prepared to work with students whose cultural and linguistic backgrounds differ from theirs. Those who work with newcomer students, particularly second language teachers and those have a good understanding of the refugee and immigrant students' needs, often feel alone due to lack of a whole school approach or the disconnection between schools and community integration agencies. (Stewart, 2011; Guo-Brennan & Guo-Brennan, 2019, p. 76)

We spoke with two primary educators in Northern Ireland who offered us a combined vignette rich with their shared experience.

Context: I'm the vice principal, and I've been here for about 6 to 7 years, but I've been teaching for over 20 years in all inner-city schools. I take small groups of asylum seekers and newcomer children. I'm also in charge of pastoral care and protection assessment and many other different things.

I'm a class teacher up in the school at the moment. I'm working with a primary class. I'm ICT coordinator at the school, and I've been here for more than ten years. We are Catholics, even though we welcome the children of all. We have students from about 30 countries including a large population of newcomers.

> We are sanctuary school. I think the great thing about our school is that it is built upon the ethos that is throughout the whole school. The ethos of the whole school has always been about giving everybody the best opportunity. Everybody who comes into our school says it's just such a welcoming place. We've sort of developed a bespoke program, along with the help of the Inclusion Education Service to develop language. We do get some extra money for newcomer children, and we will purposely use some money to develop their language skill. Initially, it's just all about getting to know the children and their families, and it is really to see if we can help them in any way. We run a foodbank with the local supermarket, and we leave the food in the foyer. They can come and help themselves if they are struggling with anything.
>
> If you were to come into my classroom, what would I be proud of in the classroom? There are two things, the visual aspect of the classroom and the atmosphere in the classroom. It's a warm bright classroom, all the children's works being celebrated in all the buildings. And instead of school rules, we have our class charter. Every classroom has a class charter as opposed to a set of class rules. It's based on every child's right to be heard and enjoy school, be safe, and then what are our responsibilities to achieve them. And then the atmosphere in the classroom, the standards one of people being able to take risks, and to support each other. If you're actually in the classroom and seeing me teach, you would see there's a lot of integration. I'm really proud of the pupils in our classroom. They are so caring and empathetic towards newcomer pupils and support the pupils who are coming in from different countries. I'm, of course, the main area of support, but I'm really proud of the levels of support the children are able to give each other as well.

Unique contexts, global principles

These Northern Irish educators spoke with great pride about their school environment and purpose. While they offered numerous ways to develop belonging, they also drew attention to the fact that belonging cannot occur unless safety and basic human needs are met. The school personnel provide food to any student's family in the community who may need it, and they have crafted a classroom charter that focuses on safety, all children having a voice, and the right to enjoy school. At its core, this school is about giving every unique student their best opportunity to flourish, and they have created this environment by working with outside experts to craft high-quality language learning approaches. Unlike providing food and safety, helping students to have a voice requires they begin to understand and be able to contribute vocally to the classroom. The teachers also spoke proudly about honouring and celebrating students by covering classroom walls with 'all the children's works' and integrating their culture and experiences into their lessons. A seemingly small gesture, showcasing student works sends a message of belonging. While these teachers see themselves as the key people for classroom integration, they also rely heavily on their students to welcome and support newly arrived students.

Creating belonging for students with refugee and asylum-seeker backgrounds is a purposeful process for classroom teachers. As Berry (1990) indicates, newly arrived students can shed their home cultures for the host culture, cling only to their home cultures or, even worse, lose touch with any culture at all. Teachers must find ways to integrate students in a manner that celebrates them as individuals. Weaving their experiences and home cultures into lessons, displaying their work alongside their peers and creating classroom environments where newly arrived students have an equal voice are ways to foster belonging. But belonging cannot exist without first meeting students' foundational human needs of safety and security and having a voice. Schools must see the provision of delivering high-quality language instruction as a priority and work with regional experts as needed to develop these programmes. This Northern Irish school intentionally reaches outward to support families, provides food assistance to all in need and has created a cohort of students who recognise their rights and responsibilities as good classroom citizens. By including all students in the work of integrating children with refugee and asylum-seeker backgrounds, not only is the teachers' power to effect change expanded, but the importance of belonging becomes a part of the classroom ethos.

Positivity

The creation of positive school and classroom environments is not only supportive of social and emotional wellbeing. It is critical for cognitive safety and effective learning (Immordino-Yang & Feath, 2010; Sousa, 1995; Willis, 2010). Cognition is ruled by emotion, and students in classrooms where they feel emotionally safe, valued and respected develop the capacities they need to learn effectively more readily in these positive environments. This is reflected not only as behaviours conducive to effective learning but also as the brain's potential to think laterally, be more open to new ideas, make conjecture and become more adventurous in their learning. Fredrickson (2000, 2001) determined that positive emotion created a great potential for these learning potentials to be activated in the brain as a result of eliciting positive emotions. Using *fMRI* scanning, she discovered that the neural activity in the brain considerably increased when her participants were engaged with watching various types of media which elicited positive emotions of love, hope, joy, pride and interest. Conversely, when exposed to material that created negative emotions, such as anger, fear, shame and distress, the neural activity decreased, and was limited to smaller, less interconnected areas of the brain. The impact of these experiences was evident in the tutorial activities which followed the *fMRI* scanning episodes. After experiencing the positive stimuli, the participants were more actively engaged, had a readiness to explore new perspectives and problem-solving strategies and provided more creative solutions to the issues raised. However, after they were exposed to the materials that created the responses of negative emotions, they were unable to be innovative, reluctant to engage and generally appear to be 'shut down' during the tutorial activities that followed.

This 'Broaden and Build' model of positive emotions helps explain the success of the *Positive Psychology* group and the findings of Csikszentmihalyi (1988); (Csikszentmihalyi, 1991; Moneta & Csikszentmihalyi, 1996; Nakamura & Csikszentmihalyi, 2002; Shernoff et al., 2003) and his description of autotelic motivation which he defined as *'flow'*. By engaging school dropouts in activities and projects in which they had a deep interest, Csikszentmihalyi (1988) was able to monitor their level of positive experience during the tasks, establishing that they were so fully engrossed in their activities that they were oblivious to outside distractions, including the passage of time. The development of the *PERMA* model (Seligman, 2002; Seligman et al., 2005; Seligman et al., 2009) combined the findings of several investigations in positive psychology, explaining the foundations for creating and maintaining positivity as the vital component of wellbeing. This model comprises five 'pillars' of wellbeing, each of which shares the same three characteristics: they are independent of each other, are pursued for their own sake and contribute to overall wellbeing. Unpacking the acronym: *P* is positive emotions; *E* is engagement in activities which produce the *flow* experience; *R* is for positive relationships, acknowledging that very little that is accomplished is essentially a solitary activity and so the role of others is important; *M* is meaning, belonging to and serving something that is 'bigger' than self; and *A* is achievement or accomplishment, pursuing or mastering something for its own sake and not for any reward. The *PERMA* model has been integrated into many classrooms since its inception, and aspects of these 'pillars' were evidenced in the responses provided by the research participants. While it is not possible or preferable to dismiss past, or even current, student experiences which result in negative emotions, deep trauma and lasting distress, the teachers in this research project who created positive and accepting classroom environments with sensitivity had the potential to participate in the social and emotional healing that was critical for effective learning, both socially and cognitively.

> …any kind of insensitivity culturally or politically by the host nations' educational systems can lead to student failure and social deviancy. Without any guarantees, education has the exclusive power to reshape children's and adults lives (Harrington, 2016; Hatton, 2017; Thomas, 2016) and to free them from the adverse effects of trauma and catastrophic life events while creating opportunities for a better future…Educators have the critical role of creating conditions of equity, high academic expectations and social justice in such contexts of demographic transformation (Brooks and Watson, 2019; Liou & Hermanns, 2017). (Arar et al., 2019b, p. 3)

We spoke with a veteran teacher who works across schools in a major Australian city to help build the capacity to support children and families with refugee and asylum-seeker backgrounds.

Context: I've taught for over 30 years, and I've always had a passion to support students from EAL/D backgrounds, which is English as Additional Language or Dialect. In my first school, there was 99.95% children from language background other than English and lots of the students needed EAL/D support. This year, I am an EAL/D Education Leader, so I'm working as a refugee support leader in an area network of primary and high schools to support and build the capacity of the schools' leadership teams, the teachers, the school learning support officers, the office staff, everybody about supporting EAL/D students, including students and families from refugee background. I just love what I do.

> Because they've been impacted by what they've gone through, they need to feel that this is a safe place for them and their children. They might go to two or three different schools in a year. So, change happens, but it's the idea of transition and that's helping them with what happens in their mind. So, we could understand that we need to support them. As for the safety aspect, predictable routines, visual timetables with photos of people, coming into the classroom, developing that trust. The worst thing is fire drills. I often warn the children that's a fire drill but there's no fire. We have to practice this. We make sure that they feel safe. You have to do it, but it can be traumatic. We warn them and that trust is so important.
>
> Develop attachment by making sure you have the pronunciation of their names. And teach responsibility that they care for their resources, making choices, acknowledging that choice and then skills. That's what I would stress to teachers, because a child hiding under the table is not going to learn. A child who's running away is not going to learn. They're not feeling safe and that's where we use all the strategies in the STARTS model. And, of course, this impact of trauma on learning...we've got to acknowledge that they might be having sleepless nights and nightmares. It's like they can't concentrate, acknowledging that, and then strategies to support them.
>
> I just want to stress that firstly in my new arrivals class, I get the children to teach me Dari or Arabic. I am really bad at that so there's a lot of laughter. This is a safe place to learn, because if you want to learn a new language you need to take risks. So, I think it makes a safe environment for them to speak. They have the school learning support officer, the bilingual individual who is giving them the language that they need. And it's also in small groups, in pairs or small groups, so they feel safe to practice their language. I try my best to make the students feel safe, that this is a safe place for them to be. I make sure they are achieving success, and they want to learn more, and they laugh at me when I try to teach them English. I try to teach them as much vocabulary as I can. And I mean you got to be in awe of these students. They've been forced to flee. They have to learn a new language, and they've had to leave friends, they've had to leave their pets, and we just want to make this a safe place for them. We just want them to feel welcome and belong and their families, as well.

Do you know the migration U curve? When children leave their country they go to a new school, and they feel they don't know the language and they don't have friends and they can keep on going down like this [downward motion with hand]. But with the schools and agencies and all the intense practices that the teachers are doing, they might instead of going down, they can go like that [uses hand to show upward motion]. It helps them, but it doesn't mean they're going to get better all the time, because something happens like the recent crisis in Afghanistan, and it's going to be like this [gestures downward]. But we can give them that support during this time. They might be happy at school, but their parents may be very sad, they might be missing families. They've got so many challenges and they're just resilient, and we've got to acknowledge that. So that's called the Migration U Carve and that's why those best practices are so important.

Unique contexts, global principles

This veteran teacher is profoundly aware of the trauma her students have experienced and in awe of their resilience, having left behind family, friends and pets in their home countries. She recognises the importance of a positive and predictable classrooms. She ensures that students understand routines and rules by explicitly teaching them as they join the classroom, and she uses photos and visuals to ensure important information is accurately conveyed. She is insistent that teachers learn how to pronounce their students' names as she believes it helps build strong relationships. She also ensures that students know what their responsibilities are in the classroom and how to treat the instructional resources they are provided. This teacher stresses the importance of creating safe and fun places for learning, and one way she does this is by allowing her students to teach her their home language. Demonstrating the challenge of learning a new language and making the experience humorous sets a wonderful tone. She is also purposeful about having children work in small groups where they are more comfortable taking risks. While she strives to create an environment where students increasingly feel safe and connected, she is also mindful that children live in a broader world where global events or parents dealing with their own anguish can trigger renewed issues.

For a child who has been forcibly displaced, suffered great loss, perhaps lived in a refugee camp, travelled around the world to a new home in an unfamiliar country, coming to a new school is likely to add to his or her trauma. Teachers can minimise this by reducing uncertainty and purposefully teaching newly arrived students the many routines and expectations that make up the school experience. Teachers can also craft a psychologically safe environment by demonstrating risk-taking and laughing at their own failures. Allowing students to see that it is okay to take risks and come up short creates an understanding that trying is valued. Also, enabling students to work in small groups and with empathetic classmates is a way to further build a feeling of safety. A simple yet incredibly important act by teachers that must occur is to learn the accurate pronunciation of student names. Doing so tells students they are valued. This Australian teacher is rightfully impressed with the resilience of her students with refugee and asylum-seeker backgrounds, yet she understands their developing perceptions of feeling safe and belonging can be side-tracked at any time with a triggering event. Maintaining a positive and safe learning environment requires teachers to stay mindful and attuned to the feelings and actions of their students and their students' families. A happy environment is the building block for student safety, creativity and learning.

Conclusion

The inclusion of students with refugee and asylum-seeker students into mainstream classrooms in western, English speaking countries is challenging. However, as the participants of this study have evidenced, it is not outside the capacities of caring teachers who are professionally dedicated to their work with students, who stay open to difference and diversity and who are willing to share strategies and be informed by research. Teaching is organic process, and the ways in which teachers respond authentically to the learning needs of their students, appreciating the multiple complexities and, often, sadness in their lives, does not simply support academic learning outcomes. It can enable these students and their families to take steps towards healing the impacts of trauma and learning to belong to two cultures simultaneously.

References

Ahmadzadeh, H., Corabatir, M., Hashem, L., Al Husseini, J., & Wahby, S. (2014). *Ensuring Quality Education for Young Refugees from Syria*. Refugee Studies Centre.

Arar, K., Brooks, J., & Bogotch, I. (2019a). *Education, Immigration and Migration Policy, Leadership and Praxis for a Changing World*. Emerald Publishing.

Arar, K., Örücü, D., & Ak Küçükçayır, G. (2019b, November). Culturally relevant school leadership for Syrian refugee students in challenging circumstances. *Educational Management Administration & Leadership, 47*(6), 960. http://ezproxy.newcastle.edu.au/login?url=http://search.ebscohost.com/login.aspx?direct=true&db=edb&AN=139308648&site=eds-live

Barrett, N., & Berger, E. (2021). Teachers' experiences and recommendations to support refugee students exposed to trauma. *Social Psychology of Education*. https://doi.org/10.1007/s11218-021-09657-4

Bartlett, J. D., Griffin, J. L., Spinazzola, J., Fraser, J. G., Noroña, C. R., Bodian, R., Todd, M., Montagna, C., & Barto, B. (2018). The impact of a statewide trauma-informed care initiative in child welfare on the well-being of children and youth with complex trauma. *Children and Youth Services Review, 84*, 110–117. https://doi.org/10.1016/j.childyouth.2017.11.015

Beers, S. R., & De Bellis, M. D. (2002). Neuropsychological function in children with maltreatment-related posttraumatic stress disorder. *American Journal of Psychiatry, 159*(3), 483–486. https://doi.org/10.1176/appi.ajp.159.3.483

Berry, J. (1997). Immigration, acculturation, and adaptation. *Applied Psychology: An International Review, 46*(1), 5–68.

Berry, J. (2001). A psychology of immigration. *Journal of Social Issues, 7*(3), 615–631.

Berry, J. W. (1990). Acculturation and adaptation: A general framework. In W. Holtzman and T. Bornemann (Eds.), *Mental Health of Immigrants and Refugees* (pp. 90–102). Hogg Foundation for Mental Health.

Berry, J. W., Horenczyk, G., & Kwak, K. (2006). *Immigrant Youth in Cultural Transition: Acculturation, Identity, and Adaptation across National Contexts*. Lawrence Erlbaum Associates. http://newcastle.eblib.com/patron/FullRecord.aspx?p=331698

Bonanno, G. A. (2004, Jan). Loss, trauma, and human resilience: Have we underestimated the human capacity to thrive after extremely aversive events? *American Psychologist, 59*(1), 20–28. https://doi.org/10.1037/0003-066X.59.1.20

Bond, B. B. (1963, October 1). Some aspects of educating the Cuban refugee student. *The Clearing House: A Journal of Educational Strategies, Issues and Ideas, 38*(2), 77–79. https://doi.org/10.1080/00098655.1963.11475946

Bradley, M., & Sellars, M. (2020). Parent cafe reflections. In M. Ruby, M. Angelo-Rocha, M. Hickey, & V. Agosto (Eds.), *Making a Spectacle: Examining Curriculum/Pedagogy as Recovery from Political Trauma* (pp. 183–190). Information Age Publishing.

Brooks, J., & Watson, T. (2019). School leadership and racism: An ecological perspective. *Urban Education, 54*(5), 631–655. https://doi.org/10.1177/0042085918783821

Csikszentmihalyi, M. (1988). The flow experience and its significance for human psychology. In M. Csikszentmihalyi & S. Csikszentmihalyi (Eds.), *Optimal Experience: Psychological Studies of Flow in Consciousness* (pp. 3–37). Cambridge University Press.

Csikszentmihalyi, M. (1991). Work as flow. In W. Holtzman & T. Bornemann (Eds.), *Flow: The Phsycology of Optimal Experience* (pp. 143–163). Harper Perennial Modern Classics.

De Bellis, M. (2005). The psychobiology of neglect. *Child Maltreatment*, May(2), 150–172.

De Bellis, M. (2010). Developmental traumatology: A commentary on the factors for risk and resiliency in the case of an adolescent Javanese Boy. In C. Worthman, P. Plotsky, D. Schechter, & C. Cummings (Eds.), *Formative Experiences: The Interaction of Caring, Culture and Developmental Psychbiology* (pp. 390–398). Cambridge University Press.

Dobson, S., Agrusti, G., & Pinto, M. (2021). Supporting the inclusion of refugees: Policies, theories and actions. *International Journal of Inclusive Education, 25*(1), 1–6. https://doi.org/10.1080/13603116.2019.1678804

Doná, G., & Berry, J. W. (1994). Acculturation attitues and acculturative stress of Central American refugees. *International Journal of Psychology, 29*(1), 57–70.

Easton-Calabria, E., & Omata, N. (2018). Panacea for the refugee crisis? Rethinking the promotion of 'self-reliance' for refugees. *Third World Quarterly, 39*(8), 1458–1474. https://doi.org/10.1080/01436597.2018.1458301

Ehntholt, K. A., Smith, P. A., & Yule, W. (2005). School-based cognitive-behavioural therapy group intervention for refugee children who have experienced war-related trauma. *Clinical Child Psychology and Psychiatry, 10*(2), 235–250. https://doi.org/10.1177/1359104505051214

Fredrickson, B. (2000). Cultivating positive emotions to optimize health and well being. *Prevention and Treatment, 3*. Retrieved September 3, 2013, from http://www.unc.edu/peplab/publications/Fredrickson_2000_Prev&Trmt.pdf

Fredrickson, B. (2001). The role of positive emotions in positive psychology. *American Psychologist* March (56, 3), 218–226.

Gabowitz, D., Zucker, M., & Cook, A. (2008). Neuropsychological assessment in clinical evaluation of children and adolescents with complex trauma. *Journal of Child & Adolescent Trauma, 1*(2), 163–178. https://doi.org/10.1080/19361520802003822

Guo-Brennan, M., & Guo-Brennan, L. (2019). Building welcoming and inclusive schools for immigrant and refugee students: Policy, famework and promising praxis. In K. Arar, J. Brooks, & I. Bogotch (Eds.), *Education, Immigration and Migration: Policy, Ledaership and Praxis a Changing World* (pp. 54–73). Emerald Publishing Limitied

Harrington, C. (2016). *Politicization of Sexual Violence*. https://doi.org/10.4324/9781315601243

Hatton, T. J. (2017). Refugees and asylum seekers, the crisis in Europe and the future of policy. *Economic Policy, 32*(91), 447–496. https://doi.org/10.1093/epolic/eix009

Hek, R. (2005). The role of education in the settlement of young refugees in the UK: The experiences of young refugees. *Practice, 17*(3), 157–171. https://doi.org/10.1080/09503150500285115

Imig, S., Sellars, M., & Fischetti, J. (2021). *Creating Spaces of Wellbeing and Safety for Students with Refugee and Asylum Seeker Experiences: Lessons from School Leaders*. Routledge.

Immordino-Yang, H., & Feath, M. (2010). The role of emotion and skilled intuition in learning. In D. Sousa (Ed.), *Mind, Brain and Education: Neuroscience Implications for the Classroom* (pp. 69–85). Solution Tree Press.

Lawson, D. M., & Quinn, J. (2013). Complex trauma in children and adolescents: Evidence-based practice in clinical settings. *Journal of Clinical Psychology, 69*(5), 497–509. https://doi.org/10.1002/jclp.21990

Lee, F. (2019). Cultivating a culture of peace and empathy in young children while empowering refugee communities. *Childhood Education, 95*(1), 16–23. https://doi.org/10.1080/00094056.2019.1565751

Liou, D. D., & Hermanns, C. B. (2017). Preparing transformative leaders for diversity, immigration, and equitable expectations for school-wide excellence. *International Journal of Educational Management, 31*, 661–678.

Madziva, R., & Thondhlana, J. (2017, November 02). Provision of quality education in the context of Syrian refugee children in the UK: Opportunities and challenges. *Compare: A Journal of Comparative and International Education, 47*(6), 942–961. https://doi.org/10.1080/03057925.2017.1375848

McDonald, M. K., Borntrager, C. F., & Rostad, W. (2014). Measuring trauma: Considerations for assessing complex and non-ptsd criterion a childhood trauma. *Journal of Trauma & Dissociation, 15*(2), 184–203. https://doi.org/10.1080/15299732.2014.867877

McLachlan, M. (1997). *Culture and Health*. John Wiley & Sons Ltd.

Moneta, G., & Csikszentmihalyi, M. (1996). The effect of perceived challenges and skills on the quality of subjective experience. *Journal of Personality, 64*(2), 275–310. https://doi.org/10.1111/j.1467-6494.1996.tb00512.x

Nakamura, J., & Csikszentmihalyi, M. (2002). The concept of flow. In C. Snyder & S. Lopez (Eds.), *Handbook of Positive Psychology* (pp. 89–105). Oxford University Press.

Pearlman, L. A., & Caringi, J. (2009). Living and working self-reflectively to address vicarious trauma. In C. A. Courtois & J. D. Ford (Eds.), *Treating Complex Traumatic Stress Disorders: An Evidence-Based Guide* (pp. 202–224). The Guilford Press.

Purkey, A. L. (2013). A dignified approach: Legal empowerment and justice for human rights violations in protracted refugee situations. *Journal of Refugee Studies, 27*(2), 260–281. https://doi.org/10.1093/jrs/fet031

Renzaho, A. M. N. (2009). Immigration and social exclusion: Examining health inequities of immigrants through acculturation lenses. In A. Taket, B. Crisp, A. Nevill, G. Lamaro, M. Graham, & S. Barter-Godfrey (Eds.), *Theorizing Social Exclusion* (pp. 117–126). Routledge.

Sam, D. L., & Berry, J. W. (2010). Acculturation. *Perspectives on Psychological Science, 5*(4), 472–481. https://doi.org/10.1177/1745691610373075

Sanggaran, J. P., Haire, B., & Zion, D. (2016, Feb). The health care consequences of Australian immigration policies. *PLoS Med, 13*(2), e1001960. https://doi.org/10.1371/journal.pmed.1001960

Schoultz, I. (2016). The state's mishandling of immigration to Sweden – How bodies controlling the state frame the problem. *Crime, Law and Social Change, 68*(1–2), 29–46. https://doi.org/10.1007/s10611-016-9675-x

Seligman, M. (2002). *Authentic Happiness: Using the New Positive Psychology to Realize Your Potential for Lasting Fulfillment*. Free Press.

Seligman, M., Ernst, R., Gillham, J., Reivich, K., & Linkins, M. (2009). Positive education: Positive psychology and classroom interventions. *Oxford Review of Education, 35*(3), 293–311.

Seligman, M., Park, N., & Peterson, C. (2005). Positive psychology progress: Empirical validation of interventions. *American Psychologist, 60*(5), 410–421.

Sellars, M. (2012). Exploring executive function: Multiple Intelligences' personalised mapping for success. *International Journal of Learning, 18*(3).

Sellars, M. (2020). *Educating Students with Refugee and Asylum Seeker Experiences: A Commitment to Humanity*. Verlag Barbara Budrich.

Sellars, M. (2021a). Belonging and being: Developing inclusive ethos. *International Journal of Leadership in Education*, 1–24. https://doi.org/10.1080/13603124.2021.1942994

Sellars, M. (2021b). Integrating students with refugee and asylum seeker backgrounds into school: Teachers perspectives. In M. Carmo (Ed.), *Education Applications and Developments VI* (Vol. VI, pp. 291–300). InScience Press.

Shernoff, D., Csikszentmihalyi, M., Schneider, B., & Shernoff, E. (2003). Student engagement in high school classrooms from the perspective of flow theory. *School Psychology Quarterly*.

Sousa, D. (1995). *How the Brain Learns*. National Association of Secondary Principals.

Stewart, J. (2011). *Supporting Refugee Children: Strategies for EDucators*. University of Toronto Press.

Thomas, R. L. (2016). The right to quality education for refugee children through social inclusion. *Journal of Human Rights and Social Work, 1*(4), 193–201. https://doi.org/10.1007/s41134-016-0022-z

Van der Dussen Toukan, E. (2018). Refugee youth in settlement, schooling, and social action: Reviewing current research through a transnational lens. *Journal of Peace Education*, 1–20. https://doi.org/10.1080/17400201.2018.1481020

Ward, C., & Kus, L. (2012). Back to and beyond Berry's basics: The conceptualization, operationalization and classification of acculturation. *International Journal of Intercultural Relations, 36*(4), 472–485. https://doi.org/10.1016/j.ijintrel.2012.02.002

Willis, J. (2010). The current impact of neuroscience on teaching and learning. In D. Sousa (Ed.), *Mind, Brain and Education: Neuroscience Implications for the Classroom* (pp. 44–66). Solution Tree Press.

Youssef, N. A., Lockwood, L., Su, S., Hao, G., & Rutten, B. P. F. (2018, May 8). The effects of trauma, with or without PTSD, on the transgenerational DNA methylation alterations in human offsprings. *Brain Science, 8*(5). https://doi.org/10.3390/brainsci8050083

3 Learning the language and differentiation

Introduction

The previous chapter highlighted the importance of developing a sense of belonging for students, in contrast to focusing on their capacities to 'fit into' new environments, academic demands and social and emotional interactions and relationships. This chapter discusses the ways in which teachers in diverse contexts have utilised their creativity and other resources to accommodate their students with refugee and asylum-seeker backgrounds and to adapt their own practices to better suit the learning needs of their different cohorts in their care. They have investigated and trialled the various ways in which differentiated tasks can add to their understandings of their students' relative strengths and the ways in which they can introduce them to new learning materials, experiences and concepts in ways that are non-threatening and which provide opportunities for success.

Differentiation

Differentiation can take many forms as is it is basically the task of changing the content, pedagogy or learning environment to allow the learning to become more personalised and accessible to the students in the class (Tomlinson, 2000; Tomlinson, 2000b). Differentiated tasks retain an achievable level of challenge and are not repetitious engagement of only that which students have already mastered (Dixon-Krauss, 1996; Vygotsky, 1968). The most used strategy in many classrooms, especially for language learning, is differentiation of content. This requires teachers to be skilled at assessing learner capabilities and planning for new learning that builds on what is already known whilst simultaneously calculating the degree of new skill, knowledge or strategies that students can reach as an achievable challenge. Many language programmes have content that can be adapted to allow for tasks that are more complicated and increasingly longer in duration in measurable steps or degrees, whilst others can be changed to adapt or regulate the degree of cognitive complexity required to complete a task using a theoretical taxonomy such as Revised Bloom's Taxonomy (Krathwohl et al., 2001). These adapted tasks are frequently and most successfully implemented within the confines of a single classroom space, without students being 'withdrawn' from the class group or arranged into groups based on so-called 'ability'. In these learning contexts, the 'big idea' or

DOI: 10.4324/9781003207900-4

common concept that is the overall learning goal for the entire group provides a common conversation about the learning.

These content modifications are highly dependent for their success in classrooms where the school ethos is built on some foundational components of multicultural education (Banks & Banks, 2010; Howard, 2006). School ethos can be understood as the rather nebulous component of school policies and procedures. Schools which have an appreciation for diverse and multicultural perspectives integrated as an essential part of their policies and practices are more likely to have teachers who understand and appreciate the value of different ways of knowing and doing (Rauland & Adams, 2015). Banks and Banks (2010) identify five essential characteristics of schools that effectively manage multicultural education, which may be necessary as the result of immigration, students with refugee and asylum-seeker experiences and other newcomers who have diverse cultural, social and religious customs. These are categorised by Banks and Banks (2010) as follows: (i) content integration – the use of strategies to find the links between the subjects taught, the skills, knowledge and strategies that they comprise, and to connect these links to the out-of-school experiences of their students; (ii) employ 'knowledge construction' pedagogical processes – allowing students opportunities to construct their knowledge in their own ways and engaging teachers who understand that there may be multiple interpretations and ways of making meaning in their classrooms; (iii) a focus on reducing prejudice – this requires teachers who are sensitive to the fact that their own opinions and perspectives may not be shared by students and that students needing to learn differently would be accepted and respected; (iv) use of equity pedagogies – this is critical in the selection and use of resources: many books, along with other media, music and other equipment used to support language teaching and learning in classrooms prioritise the promotion of white, middle-class Eurocentric vocabulary and idiom, illustrations and acceptable cultural belief and behaviours which are frequently at odds with the diversity of student experiences; and (v) an empowering school culture – whilst the efforts of individual teachers to be supportive of difference, accepting of diverse ways of

> While it is important to develop cultural sensitivity and work respectfully with groups of students and their families whose perspectives on childcare, education, the role of the teacher and other related issues, it is also critical to remember that cultural, social, and religious norms are those applied generally the specific groups of people, there is another very realistic complication for those working directly with these communities. Irrespective of the research generalities, each family and student have their own personal preferences, opinions, concerns, customs, and habits. These may also apply to language in the form of dialects, accents, vocabulary variation, colloquiums and subtleties of language expression which may differ from group to group, village to village and which may not exactly correlate with the formal use of their standard language.

knowing and doing, and adept at differentiating tasks for their students make a difference in their classrooms, the power of a school culture that authentically embraces all five of these characteristics provides an environment where all students can thrive, irrespective of multiple degrees of difference (Sellars, 2021a, 2021b, 2021c; Sellars & Imig, 2021; Sellars & Murphy, 2018).

Research findings

We spoke with a primary school teacher in regional Australia who works in one of the nation's most diverse schools. It is a school with a long history of serving children and families with refugee and asylum-seeker backgrounds.

Context: I've been at this school since 2017. It's a very multicultural school (grades K–6) in a regional centre with around 200 students, and 70% of them are EAL/D background. Our student population is diverse, for example, we get some who have highly educated parents that are studying PhDs, and some who might have been in a refugee camp for years and might not have seen any formal schooling at all. We've got a strong cohort of Afghani students, we've got Syrian refugees that have come out of Syria, and then we've got some African families.

> It's really just being around language. In the beginning, it might be half their first language and half the English language, and then from there, it starts building everything at a really simple level. We write stories that obviously start with words. Then, from words, we get to the sentences and from sentences, we get to numerous sentences. But it just starts right at the basic level. Even if they came in year four or five, they still need to be immersed in what we would be learning in kindergarten. But you still have to make it so it has meaning to their lives. I don't want them feeling like they're doing childish work. So, I guess that's part of the challenge; finding those texts that they can read and be interested in without it being a four-year old book. It all starts with literacy. Math tends to be a little bit less of a block because numbers are more universal. Some of them don't have any formal schooling at all, but they'll have some type of general knowledge of numbers which is a little bit of a universal subject for us. Because we can make inroads and start using the language of mathematics to start building vocabulary that way. So, I guess math and literacy are the keys. When they initially come in, they still participate in the other lessons. But we're focusing on them to build the oral language first and then from there, we can extend to starting to get the formal written language.
>
> It's almost like you might be teaching year three or four, but you still need to have those fundamentals that might be given to our students that are here from the start at a kindergarten level. So, it's going back to phonics, understanding what phonemes are, sounding out and breaking apart words and just getting a breadth of vocabulary. If they can get the oral language, they can start learning to write it. So, oral language is a massive thing. If you're a new teacher, you may see some of them make the mistake of just trying to go too quickly. There's a lot of pressure with the department to put in all the

standards and expectations. But you just need to take your time with them because they will learn the language. They will catch up eventually, but it will take them a little bit longer. It might take five years for them to get that basic structure to get to that level where they feel comfortable to participate. And again, every individual is different.

Unique contexts, global principles

This Australian primary teacher was very clear about the path he takes with non-English-speaking students. Building oral language is the first order of business, and he does this by exposing newly arrived students to English for as much as half of their class time. He methodically incorporates the writing of single words, then sentences, then multiple sentences as he helps his students navigate a new language. He is mindful that all teachers in his environment must possess the core skills of reading instruction, and he is clear that this process must be engaging and age-appropriate for students. He uses mathematics to find common understandings and develop a common vocabulary among his students. This teacher works hard to find texts for his students, some who have no schooling experience at all, and who are engaging and relatable but basic in their reading level. He is concerned that many of his novice colleagues push newly arrived students too hard or too fast, and he is frustrated by the pressure the state's Department of Education places on teachers to hold students accountable for all grade-level standards and expectations. His experience gives him a clear understanding that 'every individual is different', and it can take up to five years for children with refugee and asylum-seeker backgrounds to have enough confidence in their language abilities to actively engage with the class.

Entering a new classroom with new expectations is a daunting experience for any student. But imagine entering a classroom where you don't speak a word of the language and where you may not even understand the fundamental workings of a school. That must truly be a terrifying experience for many students. The development of oral and then written language is the key to help newly arrived students begin to feel a sense of safety and belonging amongst their new peers. Teachers need to overcome the language gap by grabbing student interest and finding commonalities. Mathematics for many students is a universal language and can help spark oral language development. As our Australian teacher stressed, finding books with a high level of interest but with an appropriately challenging reading level is a must. Differentiating materials and approaches is vital but teachers must recognise that newly arrived students are each unique and cannot also be treated as a homogenous group. Having high expectations for children with refugee and asylum-seeker experiences is certainly warranted given the resilience they have shown in their life journey, yet it is important to remember that language learning can be a long process that looks very different for every child. To support this process, it is impingent upon all teachers who work with this population to understand and be capable of supporting foundational language development.

Different pathways

One of the most compelling aspects of any culture is the capacity for communicating through the arts. There are multiple ways in which language acquisition can be developed in less formal and more personally responsive learning opportunities provided by school-based activities in art, dance, music interpretation and analysis, drama sessions and engagement with media, including film and technological tools for animation. All these pursuits have language opportunities which may engage students with trauma-related backgrounds such as students with refugee and asylum-seeker experiences with vocabulary to express their most personal thoughts, their fears and their dreams and ambitions. These lessons frequently engage students in collaborative tasks, providing an avenue through which they may develop language skills from their peers, in addition to building positive relationships and new skills. This more open and inclusive language approach has been steadily growing in English-speaking learning contexts in which English language learners are educated (Anderson, 2008). Visual imagery has long associated with language development (Arizpe et al., 2014), and music has been identified as a major tool, not only for language development but also for therapy for newly arrived families and individuals with refugee backgrounds (Baker & Jones, 2006). Engaging with innovative and creative activities certainly offers more possibilities than segregated language learning groups based on English language competencies. Bal (2014) discovered that the segregated, 'ability based' groups to which newly arrived Muslim Turkish students were allocated not only significantly damaged their academic identities but in practice reduced them to the levels of learners with special cognitive needs. Conversely, several other studies found that using arts-based pedagogies not only supported the English language development of students but was powerful in changing perspectives of prejudice and bias.

Danzak (2015) found that engaging multicultural students in a photography project had multiple benefits. It changed the student's perspectives of 'difference', acknowledging that instead of being a negative aspect of collaborative activity it was immensely positive; it introduces the students to new technical skills and fostered creativity while simultaneously engaging them in effective language communications. Sellars (2021a) recorded how an arts programme in an Australian primary school specifically designed for newly arrived students with refugee and asylum-seeker backgrounds supported the English language development of the young learners and provided an avenue for telling their stories in the pictures they created. Storytelling (De La Mare, 2014), circle sharing (Emert, 2014) and conversation clubs (Sorgen, 2015) were also powerful tools for language development, immersing those who were sharing and those who were listening in language as expressed by their peers, reinforcing the importance of skills in oracy (Coultas, 2015; Gibbons, 2014) and the learning opportunities of story and dramatic expressions for students with backgrounds of oracy. Emert (2013) also explored the positive impact of digital storytelling and poetry with boys of refugee backgrounds. Several studies evidenced the impact of music on English language acquisition. Fonseca-Mora et al. (2015) combined music with phonological input for young language learners, Ludke et al. (2014) reported evidence that singing can enhance

English language development, and Moreno et al. (2015) reported that music training and learning another language provided lasting changes in the functional networks of the brain, essential for effective learning. Interestingly, Baker and Jones (2006) found that music therapy was effective in influencing the classroom behaviours of students with refugee backgrounds, providing further evidence of the impact of music on the brain and validating the positive impacts of arts pedagogical strategies for these groups of students.

> Naar de Markt (To the Market 2017) by Noëlle Smit suggested for students aged 4–7 to explore celebrating diversity (a subtheme of living together) contains several levels of signs of diversity...: From whose perspective is the visual story created? Each picture showing what is going on at the market reveals the interests of different groups of people. Stallholders want to sell their products so they are advertising them. Customers want to buy the best food and are watching the sellers and examining the food. Birds want to steal some of the food on display. Yet, the story focuses on a small girl, the only child in most of the pictures. The girl is not interested in the actions of the sellers and buyers since all of her attention is concentrated on the events on the ground: the dogs or cats who are running nearby and the birds that are eating the fish. In the book, the market is full of life, energy, and colors, which all emphasize the cultural diversity of the scene(s). The illustrations depict people with different ethnic back-grounds, skin colors, and styles of dress. This book, and its imagery of peaceful everyday life uniting people with different interests and ethnic backgrounds into a harmonious whole, can be used to discuss celebrating diversity based on equality and human rights. In the CLLP, the lesson based on To the Market included three optional tasks for the students. In one of these tasks, the teachers and students were asked to consider the sonic aspects of the scenes via questions such as: What sounds do you hear? What do people say? What languages do you hear? What sounds do animals or objects make? To create these soundscapes, students had to change the semiotic mode of the story from visual to auditory. In another task, students were asked to create a visual response to the story by identifying with the stallholders and imagining selling items at the market. In this task, the instructions directed the students to make a drawing responding to the question: What kind of goods do you decide to put on display and sell? This task was thus based on the same semiotic mode as the picture book. Students' visual response to the book in their artifacts was to present food items familiar to them, including traditional local or national dishes. (Lähdesmäki et al., 2021 p. 36–37)

Research findings

An Australian primary school teacher offered keen insights into the power of art to help foster language and relationship development for newly arrived students.

Context: I used to teach at an Australian regional primary school, with around 170 students. Before this, I was a high school teacher in special education, but also taught English and history, but I was also originally art-trained. My school received the first cohort of Afghani refugees in the region. We had 24 students arrive in two weeks. We had Pashto, Dari and Farsi speakers, Turkmans, and children who lived in Pakistan, but they were all from one country. Some of the children had been transmitted through Iran, and some came through refugee camps. Even though they were all from the same cultural background, they had different journeys.

I found art was the way that we set up the intensive English. There was a lot of art which was for their voice and that was good in terms of the writing. The ability to play in some detail drawings, the ability for me to help give English labels to some of their drawings and to tie between what they know in the English language that I needed them to start to use. It was a very powerful tool. It was everything from colours all the way through. The pictures that they were drawing allowed them to voice some of their stories through pictures and to communicate in a very basic way. It is a tool that could remain with them until they are very sophisticated in their English language. It's a universal tool for all of the students regardless of their individual trajectories, journeys and histories. It actually makes them feel the same. It helps to create that belonging because they're not different from their peers. It helps to unify the classroom and developed commonalities because of the approaches. It helps them in the labelling and the capacity to start to pull up language. If we're reading, they could draw their understanding of what actually occurred. That helps them to transfer between languages and capacity to 'if I can think I can say it, if I can say it, I can write it, if I can write it off and read it, and so can others.' That sort of thing helps them to learn to translate into, think of the English and label with English words initially before we get into the deep structures and grammars of formal English. I think writing in formal English is probably one of the most powerful gifts we can give children in the classroom.

One of my other main beliefs is experience before explicit, so I did a lot of excursions. A lot of schools do the unit of work and then the excursion at the end of it. We are doing excursion at the beginning. It's a common experience that helps them to be able to build the background knowledge. It's place-based learning and helps them learn when they are out in the real world. To have experiences that they haven't had before, and then back into the classroom and say, "remember when". They've been there, they've smelt it, they tasted it, they felt it, they walked there, they've moved through it. That adds to the geographies of self. So those sorts of things in terms of the experiences allow us to help to label everything.

Unique contexts, global principles

This teacher had a very clear process and rationale for using art with his students. With a classroom comprised of multiple children with refugee and asylum-seeker backgrounds, he used art-making as an opportunity to explicitly teach English, as a form of therapy, and to help his students feel a sense of connection in the classroom. He purposefully situated himself among his students as they created art so he could point to drawn images and label them in English, perhaps ask students to pass him a 'red marker' and question students about what they produced. He was able to extend the purpose of drawings to ask students to illustrate their perceptions of readings or discussions, and this created another opportunity to observe his students' understandings. In terms of introducing curriculum, he is adamant that experience should precede explicit instruction. Engaging in a whole-class field trip prior to learning about a topic offers his students a set of shared experiences that will inform their understanding as they then engage with and label the related concepts in class. In addition to the benefits for language development, this teacher is passionate about building belonging in his classroom, and he sees shared experiences as key to this.

The power of art-making for students with refugee and asylum-seeker backgrounds should not be underestimated. In accountability-driven school systems, art-based classroom activities are often minimised or eliminated from classroom practice, and this is unfortunate for numerous reasons. As our Australian teacher illustrates, art can support foundational language learning; it can be used to assess understandings, and it can offer newly arrived students vital opportunities to feel equal to their peers. Art allows all children to engage with the process and reduces the isolation felt by newly arrived children wrestling with the language. Further, as Danzak (2015) found, art can even provide opportunities to highlight and celebrate the difference life experiences and cultures that newly arrived students often bring. In all forms of art-making, it is necessary for teachers to purposively play a role in the process. Whether it is visual arts, making music, acting, or dancing, the classroom teacher must imbed himself/herself in the art-making to promote language development. As art offers an opportunity to give students a look into the lives of newly arrived classmates, engaged teachers can also use the process as a means to address biases and develop understandings.

Personalising language learning

There are two common ways of personalising learning that can be used to promote languageacquisition and development. These are Individual Language or Learning Plans (IEPs) or individual goal setting plans. IEPs are frequently designed for a wide range of students who have particular learning needs. These learning needs may be academic, but also may be founded in socio-emotional learning. In the case of literacy learning, these plans may be developed for students with refugee experiences who have not had the opportunity to have any school experiences in their homelands, have particular disadvantages which impact on their capacity to learn effectively in the regular differentiated interactions in class (for example, those who have sight or hearing impairments, cognitive impairments or physical damage or losses). These plans can also be collaboratively designed so that interactions with support agencies such as speech pathologists, paediatric therapists and other professionals who may be working with individual students to support their learning can use the specialist knowledge to advise and inform the planning and strategising. One of the many benefits of collaborative planning is that it regularly invites parental contributions in addition to the professional perspectives on the suitability of the planning, the appropriateness of the strategies implemented to achieve the focus learning of the plans and provides common purpose and approaches amongst all those invested in supporting the learning of the student. In cases of students with refugee and asylum-seeker experiences, these individual language plans may involve interactions with school psychologists and a range of support staff so students can acquire the language to express emotions and past experiences. The overall aim of these IEPs, however, is that the students are included as the focus of the teaching and learning in the classroom.

The second plan for individual language learning is more student centred as it involves the students themselves determining a language goal that they would personally like to achieve. These are frequently achieved goals and are planned on a framework that allows students to consider the practicality and potential of their goals. These goals are essentially different to 'ego' goals where students may aim to be the 'best' or be 'better than' others and are an introduction to self-regulated, autonomous learning that may transform their perceptions of themselves as learners (Onsando & Billett, 2009; Ridley et al., 1992; Sullivan et al., 2009; Vrugt & Oort, 2008). A *SMART* goal framework is often used in schools to facilitate the development of these goals by students. The acronym may be customised for educational contexts and can be implemented as S – specific tasks or goals that individual students would like to complete successfully, M – meaningful for the student as a valued activity or skill, A – achievable by the student as tasks that are too distant from the current competent levels are likely to be discouraging and unsuccessful, R– relevant to improvement in the area of learning on which it is focused and T – timed so aspects or increments of the task can be regularly self-monitored for progress towards task completion. SMART goals have been credited with not only strengthening the cognitive skills of executive function (Meltzer, 2007; Meltzer et al., 2007) but also providing opportunities for students to develop self-knowledge about their own learning strengths, strategies and capacities known as metacognition (Carretti et al., 2014; Cornoldi et al., 2015; Kuhn & Dean, 2004). Setting *SMART* goals is a particularly useful strategy for students with refugee and

> Many tutors spoke of the lack of consideration shown by classroom teachers for these students. "There was no kind of consideration for the fact that they had only been at the school for a short time, or that they had issues or anything like that. It was just like 'you are going to get zeros, but try and get it done and get an award." Other tutors mentioned the number and complexity of the assignments refugee students were given. "They were bombarded with assignments. …every week they had two or three assignments to complete, and knowing that they have literacy difficulties that was very hard to overcome." Other tutors spoke of the challenges involved in explaining concepts, ideas or words for which the students have no cultural context. For example, you read through a passage and you expect them to understand

> particular things, but how do you explain Snow White to someone or the cultural significance of it, or the associated meaning?
>
> In these passages we see examples of the defamiliarization King (2004) identified as critical to transformational learning. Defamiliarization is the process by which what is known and familiar becomes strange, and what is strange becomes familiar. We see the switch that has occurred as the tutors speak quite heatedly of the difficulty of the assignments given to students, and the indifference of many teachers to the learning needs of refugee students......Although they were committed to learning and initially highly motivated, once they were moved from the IEC into regular classrooms, they found that they didn't understand the subjects being discussed, the implicit knowledges underlying the lessons, or the language used in the assignments. Some of them became extremely frustrated. (Vickers & McCarthy, 2010 p. 206)

asylum-seeker experiences. Their past experiences may have proven to be traumatic, but for many they also promoted the personal traits of resourcefulness, persistence in the face of difficulty and resilience, all of which are critical to self-regulated learning. All students are influenced by social and cultural motivators when setting and strategising their learning goals, and employ their relative strengths as a means to achieving them (Sellars, 2003). For students with dissimilar backgrounds and language experiences, goal setting provides opportunities for diverse ways of thinking and learning to achieve language competencies.

Research findings

We spoke with a teacher in the United States who works in a large high school outside of a major city that serves a very diverse and low-income population of students. This school has adopted a consistent approach across classes and grades to develop student skills.

Context: I teach ninth and tenth grades at a high school in the US. This is my seventh year in teaching. Our population is 85% Latino students with the majority coming from Central America. Our largest population this year is Guatemalan followed by Salvadorean and Honduran, and, then, it kind of goes down from there. And then our second largest group is of refugee students. So they represent Afghanistan, Iraq and Syria and we have a little bit of a smaller population that are some of the African countries from East and West Africa, Ethiopia and Congo. Roughly 95% of our student population identifies as low income and receives free and reduced lunch.

> We are a competency-based school. We teach students based on a core skill set. We have rubrics, the critical thinking skills, content skills, and language skills. So, I don't teach from a set curriculum, but my colleagues who teach math, science and social studies have the State curriculum that they have to

follow. Our goal is to create projects and more hands-on experiences for students to touch on those skills and give students a chance to show mastery in a skill without language getting in the way.

An example of this for math might be like designing a theme park. They have to go through the steps of the couple of different days of math to decide "how big does my grid have to be? what's the scale of my slide? if I want this to fit here?" Conversely, the science teacher might also try to be involved in something similar. The science teacher might think of "well, what's some of the physics that has to go along with that?" So, students are kind of getting it across.

So, we all use the same rubric. For example, a rubric for the skill of 'compare and contrast' is going to be identical in my class and their science class and their math class. It's never going to change the requirement there, so they know what they have to do. We follow that to build our projects and curriculum. We also have similar structures that we follow for language like writing or writing processes which is called Statement Evidence Analysis (SEA). When they get a little older in the 11th grade, they add an 'L' and call it (SEAL), and it's linking back to the beginning. We also have phrases like 'restate the question'. These are common practices that we all use.

We also have a phrase called "level up" that was started in our language classes from ESL to push kids to the next level in their language. We use our language rubric of like "Okay, now you want to write and say more, let's level up. Here's what you need to do. You need to have compound and complex sentences. You need to have longer paragraphs. I need to hear your own voice." We applied that across the school. So, now other teachers use that language to level up. A project will have a level up option. We say, "you have some outside sources in your compare and contrast and you're hitting this part of the history content that you have to hit. Now, let's try to level up. Can you apply this to a real-world situation for something in the skill of compare and contrast?" Our rubrics are one to five, with five being college and career ready. So, in that way, we are all following the same practices for the rubric.

Unique contexts, global principles

This teacher works in a school that has embraced a 'whole of school' approach to supporting and measuring student learning. With a shared language, shared rubrics and some shared projects, this teacher and her colleagues have created a culture where students know what is expected, and they play an active role in their own learning. She is purposeful in her curriculum development to provide opportunities for students to demonstrate skills without their lack of English getting in the way. This was illustrated by having her students develop a theme park. This hands-on and creative project enabled them to demonstrate mastery of multiple math and science concepts without the need for English explanations. Additionally, by having a shared rubric across subjects and a shared language (e.g. 'level up'), students can demonstrate mastery and self-monitor across classes. It's notable that the language learning rubric described by the teacher expands as students matriculate through the years. Such a tool ensures that the cross subject collaboration that occurs at this unique school is also a cross-grade collaborative process. It is also important to note the rubric used across this school has an endpoint equivalent to 'college and career ready' sending a powerful message to students about their own potential and the school's commitment to their future.

Goal setting has been found to be particularly useful for children with refugee and asylum-seeker backgrounds. This may be a by-product of being resilient, or it may be an attempt by these children to find order when there are so many uncertainties in life. Regardless, providing students opportunities to clearly know what is expected and offering ways to plot their own growth is a powerful motivator for learning. Further, when coupled with projects and learning opportunities that do not penalise students for having limited English language abilities, this approach can be empowering for students. Our US high school teacher works in a school that has embraced a common language and common measures across grades and subjects. This whole-school approach to monitoring student learning promotes shared understandings among all staff – something that is truly rare in many large high schools. The flow-on effects of consistent expectations and collaborative educators is a school environment that helps to reduce anxiety, promotes risk-taking and sparks creativity for all children.

Conclusion

Despite the many accountabilies and responsibilities which are loaded on teachers daily and at an increasing rate as neoliberalised education increases its influence on the teaching and learning interactions in classrooms, students with refugee and asylum-seeker experiences are entitled to an education from which they can glean meaning, grow intellectually and find multiple ways of knowing and doing. Differentiation is not difficult in many educational contexts. The participants in this were working in ways that they found were advantageous for their students whilst fulfilling the mandates of systems. All students can learn. It is the professional and ethical responsibility of teachers to support learning for all students. Sometimes that means looking at the teaching and learning interactions differently.

References

Anderson, J. (2008). Towards an integrated second-language pedagogy for foreign and community/heritage languages in multilingual Britain. *Language Learning Journal*, 36(1), 79–89. https://doi.org/10.1080/09571730801988553

Arizpe, E., Bagelman, C., Devlin, A. M., Farrell, M., & McAdam, J. E. (2014). Visualizing intercultural literacy: Engaging critically with diversity and migration in the classroom through an image-based approach. *Language and Intercultural Communication*, 14(3), 304–321. https://doi.org/10.1080/14708477.2014.903056

Baker, F., & Jones, C. (2006). The effect of music therapy services on classroom behaviours of newly arrived refugee students in Australia—a pilot study. *Emotional and Behavioural Difficulties*, 11(4), 249–260. https://doi.org/10.1080/13632750601022170

Bal, A. (2014). Becoming in/competent learners in the United States: Refugee students' academic identities in the figured world of difference. *International Multilingual Research Journal, 8*(4), 271–290. https://doi.org/10.1080/19313152.2014.952056

Banks, J., & Banks, C. (2010). *Multicultural Education: Issues and Perspectives* (10th ed.). Wiley.

Carretti, B., Caldarola, N., Tencati, C., & Cornoldi, C. (2014, June). Improving reading comprehension in reading and listening settings: the effect of two training programmes focusing on metacognition and working memory. *British Journal of Educational Psychology, 84*(Pt 2), 194–210. https://doi.org/10.1111/bjep.12022

Cornoldi, C., Carretti, B., Drusi, S., & Tencati, C. (2015). Improving problem polving in primary school students: The effect of a training programme focusing on metacognition and working memory. *British Journal of Educational Psychology, 85*(3), 424–439. http://ezproxy.newcastle.edu.au/login?url=http://search.ebscohost.com/login.aspx?direct=true&db=eric&AN=EJ1071494&site=eds-live http://dx.doi.org/10.1111/bjep.12083

Coultas, V. (2015). Revisiting debates on oracy: Classroom talk – moving towards a democratic pedagogy? *Changing English, 22*(1), 72–86. https://doi.org/10.1080/1358684x.2014.992205

Danzak, R. L. (2015). "Sometimes the perspective changes": Reflections on a photography workshop with multicultural students in Italy. *International Journal of Multicultural Education, 17*(3), 56–75. http://search.ebscohost.com/login.aspx?direct=true&db=ehh&AN=111174234&site=eds-live

De La Mare, D. M. (2014). Communicating for diversity: Using teacher discussion groups to transform multicultural education. *Social Studies, 105*(3), 138–144. https://doi.org/10.1080/00377996.2013.859118

Dixon-Krauss, L. (1996). *Vygotsky in the Classroom: Mediated Literacy Instruction and Assessment*. Longman Publishers USA.

Emert, T. (2013, 08/01). 'The Transpoemations Project': Digital storytelling, contemporary poetry, and refugee boys. *Intercultural Education, 24*(4), 355–365. https://doi.org/10.1080/14675986.2013.809245

Emert, T. (2014). "Hear a Story, Tell a Story, Teach a Story": Digital narratives and refugee middle schoolers. *Voices From the Middle, 21*(4), 33–39. http://search.proquest.com/docview/1519055930?accountid=10499

Fonseca-Mora, M. C., Jara-Jiménez, P., & Gómez-Domínguez, M. (2015). Musical plus phonological input for young foreign language readers. *Frontiers in Psychology, 6*, 1–9. https://doi.org/10.3389/fpsyg.2015.00286

Gibbons, S. (2014). The importance of oracy. In S. Brindley & B. Marshan (Eds.), *MasterClass in English education: Transforming teaching and learning* (pp. 186–193). Bloomsbury Publishing. http://site.ebrary.com/lib/newcastle/docDetail.action?docID=10962762

Howard, G. (2006). *We Can't Teach What We Don't Know* (2nd ed.). Teachers College Press.

Krathwohl, D. R., Anderson, L. W., & Bloom, B. S. (Eds.). (2001). *A Taxonomy for Learning, Teaching, and Assessing: A Revision of Bloom's Taxonomy of Educational Objectives* (complete ed.). Longman.

Kuhn, D., & Dean, D. (2004, Autumn). Metacognition: A bridge between cognitive sychology and educational practice. *Theory Into Practice, 43*(4), 268–274.

Lähdesmäki, T., Baranova, J., Ylönen, S., Koistinen, A., Mäkinen, K., & Zaleskienė, V. (2021). *Learning Cultural Literacy throughCreative Practicesin Schools: Cultural and Multimodal Approaches toMeaning-Making*. Palgrave Macmillan. https://doi.org/10.1007/978-3-030-89236-4

Ludke, K., Ferreira, F., & Overy, K. (2014). Singing can facilitate foreign language learning. *Memory & Cognition, 42*(1), 41–52. https://doi.org/10.3758/s13421-013-0342-5

Meltzer, L. (2007). Executive function: Theoretical and conceptual frameworks. In L. Meltzer (Ed.), *Executive Function in Education: From Theory to Practice* (pp. 1–4). The Guildford Press.

Meltzer, L., Pollica, L., & Barzillai, M. (2007). Executive function in the classroom: Embedding strategy into everyday teaching practices. In L. Meltzer (Ed.), *Executive Function in Education: From Theory to Practice* (pp. 165–193). The Guildford Press.

Moreno, S., Lee, Y., Janus, M., & Bialystok, E. (2015, March–April). Short-term second language and music training induces lasting functional brain changes in early childhood. *Child Development, 86*(2), 394–406. https://doi.org/10.1111/cdev.12297

Onsando, G., & Billett, S. (2009, 12/01). African students from refugee backgrounds in Australian TAFE institutes: A case for transformative learning goals and processes. *International Journal of Training Research, 7*(2), 80–94. https://doi.org/10.5172/ijtr.7.2.80

Rauland, C., & Adams, T. (2015, Winter). A stronger smarter future: Multicultural education in Australia. *Reclaiming Children & Youth, 23*(4), 30–35. http://ezproxy.newcastle.edu.au/login?url=http://search.ebscohost.com/login.aspx?direct=true&db=ehh&AN=101298274&site=eds-live

Ridley, D. S., Schutz, P. A., Glanz, R. S., & Weinstein, C. E. (1992). Self-regulated learning: The interactive influence of metacognitive awareness and goal-setting. *The Journal of Experimental Education, 60*(4), 293–306. https://doi.org/10.1080/00220973.1992.9943867

Sellars, M. (2003). *Using Students' Strengths to Support Learning Outcomes: A Study of the Development of Gardner's Intrapersonal Intelligence to Support Increased Academic Achievement for Primary School Students*. [Research, Australian Catholic University], Sydney.

Sellars, M. (2021a). Being and belonging: Developing inclusive ethos. *International Journal of Leadership in Education.*

Sellars, M. (2021b). Integrating students with refugee and asylum seeker backgrounds into school: Teachers perspectives. In M. Carmo (Ed.), *Education Applications and Developments VI* (Vol. VI, pp. 291–300). InScience Press.

Sellars, M. (2021c). Planning for belonging: Including refugee and asylum seeker students. *Journal of Refugee Studies, May*, 1–13. https://doi.org/10.1093/jrs/feab073

Sellars, M., & Imig, S. (2021). School leadership, reflective practice, and education for students with refugee backgrounds: a pathway to radical empathy. *Intercultural Education*, 1–13. https://doi.org/10.1080/14675986.2021.1889988

Sellars, M., & Murphy, H. (2018). Becoming Australian: A review of southern Sudanese students' educational experiences. *International Journal of Inclusive Education, 22*(5), 490–509. https://doi.org/10.1080/13603116.2017.1373308

Sorgen, A. (2015). Integration through participation: The effects of participating in an English conversation club on refugee and asylum seeker integration. *Applied Linguistics Review, 6*(2), 241–260. https://doi.org/10.1515/applirev-2015-0012

Sullivan, P., Youdale, R., & Jorgensen, R. (2009). Knowing where you are going helps you know how to get there. *Australian Primary Mathematics Classroom, 14*(4), 4–10. http://0-web.ebscohost.com.library.newcastle.edu.au/ehost/detail?vid=6&sid=4c8786f5-424e-46c9-8006-c77b8a6d726e%40sessionmgr115&hid=123&bdata=JnNpdGU9ZWhvc3QtbGl2ZQ%3d%3d#db=a9h&AN=48850959

Tomlinson, C. (2000). Differentiation of instruction in the elementary grades. *Eric Digest*. Retrieved December 12, 2012, from http://ecap.crc.illinois.edu/eecearchive/digests/2000/tomlin00.pdf

Tomlinson, C. A. (2000b). Reconcilable differences? *Educational Leadership, 58*(1), 1–7.

Vickers, M. H., & McCarthy, F. E. (2010). Repositioning refugee students from the margins to the centre of teachers' work. *International Journal of Diversity in Organisations,*

Communities & Nations, *10*(2), 199–210. http://search.ebscohost.com/login.aspx?direct=true&db=sih&AN=65534342&site=eds-live

Vrugt, A., & Oort, F. J. (2008). Metacognition, achievement goals, study strategies and academic achievement: Pathways to achievement. *Metacognition and Learning, 3*(2), 123–146. http://www.scopus.com/inward/record.url?eid=2-s2.0-47149085611&partnerID=40&md5=5ad9cec1eb072e1261b7de22f1c8bb91

Vygotsky, L. S. (1968). *The Problem of Consciousness*. Retrieved August 23, from http://www.markists.org/archive/vygotsky/works/1934/problem-consciousness.htm

4 Communicating effectively

Introduction

Learning the language of the new homeland has been a priority for students with refugee and asylum-seeker backgrounds (Anders, 2012; Creagh, 2016; Due et al., 2015; Naidoo, 2009; Osterling, 1998; Sanatullov & Sanatullova-Allison, 2012; Taylor, 2008). While this is undoubtedly critical to integration, communicating effectively requires more than the knowledge of and structure of a language. Ranta and Harmawati (2017, p. 1) define communicating as 'simply the act of transferring information from one place to another'. They emphasise the critical importance of verbal and non-verbal language in classroom interactions, determining that both the teacher and the students engage in both to communicate effectively with each other. Languages such as English have many idiomatic phrases that are dependent on the context for interpretation. It also has many words that are visually and phonetically identical but have different meanings in diverse circumstances. To add to the complexity, English is, like other languages, dependent on the tone of the spoken word and text, the ways in which the interaction is conducted and demeanour of those participating, illustrating the need to understand the role of non-verbal communicative actions and postures in addition to mastering the complexity of the language itself. Communicating effectively with communities and students with refugee and asylum-seeker backgrounds is complex and requires sensitivity and skill, bodily awareness and an emphatic approach to ways in which the mood and tone of the communication is interpreted by those whose experiences include displacement, trauma and, frequently, extreme violence and persecution. In many instances, the critical components of effective communication are being perceptive regarding cultural variations in the interpretation of body language and facial expression, self-discipline in the ways interactions are conducted and the ongoing process of building respectful, positive relationships.

Cultural differences

While some educational systems encourage schools in their jurisdiction to simply identify their students with refugee and asylum backgrounds merely as 'new arrivals', it is important for the teachers who interact with these students and their

DOI: 10.4324/9781003207900-5

communities to have some knowledge, not only of their language needs but also of their homelands, their customs and their ways of communicating respectfully. Much of this cultural difference may be expressed through religious beliefs which impact on the ways in which communication can be observed as appropriate and courteous. Explaining some of the most taken-for-granted aspects of school life may take considerable tact and diplomacy. English-speaking countries, despite claiming to be multicultural in various degrees, are heavily influenced by Christian beliefs and values. These permeate the school systems, not only in policies but also with respect to holidays and celebrations. Communicating these routines and mandatory practices to non-Christian groups, many of whom may have had unpleasant experiences with Christian militants in ways that are respectful and accepting of their religious and cultural beliefs and values, their traumatic experiences, and their hopes for inclusion in these school communities often require more than carefully selected words (Collet, 2014; Nawyn, 2006; Ní Raghallaigh & Sirriyeh, 2015; Wilding, 2012). It necessitates that even the most simple and basic communicative gestures are carefully considered and that situations that challenge teachers' own beliefs and values are met with understanding and acceptance. Arguably, those particularly at risk of inadvertently communicating disapproval or distaste may be teachers who are female and are attempting to communicate effectively with parents who have strict religious codes or are from highly patriarchal societies that challenge the rights and status that western women have worked to establish for decades. There are many examples of common western practices which may challenge or offend those from other cultural beliefs. Some Islamic groups, for example, cannot accept an outstretched hand for a handshake, particularly from a female teacher or principal. Other cultural and religious systems of hierarchy frown upon women taking the lead in conversation, having questions addressed specifically to them and even meeting with anyone in authority without a significant male accompanying them as a spokesperson. While it may be commonplace for young Muslim girls to wear a hijab once they reach puberty, conversations around this convention, whether initiated by classroom peers or teachers, should effectively focus on the rights of these girls to modesty and feminine identity (Al Wazni, 2015). Other religious clothing may also need to be discussed in terms of religious freedom and identity. For example, it is offensive to Sikh groups to have others touch their turbans, or head coverings and top knots for younger Sikhs, because it is a religious article of clothing and so needs the permission of the wearer. Young Sikhs from about the age of 13 years frequently wear full turbans. Many cultural views on child-rearing confront western ways of interacting with children and young people (Hall, 1976). Notions of praise and discipline can frequently be very different to those employed in school communities in the new homelands of students with refugee and asylum experiences (Gustafson & Iluebbey, 2013; McInnis, 1991; McMichael et al., 2011). The lack of physical punishment, the helplessness of teachers to regulate behaviours and the resultant discord between student and community expectations and regulations in western schools not only create an unwelcome perspective regarding western schooling for some communities with refugee and asylum-seeker experiences but also necessitate clear, non-judgemental, effective communication (Sanatullov & Sanatullova-Allison, 2012).

> Whilst interpreters are a critical support in the initial meetings with teachers and principals and may retain this role for quite some time, they must also be aware of the need to communicate effectively. As trained professionals, they need to be qualified to mimic the tone and content of the conversation authentically without personal input and with an accuracy of the language that demonstrates an understanding of the complexity of the language, idioms and colloquialisms. They must also be able to advise and implement traditional ways of communicating respectfully. Examples of cultural ways of engaging in conversation include prefacing any serious business with several minutes of small talk and understanding the need for many women to ask permission from their male relative before venturing to speak. Additionally, there are protocols around working with an interpreter. The teacher must always maintain eye contact with the person from whom they are seeking the information. It is not considered appropriate to address the interpreter when asking questions or making comments. It is respectful to keep the communication between the teacher and the individual for whom the interpreter is employed.

Research findings

We spoke with a veteran primary teacher in regional Australia who spent many years working with newly arrived Afghan refugee students and their families.

Context: I have been teaching for nearly 18 years. Currently, I am working in assistant principal role as well as teaching. We're very well known for our highly differentiated curriculum and personalised learning goals for each student. We make lots of adjustments for the students to be successful. We have lots of EAL/D support staff to help develop our students with oral language. We do lots of professional learnings.

> I think it's really important to learn some key phrases from the languages that you're going to be having students. Phrases like 'come here, sit down, toilet, food, water'. I found that some of those basic need type phrases in their home language are extremely helpful. The next thing I would probably say is to really take note of the environment of your classroom. "Is it too chaotic? Do you have safe spaces for them to go, something like a tent? Sometimes they can even fall asleep because they're exhausted and one day probably going to have some sort of jet lag type experience?" I wouldn't even be focusing on the academic straightaway. Because there's no teaching academic, if they're not going to engage with you and they're going to shut off or stand and scream. I think relationships and making them know that they're safe is really important.
>
> Spend lots of time with them. I know they are really simple things like having toys. They're coming with nothing, and you often find that they like to sneak things into their bags because they find it so special. We really take

things for granted over here and are entitled to some degree that kids just get everything and anything. Having a few things can really make a transition into Australia really comforting.

Doing some research into their culture. For example, Sunni Muslims fighting with Shias. Or Afghans might come from the same country, but Pashto speakers have got that hierarchy over some other speakers. Just be aware of that there are some more dominant families and kids that you're going to get out of the same country compared to some others. That explains some behaviours, some back stories of some different families in terms of trauma. Just be delving big into their cultural background and then setting up your classroom to be a safe environment. Make pleasefsure there's no loud noises happening that can trigger past thoughts. You might have to allow them to be with their siblings even if they aren't in the same class, if that's what it means to for them to feel safe. Let them eat and drink whenever they want because they're not going to understand. Just be flexible to their needs. Rather than trying to get them to fit in with, you fit in with them.

Unique contexts, global principles

This Australian primary school teacher is keenly aware of meeting the foundational needs of her newly arrived students. Understanding keywords and phrases in her students' home languages, including *food, water* and *toilet* is a must. She recognises that being in a new setting, with new rules and a new language can be exhausting for her students, and she has provided a safe space, a tent, where students can escape, and rest as needed. Academic learning is not her initial concern, and she is flexible about allowing students to eat and drink when they want. She has even rearranged schedules to allow siblings in different classes and across grades to have lunch together. Her initial emphasis is on developing communication, creating a connection and learning all she can about her students. This teacher is aware that many of her students may have lost everything they owned during the migration to her classroom, and she is sympathetic to their behaviours, even behaviours like taking items from the classroom. She has learned a great deal about the home countries and cultures of her students. She understands that some of her families may be more vocal or assertive, while others may be passive and quiet, because of social hierarchies in their homeland.

Being acknowledged and understood is a foundational human need. Teachers need to prepare for the arrival of children with refugee and asylum-seeker experiences by making an effort to learn keywords and expressions in the students' home language. By meeting a newly arrived student using the correct pronunciation of his or her name and labelling a few items and behaviours in that child's home language, teachers can help alleviate anxiety and start to build a relationship. This effort must also include an exploration of basic concepts related to student's home countries and cultures. This knowledge is vital as it helps teachers understand differences among newly arrived students and explanations for the behaviours of students and their families. Our Australian teacher understands the exhaustion that can arise for children experiencing such an unfamiliar context, and she has provided a safe space in her classroom, given them flexibility and changed her schedule to meet their needs. It is not enough to provide instruction and expect newly arrived children to fit into a school culture; rather, teachers need to listen to these students and flex to meet their needs.

Not simply words

Understanding the cultural expectations of communities from other cultural backgrounds is only part of the communication process. Apart from how messages are verbally conveyed, the body language and facial expression of the teacher hold messages that may be misinterpreted and cause difficulties in the communicative process (Damonhouri, 2018). Avoiding any of these misunderstandings requires self-discipline in terms of letting negative emotions become apparent to the parents, caregivers and students themselves. It also requires a deep empathetic understanding of these communities and impacts of their experiences pre-displacement, during displacement and on the subsequent journey and arrival in their new homelands. Resat (2019) discusses the cultural differences in the ways that handshakes, hand gestures, eye contact, head movements, physical contact and sitting position are interpreted in different cultures. Knowledge of the cultural backgrounds of communities and students with refugee and asylum-seeker experiences is an important aspect of effective communication. In her detailed explanation of how each of these aspects of body language is perceived in different communities and cultures, Resat (2019) remarks on the complexity and sophistication of many of these rules, especially those pertaining to physical contact. She comments that in matters of physical contact 'the majority of those rules depend on the status, gender, profession, and ethnicity of the individual' (p. 36). Pranowo (2019, p. 42) attests that there are three types of non-verbal body language. One type can stand on its own without language and is the type of signalling often used by children who are communicating without speaking each other's language. These include sign language, symbols, gesturing, pointing and hand and eye movement. The second type is body movements that are used in a cultural context. Both he terms 'dynamic non-verbal communications'. The final type is what he terms 'static non-verbal communication', and in this category he includes body posture, facial features, hair colour and other attributes which contribute to clarifying the individual's social status and intellectual capacity. He considers non-verbal communication to be cultural behaviours, which not only clarify the communication but emphasise the need for teachers to have sound knowledge and deep understanding of the cultural background of those with whom they are communicating. Introductions to communicative events where teachers are wearing facial expressions that may convey annoyance, irritation, weariness or impatience, irrespective of the cause of that emotion, have the potential to negatively influence communication. School staff interactions with these traumatised cohorts who have learned that, in the absence of a shared language, their very survival may be dependent on interpreting the facial and body language of those with whom they must interact cannot afford to display any negativity or reluctance in their non-verbal behaviours if they seek to engage effectively with their communities and students who have refugee and asylum-seeker experiences. A conscious and disciplined effort to reflect on the experiences that brought these groups to their new homelands is critical for effective communication as an expression of acceptance and empathy (Ratcliffe, 2012).

> The principal stood in the playground chatting to some newly arrived parents. They were some of the fathers of his students with refugee and asylum seeker experiences. Always welcoming and proud of his strategies to demonstrate the inclusivity of his school community, he was trying to make these newcomers feel comfortable. Unconsciously, he changed his stance, provoking an unintended response from one of the fathers. Years of hypervigilance had made the man tense his fist and raise his arm as a reaction to the unexpected move. Whilst the incident did not have any adverse consequences, it did serve to illustrate both the need to be sensitive to the experiences of these cohorts and their subsequent interpretation of body language, in this case, as a non-verbal communication of threat or danger.

Research findings

We spoke with a passionate high school teacher in the United States who shared insights about connecting with and empowering her students, many of whom had traumatic life experiences on the way to her classroom.

Context: I've been teaching at this school for three years now. Almost all of our students are from Guatemala, Honduras and El Salvador. Many of them arrived here as unaccompanied minors. A lot of my students have experienced sexual assaults in their home countries, on their way here and then in this country as well. I teach a heterogeneous class of English with nine to ten students together in the same room. These are students who are totally across the spectrum and language level. Some of them are newcomers, some have interrupted education and some are just about to exit the ESL system.

> My approach each day with the kids, especially with such a big variety of skills, is very strengths-based. It looks at what my students can do every day instead of focusing on where they struggle or what they can't do. That's absolutely where I begin. In all of my planning, I try to make sure before I go into anything, there's some type of background building that unlocks students' prior knowledge. So, they can not only make a connection with the content and see the relevancy which can be sometimes tricky like literature, but also to get their confidence up. Especially in English class which to them is probably their most intimidating class, so that they feel confident and connected to the content before we try to dive into it. Because we do have students from various countries and educational backgrounds, I do spend probably the first month of the school year doing activities like community building and relationship building. Some of it may be mildly disguised as simple as content

stuff, sentence writing, and putting periods at the end, but that helps a lot because students are expected to collaborate a lot.

I just really love to see how much my kids grow, especially with regards to their confidence and finding a place that they can call home. When they first get here, they have so much going on in their lives. When they think of home, I'm sure their home country will always be home for them. But when we get to the point where you start to see that a classroom is becoming a home to them, their relationships they are making with peers are really genuine and their future plans that they're making are based on things that they're learning in your class. Seeing them grow socially and emotionally, not just with maturity but in general. How they're processing everything is probably the most rewarding thing and how they're finding their voice to tell their stories. There's a reason that's a big thing in my department. Not just because it turns into eventually their college application essays, but it's just an important part of being an immigrant in this country to find your voice and own your narrative and use it to empower yourself and others.

Unique contexts, global principles

This American teacher brings a uniquely positive perspective to her students and her teaching. As she plans for and delivers content to her academically diverse classes, she first looks for ways to honour students' prior knowledge and experiences in the process. As was the case with nearly every educator we interviewed, she allocates a significant amount of class time to developing relationships and communication with and among her students. She is keenly observant and attuned to the fact that her students may still long for their home countries and agonise over the families many left behind. As many of her students may have arrived unaccompanied, she works to make her classroom a home for them. She recognises that trauma continues to shape their lives, and is focused on helping her students find their voice to tell their own stories. Her academic department shares the belief that they need to help their newly arrived students understand their own cultures and experiences and own those to inspire others. This teacher's rather nonchalant observation that finding a voice helps her students complete their college essays is reflective of the strength-based approach she takes in all of her student interactions.

While students with refugee and asylum-seeker backgrounds have undoubtedly experienced great trauma and need extensive support, approaching them with an asset-based mindset offers an opportunity to immediately honour and value them as individuals. As our high school teacher in the United States demonstrated, shaping dialogue and lessons around the experiences and understandings of newly arrived students helps to draw them in and engage them with what is happening in the classroom. At its foundation, educating newly arrived students is about helping them feel safe and welcome and then building language and educational knowledge. But education is much more than these foundational practices; it is also about empowering students and helping them find their own voice uniquely shaped by their own experiences. Teachers need to remain keen observers, listeners and active participants in the classroom, and they need to stay attuned to the role they play in shaping lives. Effective communication in the classroom is more than being explicit; it is about shaping opportunities for students to demonstrate their understandings and offering appropriate verbal and non-verbal responses.

Building positive relationships

Positive relationships are important for effective communication. For classroom teachers, this means building positive relationships, not friendships, with students, their parents and, frequently, their wider communities. This is in addition to cultivating positive peer relationships with the other teachers, principal and school support staff. While friendship is recognised as a critical aspect of psychological wellbeing (Correa-Velez et al., 2010; McMichael et al., 2011; Omar et al., 2017; Seligman, 2004, 2011; Sulaiman-Hill & Thompson, 2010; Ziaian et al., 2018), it is not always possible or even desirable to be friends with everyone in a professional context. There are many reasons for this, including those relating to cultural, legal and professional standards. Anderson and Fowers (2020) found that friendships were important both in terms of companionship and life satisfaction and in helping individuals to experience a life well lived as part of their interactions. Developing positive relationships with individuals in professional contexts where there may be multiple degrees of difference in many of the interactions that are experienced requires a different perspective and an approach that relies less on developing friendships and more on following a set of guidelines that focus on the characteristics of mutual respect and acceptance. One such model which has been found to support positive interactions between all members of a school community in which multiple, diverse communities of refugee and asylum-seeker students were enrolled (Sellars, 2021) is the SCARF model (Rock, 2008, 2009; Rock & Cox, 2012).

Designed as a model to support effective business collaboration, SCARF is an acronym for the components of interactions which neuroscientific evidence has been able to establish promote positive reactions in the brain. Relationships which are developed with attention to attributing *Status* to students and parents with refugee and asylum-seeking experiences, allowing them to develop *Certainty*, promoting *Autonomy*, providing experiences of *Relatedness* and emphasising the importance of *Fairness* have proven to be particularly effective in educational settings where these cohorts may have otherwise been viewed through a rather negative lens. In classroom and school contexts, attributing *Status* to these students and their families should not be difficult. Whilst they may not initially have the language, school experiences or academic competencies of their homeland peers, they have much to teach school communities about resilience, innovation, hope and determination (Alford, 2014; Banki, 2012; Cassidy & Gow, 2005; Correa-Velez et al., 2010; Emert, 2014; Essomba, 2017; Hope, 2008; Kohli, 2006; Zsófia, 2018). The notion of *Certainty* contributes to positive relationships in a very powerful manner. It depends exclusively on the students and communities relying on the ways in which they will be greeted and treated in the classroom and in the school. It relies on teachers ensuring that they are consistent in their welcoming, their appreciation and their acceptance of diverse communities and the skills and attributes they bring to the classroom. In many instances, this is aptly demonstrated by those who engage with 'pedagogies of love' (Arar et al., 2018; Green & Tucker, 2011; Noddings, 2005; Sellars, 2020a, 2021; Sellars & Imig, 2021a, 2021b; Wilkinson & Kaukko, 2020; Zaidi et al., 2021).

Autonomy is not a characteristic which is commonly associated with western school systems (Sellars & Imig, 2020). Very little is left to choice in educational institutions (Foucault, 1977; Foucault, 1979a, 1979b). Many families and communities have had little choice but to leave their homelands. They had no choice about where and how they arrived in new homelands, which schools their children and young people attended or how they were placed when they arrived at school. The compulsory, conventional culture of many schools could easily perpetuate this situation. However, there are circumstances where appropriate pedagogical strategies and administrative processes are able to afford some degrees of autonomy to these students and their families (Arizpe et al., 2014; Dooley, 2009; Dooley & Thangaperumal, 2011; Emert, 2013; Matthews, 2008; Miller, 2009; Miller et al., 2014; Naidoo, 2009; Strekalova-Hughes & Wang, 2019; Windle & Miller, 2012). School routines around uniforms, play areas, lunchtime procedures, parent communication and involvement in teaching and learning activities are frequently based on unproven principles and traditional practice. Schools with sensitive leadership and classroom practices can readily provide opportunities for students and parents in refugee and asylum-seeker communities to regain some degree of autonomy by providing choices, altering routines and pedagogical practices to facilitate multiple ways of knowing and doing.

Involving these students and parents in the activities of the wider school community is a foundational step to facilitating a sense of *Relatedness*. Equally important are the multiple everyday practices that allow these families to feel that they are part of the community (Bradley & Sellars, 2020; Imig et al., 2022; Sellars, 2020b; Sellars & Murphy, 2017). Many teachers have their own strategies, developed as a result of understanding the ways in which these students and their families could easily feel marginalised in the context of western educational expectations and demands (Sellars, 2020a). These strategies may include learning words of greeting in the languages and dialects that are the students' first language, learning about homelands with the objective of bringing relevance to their lesson contents and to less formal occasions, organising integrated cultural activities, not as tokenistic endeavours, but as genuine reflections of the diversity of the school community. There are many actions that teachers can take to create the sense of belonging that is reflected as *Relatedness* (Antoniou & Zembylas, 2018; Correa-Velez et al., 2010; Edgeworth, 2013; Hunpage & Marston, 2006; Oikonomidoy, 2009; Sellars, 2021; Sorgen, 2015).

The concept of *Fairness* is culturally mediated and, as such, is highly dependent on effective communicative strategies during discussions about policies and the judgements and decisions that emanate from them (Green & Edwards-Underwood, 2015). In combination with the other characteristics of the *SCARF* model, this aspect depends on the student and family perceptions of how they are treated in general. In this way, the characteristics of the model impact one on the other and allow for positive communication and negotiation in matters related to *Fairness*, finding some common ground and understanding of what this important aspect of collaboration means in the context of both the system and school accountabilities and the worldviews of the diverse populations that comprise the educational community, especially the teachers who are primary educators and communicators with both parents and students.

The neuroscientific information facilitated by the development of the *f*RMI scanners which can record the metabolic functioning of the brain led to the development of the SCARF model of collaboration and communication. While it has been acknowledged that brain reacts to threat and rewards, it has been more recently confirmed that the brain reacts to social threats and rewards in addition to the traditional 'fight or flight response' of physical threat or the rewards of social acknowledgement (Lieberman & Eisenberger, 2009). It also provided evidence that the capacity to make decisions is decreased in times of stress or threat in social situations (Elliot, 2008; Fredrickson, 2000) and that the stress response is more intense, is experienced more frequently and has a negative impact on social situations (Baumeister et al., 2001). These three facts underpin the *SCARF* model (Rock, 2008), resulting in its focus on providing pleasurable, respectful collaborations and communications. This make it a very valuable tool in establishing effective communication between teachers and pupils, teachers and parents, and teachers and the wider community and for establishing positive relationships.

Research findings

We spoke with an Australian high school teacher in a major urban setting. This teacher brings a wealth of experience from working in an intensive English centre embedded within his school.

Context: We have a lot of refugee and refugee-like students from countries such as Afghanistan, Pakistan, Syria and West Africa. In our school, we try to connect our students with the community and make sure that they're part of a network that they're familiar with. We also make sure that we buddy them up in school. What we also do is make sure that they're on a similar level of Educational English.

> In the first instance, students who feel safe are the students that more ready to learn. I think one of the things that we do well in the Intensive English Centre (IEC) is trying to create that safe space for them which some of them may not be used to. Once that's established, they're going to progress through the stages of learning such that they can acquire the basics of English.
>
> We also make sure that we address the emotional needs in a group level too. We have well-being lessons and it's quite a common thread throughout

our school. We've had those things in place for ages. We might not have called it wellbeing class, but those things have been in place for a long time. Counsellors would often come in and they would run settling in programs. These specific programs allow the students to form a language or the basics of expression, such that they can communicate feelings and experiences. Because I think one of the frustrating things when you're new to a country is not being able to get it out there. A lesson might be as simple as a chart of 10 faces with different expressions and the actual identification or feelings of sad, happy, excited, scared and worried. All those kinds of adjectives are taught explicitly so that they know to use those kinds of words whether it be in a counselling situation or communicating just to a teacher.

Last term we had six students move across [to mainstream schooling]. Those students would be immediately identified as students who need extra support in the transition phase. When those enrolments occur, there is communication that goes to all their class teachers without being too specific. There is some basic information about the learning background prior to the IEC, prior to Australia, so that there's a context for how they may be learning and why they may not always encounter difficulties. So, in that sense you've got a lot of communication going on from the sending site to the receiving site and that occurs no matter what.

The other thing is the wellbeing side dealt with. Often the issues that occur pre coming to Australia and ongoing into the mainstream. We can't necessarily resolve them within a short time frame just like all human experience. Sometimes there are number of years before things can be addressed and so there's continuity there too. So, the information files are passed across the school from a counsellor to another counsellor at a confidential level so that the new counsellor or the receiving counsellor doesn't have to start fresh. They can start with a body of knowledge and understanding of what has been implemented to help the students along the way in terms of resolving any difficulties at an emotional well-being level or from trauma backgrounds.

Unique contexts, global principles

This teacher's school has developed an intensive English centre for newly arrived students that is housed within a traditional high school. Students in the centre are buddied with peers who have similar levels of English, and they are also connected with members of the community who have experienced similar journeys to Australia. These connections are intended to build relationships and promote a sense of belonging. Focusing on safety and wellbeing are priorities in this school, and counsellors embed self-care lessons across the curriculum. Having the ability to verbalise feelings is seen as exceptionally important, and the vocabulary for common emotions is explicitly taught when students arrive. As students move from the centre to the mainstream school environment, they are identified as needing support in the transition, and their life experience is shared with their new teachers. There is also a transfer of records between counsellors as students matriculate through the school. As this teacher indicated, the school staff recognises issues related to wellbeing and trauma are ongoing and not easily resolved. This school has systems in place to label, transition and monitor students as they move across grades and settings.

Regardless of school size, level or structure, having formal programmes and plans in place to meet the needs of newly arrived students is a way of ensuring they remain visible and cared for. To place students in buddy relationships with classmates and community members, as this Australian school does, is a purposeful process to help students develop belonging. Further, offering whole class workshops on wellbeing and developing clearly articulated transition plans between teachers and counsellors are also steps to build certainty for students. Providing students with foundational vocabulary to express themselves and to share their feelings is a way to respect them. With nearly 80 million current refugees, it is likely schools in every corner of the world will find themselves having to meet the needs of children and families who meet this designation. Educators must engage with this work at a school level; they need to develop plans for welcoming, supporting and transitioning children and their families. By collaborating on this planning, and using a quality framework like the SCARF model, teachers can support the families who have arrived and prepare for those yet to come.

Conclusion

There is a great deal to learn about communicative practices in different cultures. The differences may be subtle but often ignoring these or minimizing their importance may lead to misunderstandings to the detriment of building the positive relationships and developing the inclusive environment that is so important to the successful integration of these students in schools. As will be highlighted in the following chapter, language is multifaceted in that it conveys layers of meaning, and, especially in the case of the English language, word meanings differ when used in varying contexts and sayings or phrases may hold very different interpretations to the words from which they are constructed.

References

Al Wazni, A. B. (2015). Muslim women in America and Hijab: A study of empowerment, feminist identity, and body image. *Social Work, 60*(4), 325–333. https://doi.org/10.1093/sw/swv033

Alford, J. H. (2014). "Well, hang on, they're actually much better than that!": Disrupting dominant discourses of deficit about English language learners in senior high school English [Article]. *English Teaching: Practice & Critique (University of Waikato), 13*(3), 71–88. http://search.ebscohost.com/login.aspx?direct=true&db=ehh&AN=108368025&site=eds-live

Anders, A. (2012). Lessons from a postcritical ethnography, Burundian children with refugee status, and their teachers. *Theory Into Practice, 51*(2), 99–106. http://dx.doi.org/10.1080/00405841.2012.662850

Anderson, A. R., & Fowers, B. J. (2020). An exploratory study of friendship characteristics and their relations with hedonic and eudaimonic well-being. *Journal of Social and Personal Relationships*, *37*(1), 260–280. https://doi.org/10.1177/0265407519861152

Antoniou, P., & Zembylas, M. (2018). Conceptualizing and contextualizing the concept of refugee in education: A phenomenological study of teachers' and students' perceptions in a conflict-affected society. *Diaspora, Indigenous, and Minority Education*, November, 1–16. https://doi.org/10.1080/1E5595692.2018.1538045

Arar, K., Orucu, D., & Kucukcayir, G. (2018). These students need love and affection: Experience of a female school leader with the challenges of syrian refugee education. *Leading and Managing*, *24*(2), 28–43.

Arizpe, E., Bagelman, C., Devlin, A. M., Farrell, M., & McAdam, J. E. (2014). Visualizing intercultural literacy: Engaging critically with diversity and migration in the classroom through an image-based approach. *Language and Intercultural Communication*, *14*(3), 304–321. https://doi.org/10.1080/14708477.2014.903056

Banki, S. (2012). Refugees as educators: The potential for positive impact on educational systems. In F. McCarthy & M. Vickers (Eds.), *Refugee and Immigrant Students: Achieving Equity in Education* (pp. 43–64). Information Age Publishing, Inc.

Baumeister, R., Bratslavsky, E., Finkenauer, C., & Vohs, K. (2001). Bad Is Stronger Than Good. *Review of General Psychology*, *5*(4), 323–370. https://doi.org/10.1037//1089-2680.5.4.323

Bradley, M., & Sellars, M. (2020). Parent cafe reflections. In M. Ruby, M. Angelo-Rocha, M. Hickey, & V. Agosto (Eds.), *Making a Spectacle: Examining Curriculum/Pedagogy as Recovery from Political Trauma* (pp. 183–190). Information Age Publishing.

Cassidy, E., & Gow, G. (2005). Making up for lost time: The experiences of Southern Sudanese young refugees in high schools. *Youth Studies Australia*, *24*(3), 51–55.

Collet, B. (2014). Sites of refuge: Refugees, religiosity, and public schools in the United States. *24*, 1. https://doi.org/10.1177/089590480354726

Correa-Velez, I., Gifford, S. M., & Barnett, A. G. (2010, Oct). Longing to belong: social inclusion and wellbeing among youth with refugee backgrounds in the first three years in Melbourne, Australia. *Social Science & Medicine*, *71*(8), 1399–1408. https://doi.org/10.1016/j.socscimed.2010.07.018

Creagh, S. (2016). 'Language Background Other Than English': A problem NAPLAN test category for Australian students of refugee background. *Race Ethnicity and Education*, *19*(2), 252–273. https://doi.org/10.1080/13613324.2013.843521

Damonhouri, M. (2018). The advantages and disadvantages of body language in Intercultural communication. *Khazar Journal of Humanities and Social Sciences*, *21* (1), 68–82. https://doi.org/10.5782/2223-2621.2018.21.1.68

Dooley, K. (2009). Re-thinking pedagogy for middle school students with little, no or severely interrupted schooling [Article]. *English Teaching: Practice & Critique (University of Waikato)*, *8*(1), 5–19. http://search.ebscohost.com/login.aspx?direct=true&db=ehh&AN=47084174&site=eds-live

Dooley, K., & Thangaperumal, P. (2011). Pedagogy and participation: literacy education for low literate refugee students of African origin in a western school system. *Language and Education*, *25*(5), 385–397.

Due, C., Riggs, D. W., & Mandara, M. (2015, August 1). Educators' experiences of working in Intensive English Language Programs: The strengths and challenges of specialised English language classrooms for students with migrant and refugee backgrounds. *Australian Journal of Education*, *59*(2), 169–181. https://doi.org/10.1177/0004944115587365

Edgeworth, K. (2013). *Refugees in Rural Schools: Issues of Space, Racism and (un) Belonging* Australian Association for Researc in Education Conference, Adelaide, South Australia.

Elliot, A. (2008). Approach and avoidance motivation. In A. Elliot (Ed.), *Handbook of Approach and Avoidance Motivation* (pp. 3–14). Pyschology Press.

Emert, T. (2013). 'The Transpoemations Project': Digital storytelling, contemporary poetry, and refugee boys. *Intercultural Education, 24*(4), 355–365. https://doi.org/10.1080/14675986.2013.809245

Emert, T. (2014). "Hear a Story, Tell a Story, Teach a Story": Digital narratives and refugee middle schoolers. *Voices From the Middle, 21*(4), 33–39. http://search.proquest.com/docview/1519055930?accountid=10499

Essomba, M. À. (2017). The right to education of children and youngsters from refugee families in Europe. *Intercultural Education, 28*(2), 206–218. https://doi.org/10.1080/14675986.2017.1308659

Foucault, M. (1977). Panopticism (A. Sheridan, Trans.). In *Discipline and Punish: The Birth of the Prison* (pp. 195–228). Vintage Books. http://foucault.info/documents/disciplineAndPunish/foucault.disciplineAndPunish.panOpticism.html

Foucault, M. (1979a). *Discipline and Punish*. Peregrine.

Foucault, M. (1979b). *Power, Truth, Strategy*. Feral Publications.

Fredrickson, B. (2000). Cultivating positive emotions to optimize health and well being. *Prevention and Treatment, 3*. Retrieved September 3, 2013, from http://www.unc.edu/peplab/publications/Fredrickson_2000_Prev&Trmt.pdf

Green, M. G., & Tucker, J. L. (2011). Tumultuous times of education reform: A critical reflection on caring in policy and practice. *International Journal of Leadership in Education, 14*(1), 1–19. https://doi.org/10.1080/13603124.2010.488701

Green, S. L., & Edwards-Underwood, K. (2015). Understanding and redefining multicultural education [Article]. *Journal of Education Research, 9*(4), 399–411. http://ezproxy.newcastle.edu.au/login?url=http://search.ebscohost.com/login.aspx?direct=true&db=ehh&AN=114759461&site=eds-live

Gustafson, D. T., & Iluebbey, V. (2013, Summer). "Traditional discipline" or domestic violence: Participatory action research with a Sudanese refugee community [Article]. *Journal of Cultural Diversity, 20*(2), 51–56. http://ezproxy.newcastle.edu.au/login?url=http://search.ebscohost.com/login.aspx?direct=true&db=sih&AN=88112432&site=eds-live

Hall, E. (1976). *Beyond Culture*. Knopf Doubleday Publishing Group.

Hope, J. (2008). "One day we had to run": The development of the refugee identity in children's literature and its function in education. *Children's Literature in Education, 39*(4), 295–304. https://doi.org/10.1007/s10583-008-9072-x

Hunpage, L., & Marston, G. (2006). Recognition, respect and rights: Refugees living in Temporary Protection Visas (TPVs) in Australia. In N. Yuval-Davies, K. Kannabiran, & U. Vieten (Eds.), *The Situated Politics of Belonging* (pp. 113–126). Sage.

Imig, S., Sellars, M., & Fischetti, J. (2022). *Creating Spaces of Wellbeing and Safety for Students with Refugee and Asylum Seeker Experiences: Lessons from School Leaders*. Routledge.

Kohli, R. K. S. (2006). The sound of silence: Listening to what unaccompanied asylum-seeking children say and do not say. *British Journal of Social Work, 36*(5), 707–721. http://search.ebscohost.com/login.aspx?direct=true&db=ccm&AN=106356318&site=eds-live

Lieberman, M. D., & Eisenberger, N. (2009). Pains and pleasures of social life. *Science, 323*(5961), 890–891. https://doi.org/10.1126/science.1170008

Matthews, J. (2008). Schooling and settlement: Refugee education in Australia. *International Studies in Sociology of Education, 18*(1), 31–45. https://doi.org/10.1080/09620210802195947

McInnis, K. (1991). Practice forum: Ethnic-sensitive work with Hmong refugee children. *Child Welfare, 70*(5), 571–580. http://ezproxy.newcastle.edu.au/login?url=http://search.ebscohost.com/login.aspx?direct=true&db=eric&AN=EJ436399&site=eds-live

McMichael, C., Gifford, S. M., & Correa-Velez, I. (2011). Negotiating family, navigating resettlement: Family connectedness amongst resettled youth with refugee backgrounds living in Melbourne, Australia [Article]. *Journal of Youth Studies, 14*(2), 179–195. https://doi.org/10.1080/13676261.2010.506529

Miller, J. (2009). Teaching Refugee Learners with interrupted education in science: Vocabulary, literacy and pedagogy. *International Journal of Science Education, 31*(4), 571–592. https://doi.org/10.1080/09500690701744611

Miller, J., Windle, J. A., & Yazdanpanah, L. K. (2014). Planning lessons for refugee-background students: Challenges and strategies [Article]. *International Journal of Pedagogies & Learning, 9*(1), 38–48. https://doi.org/10.5172/ijpl.2014.9.1.38

Naidoo, L. (2009). Refugee-centred education: Making community engagement central rather than peripheral to pre-service teacher professional development [Article]. *International Journal of Learning, 16*(5), 35–44. http://search.ebscohost.com/login.aspx?direct=true&db=ehh&AN=47479234&site=eds-live

Nawyn, S. J. (2006). Faith, ethnicity, and culture in refugee resettlement. *American Behavioral Scientist, 49*(11), 1509–1527. https://doi.org/10.1177/0002764206288462

Ní Raghallaigh, M., & Sirriyeh, A. (2015). The negotiation of culture in foster care placements for separated refugee and asylum seeking young people in Ireland and England. *Childhood, 22*(2), 263–277. https://doi.org/10.1177/0907568213519137

Noddings, N. (2005). *The Challenge to care in schools; an alternative approach to education* (2nd ed.). Teachers College Press.

Oikonomidoy, E. (2009). The multilayered character of newcomers' academic identities: Somali female high-school students in a US school. *Globalisation, Societies and Education, 7*(1), 23–39. https://doi.org/10.1080/14767720802677358

Omar, Y. S., Kuay, J., & Tuncer, C. (2017). 'Putting your feet in gloves designed for hands': Horn of Africa Muslim men perspectives in emotional wellbeing and access to mental health services in Australia. *International Journal of Culture and Mental Health, 10*(4), 376–388. https://doi.org/10.1080/17542863.2017.1324887

Osterling, J. P. (1998). Moving beyond invisibility: The sociocultural strengths of the Latino community (The case of Arlington's Salvadoran families). http://search.ebscohost.com/login.aspx?direct=true&db=eric&AN=ED424341&site=eds-live

Pranowo, P. (2019). Ethnopragmatic study on Javanese nonverbal language. *Asia Proceedings of Social Sciences, 4*(1), 41–43. https://doi.org/10.31580/apss.v4i1.556

Ranta, R., & Harmawati, D. (2017). Analyzing teacher's instructional and nonverbal communication in efl classroom. *Lingual: Journal of Language and Culture, 4*(2), 26. https://doi.org/10.24843/ljlc.2017.v04.i02.p05

Ratcliffe, M. (2012). Phenomenology as a form of empathy. *Inquiry, 55*(5), 473–495. https://doi.org/10.1080/0020174x.2012.716196

Resat, F. A. (2019). Body language of culture. *International Journal for Innovation Education and Research, 7*(8), 32–39. https://doi.org/10.31686/ijier.vol7.iss8.1639

Rock, D. (2008). SCARF: A brain-based model for collaborating with and influencing others. *Neuro Leadership Journal* (1), 1–9.

Rock, D. (2009). Managing with the brain in mind neuroscience research is revealing the social nature of the high-performance workplace. *Organizations and People*, (56), 1–12 https://www.strategy-business.com/article/09306.

Rock, D., & Cox, C. (2012). SCARF® in 2012: updating the social neuroscience of collaborating with others. *NeuroLedaership Journal* (4), 1–14. Retrieved February 24, 2020, from https://pdfs.semanticscholar.org/5f7b/37514e26877f8e0c1c156c1009f8e9970d7a.pdf

Sanatullov, M., & Sanatullova-Allison, E. (2012). Slavic-speaking refugee students in the United States public schools: Interface of language and education [Article]. *International*

Journal of Learning, 18(3), 325–341. http://search.ebscohost.com/login.aspx?direct=true&db=ehh&AN=73352801&site=eds-live

Seligman, M. (2004). *Can Happiness be Taught?* Daedalus (Spring).

Seligman, M. (2011). *Flourish: A Visionary New Understanding of Happiness and Well-being.* Free Press.

Sellars, M. (2020a). *Educating Students with Refugee and Asylum Seeker Experiences: A Commitment to Humanity.* Verlag Barbara Budrich.

Sellars, M. (2020b). Spaces of Safety and Belonging for Students with refugee and asylum seeker backgrounds.

Sellars, M. (2021). Planning for belonging: Including refugee and asylum seeker students. *Journal of Refugee Studies*, 1–13. https://doi.org/10.1093/jrs/feab073

Sellars, M., & Imig, D. (2021a). Pestalozzi and pedagogies of love: Pathways to educational reform. *Early Child Development and Care*, 1–12. https://doi.org/10.1080/03004430.2020.1845667

Sellars, M., & Imig, S. (2020). The real cost of neoliberalism for educators and students. *International Journal of Leadership in Education*, 1–13. https://doi.org/10.1080/13603124.2020.1823488

Sellars, M., & Imig, S. (2021b). School leadership, reflective practice, and education for students with refugee backgrounds: a pathway to radical empathy. *Intercultural Education*, 1–13. https://doi.org/10.1080/14675986.2021.1889988

Sellars, M., & Murphy, H. (2017). Becoming Australian: A review of southern Sudanese students' educational experiences. *International Journal of Inclusive Education, 22*(5), 490–509. https://doi.org/10.1080/13603116.2017.1373308

Sorgen, A. (2015). Integration through participation: The effects of participating in an English conversation club on refugee and asylum seeker integration [Article]. *Applied Linguistics Review, 6*(2), 241–260. https://doi.org/10.1515/applirev-2015-0012

Strekalova-Hughes, E., & Wang, X. C. (2019). Perspectives of children from refugee backgrounds on their family storytelling as a culturally sustaining practice. *Journal of Research in Childhood Education, 33*(1), 6–21. https://doi.org/10.1080/02568543.2018.1531452

Sulaiman-Hill, C. M., & Thompson, S. C. (2010). Selecting instruments for assessing psychological wellbeing in Afghan and Kurdish refugee groups. *BMC Res Notes, 3*, 237. https://doi.org/10.1186/1756-0500-3-237

Taylor, S. (2008, Third Quarter). Schooling and the settlement of refugee young people in Queensland: '…The challenges are massive' [Article]. *Social Alternatives, 27*(3), 58. http://search.ebscohost.com/login.aspx?direct=true&db=f5h&AN=34999826&site=eds-live

Wilding, R. (2012). Mediating culture in transnational spaces: An example of young people from refugee backgrounds. *Continuum, 26*(3), 501–511. https://doi.org/10.1080/10304312.2012.665843

Wilkinson, J., & Kaukko, M. (2020). Educational leading as pedagogical love: the case for refugee education. *International Journal of Leadership in Education, 23*(1), 70–85. https://doi.org/10.1080/13603124.2019.1629492

Windle, J., & Miller, J. (2012). Approaches to teaching low literacy refugee background students. *Australian Journal of Language and Literacy, 35*(3), 317–333.

Zaidi, R., Strong, T., Oliver, C., Alwarraq, H., & Naqvi, A. (2021). The understated role of pedagogical love and human emotion in refugee education. *International Journal of Qualitative Studies in Education*, 1–19. https://doi.org/10.1080/09518398.2021.1991029

Ziaian, T., de Anstiss, H., Puvimanasinghe, T., & Miller, E. (2018). Refugee students' psychological wellbeing and experiences in the Australian education system:

A mixed-methods investigation. *Australian Psychologist*, *53*(4), 345–354. https://doi.org/10.1111/ap.12301

Zsófia, N. (2018). From camps to schools: The participation of refugee children in greek public education. *Journal of Modern Greek Studies*, *36*(2), 373–399. https://doi.org/10.1353/mgs.2018.0028

5 Numeracy

Introduction

In Chapter 4, the notion of literacy as social practice was discussed. In a similar fashion, numeracy is also found in different forms and has various uses in diverse social contexts. This chapter focuses on the ways in which mathematics and numeracy are also socially constructed; the notion of ethnomathematics and varying ways in which mathematical thinking, including preparation for algebraic thinking, can be achieved using diverse media and skills. Students with refugee and asylum-seeker experiences may not have the knowledge of the symbolic, formal recording of mathematical expression, but they certainly have developed notions of measurement space and number in their original learning contexts, irrespective of the environments in which they were interacting. One of the most critical aspects of teaching students the ways in which the Hindu-Arabic is expressed and recorded is to understand it as a language, which has symbolic representation, governing rules and non-quantitative notations that dominate the ways in which story can be expressed. Understanding that mathematical thinking and logic underpins the basis of language structures, sequence and sense-making at the micro, meso and macro levels of literacy may support the development of language proficiency as negotiable, and mathematics competencies as manipulatable have the potential to mediate the rather mechanical learning of both capacities and promote the deeper understanding that is necessary for the critical appreciation and application of both disciplines (Sellars, 2017b).

Numeracy as social practice

Numeracy and mathematics practices are socially constructed (Alsina, 2009; Angier & Povey, 1999; Atweh & Brady, 2009). The types of unique numeracy practices that are utilised by discrete groups of people in their own cultural contexts are frequently identified as *ethnomathematics* (D'Ambrosio, 1985). Described as numeracy skills and understanding from which these groups make sense of their world, they are unique to the environments in which these individuals inhabit. As early as 1996, Barton (1996) discussions in educational contexts were focused on the debate which resulted from students being included in western schools with skills in ethnomathematics but not in the widely used Hindu-Arabic system which

DOI: 10.4324/9781003207900-6

dominates school curricula. There was no clear outcome of these discussions. Many mathematicians believed that understanding ethnomathematical approaches to numeracy and mathematics was important as an ethical pathway to respectful acknowledgement of culture for the many migrant and refugee students who were enrolled in schools with diverse populations. Others disagreed, arguing that using ethnomathematical knowledge as a pathway to build skills in the mathematics of the curriculum was a misuse of its integrity as an environmentally orientated, culturally founded knowledge base (Mesquita et al., 2011; Pais, 2011; Pinxten & François, 2011; Powell & Frankenstein, 1997; Rowlands & Carson, 2002; Stillman & Balatti, 2010). Irrespective of the debates that were at their most powerful a decade ago, many students have found it beneficial to their learning to be permitted to approach new ways of doing and knowing mathematically in their new environments by building on their understandings from the past. This supported the arguments of Ingram et al. (2004) that it is the right of all students to be accessible to learning in ways that allow full participation. Proponents of including mathematics as cultural practice (ethnomathematics) (see, for example, Boaler, 1993; Boaler, 2016; Zevenbergen, 2010) have many implications for the teaching and learning of mathematics in Eurocentric classrooms (Atweh & Clarkson, 2010). This is because many of these educational contexts reflect the political and economic aims of neoliberalism (Sellars & Imig, 2020), frequently to the detriment of individual learner preferences and diverse ways of knowing and doing, despite much of the mobility, whether forced or not, reflecting the impact of globalisation and political power play. For teachers of mathematics in schools who are welcoming refugee and asylum-seeker students into their classrooms, the impacts include familiarising themselves with many models of mathematics, developing new pedagogies to respect and value the knowledge that all students bring to their classrooms and engaging with culturally diverse resources and technologies.

> Finger counting, an essential activity for children learning to count in any system is typically engaged with in different ways internationally. It provides a good example of the social context of numeracy skill development. The actions themselves were frequently discouraged in the past by both parents and teachers before *fMRI* scanning demonstrated that finger counting mirrored the activity on the mental number line developed and elaborated upon by practice and the increasing complexity of manipulating numbers. Interestingly, finger counting is executed differently in many countries. There are variations to starting point of the count, the ways in which the fingers are displayed when counted and ways of using fingers to count numbers larger than ten. The latter method is common in students with heritage from the Indian continent who use the lines between the parts of the fingers to count, meaning they can count to twenty on one hand. Students from East Africa may use both hands as equally as possible, demonstrating four as two fingers on each hand and various ethnic groups use the spaces between

> the fingers to count. Some South American groups use their knuckles to count, and Chinese students show a different symbol representation using both their hands once they count over five. These are only a few of the variations of finger counting and cognitive researchers are seeking to investigate others, whilst attempting to determine how these diverse finger counting methods impact on the student's individual understanding of number.

Research findings

We interviewed a passionate primary teacher in New Zealand from one of the nation's most diverse schools. Her experiences working with children from multiple countries within the same classroom setting offer keen insights.

Context: We have 750 students from about 70 different ethnicities. About 40% of our students are Māori, more than 40% are from other ethnicities and nearly 20% identify as being New Zealand European. We have children from across the Pacific including Samoa, Tonga, Fiji, Cook Islands, Papua New Guinea, Vanuatu, Solomon Islands, Tuvalu, Niue, Naru, Tokalau, Kiribati, Micronesia, Melanesia and Polynesia. We celebrate the diversity that we have and encourage children to learn about other cultures. We try to build a culture of care and concern and aim to be culturally responsive.

> We are aware that it is difficult to cope with change and it's so easy to fall back to what has worked for you and what you have always done. So, we need to have frequent professional learning conversations with staff about the pedagogy for mainstream classes. This includes conversations about pedagogical content knowledge, scaffolding learning and teaching in meaningful authentic contexts for our English language learners. It's an ongoing process that takes time.
>
> It's really interesting. Every time we face a barrier, we always try to look at a solution. We try to use a strength-based approach. The best thing is having bilingual learning assistants. We've employed 7 bilingual learning assistants. They are my greatest resource in the school. They speak the languages of the predominant refugee families that we have. For example, when mathematics is timetabled, they will go to the classrooms with those children for the maths classes and they often explain the content, concepts, instructions, and things like that in the students first language. So, the children are able to work at the level that they're at in mathematics and it's not the English holding them back.
>
> Our whole school teaches Prime Mathematics which is a Singaporean program. When we are teaching mathematics, we are finding that there are a lot of concepts that need unpacking and also a lot of English involved to be able to do the tasks, like knowing the vocabulary and reading the examples, questions and problems. We want the students to be able to do the mathematics and not be disadvantaged because of the English required in reading the questions and understanding the teachers' instructions.

Unique contexts, global principles

This New Zealand primary teacher brings an incredibly optimistic approach to her work. Keenly aware that her newly arrived students bring unique backgrounds, cultures and languages, she is mindful not to rely on the past to shape her practice. She engages in frequent professional learning conversations with her colleagues to identify, discuss and solve challenges as they emerge. These conversations cover the complexities of teaching and delve into pedagogy, scaffolding, content and learning. Her large primary school has a staff of seven bilingual learning assistants which demonstrates a commitment to meeting the needs of the diverse students enrolled. These assistants are vital to ensure that a lack of language understanding doesn't stifle student learning. For mathematics, this school purposefully builds student schedules that allow the bilingual assistants to support non-English speakers. These teachers translate the English that underpins the learning of new concepts and explain the expectations for completing assignments and assessments. This school implements two mathematics programmes that are English-rich, and they ensure non-English speakers are not penalised as a result.

When children with refugee and asylum-seeker experiences find themselves sitting in a classroom on the other side of the planet from their home country, they are not coming as empty vessels to be filled. In the case of mathematics, many of these children come with an understanding of foundational concepts and, potentially, unique insights and approaches to the topic. As our New Zealand teacher makes clear, it is imperative that newly arrived students are not viewed as a monolithic group with the same strengths and needs. By engaging in frequent professional learning conversations, educators have an opportunity to meet challenges and honour the understandings of individual students. These conversations should be had by the range of teachers and assistants supporting these students and start from a solutions-based perspective. Funding and hiring learning assistants is one way to ensure newly arrived students can continue progressing in core subjects like mathematics without their limited English being a hurdle. By purposefully developing and then ensuring all subjects have wrap-around language support, schools can build environments where content is accessible to all students. Such an approach also enables schools to remain true to their educational philosophies and implement curriculum materials without concern that they will be inaccessible to their non-English speakers.

Arithmetic and algebraic thinking

One of the problems that was reported by the participants in this study was the difficulty of supporting some of the students with refugee and asylum-seeker backgrounds to gain the skills of algebraic thinking. There are multiple reasons for why this could be so, including lack of access to education in mathematics prior to arrival in their new homelands, different ways of thinking about arithmetic activity, transmission pedagogies which prioritised modelling and rule observance at the cost of understanding and the use of specialised algebraic language. Whilst earlier arithmetic activities such as generalising patterns, having a deep understanding of the structure of the number system in arithmetic calculations and manipulations and recognising similarities and differences in numbers, can form a sound basis for developing an aptitude for thinking algebraically, it appears to be critical that a sound understanding of the cognitive differences in these ways of working and understanding mathematically is clearly articulated. Nogueira de Lima and Healy (2010) suggest that difficulties with learning in algebra is student difficulty moving from the embodied (arithmetic thinking) to the conceptual, suggesting that perhaps limited exposure to ethnomathematical thinking or numeracy practices in the home may present some initial algebraic difficulties (Baker et al., 2003). Bal (2016) stressed the importance of differentiated teaching strategies in algebra, indicating that this produced improved cognition and affective status for the students. Tall et al. (2014) recommended a three-strategy framework, indicating that there are examples of liner equations in algebra which may be solved using arithmetic strategies and knowledge, producing a solution which was a known quantity. They explored examples which could be manipulated by the 'doing the same to both sides' strategies and then also by identifying those problems which required the phenomenon known as the 'didactic cut' (Filloy & Rojano, 1989). This term refers to the process by which arithmetic thinking is dismissed and a more complex set of cognitive processes are brought to bear on algebraic situations, suggesting that students are made explicitly aware of the limitations and problematic thinking that they may have about working mathematically in arithmetic thinking, and, by literally cutting out that type of thinking, they can engage cognitively in the more complex cognition of working conceptually with symbolic relationships in algebra (Booker, 2011; Pournara, 2020; Siemon et al., 2013). The capacity to think conceptually in the contexts of algebraic thinking and algebraic modelling is considered to be critical in the twenty-first century as the world becomes increasingly technological and the gap between abundance and poverty spreads to increasingly large proportions (Blair & Getz, 2011; Gutstein & Peterson, 2005; Skovsmose, 1994, 2012; Skovsmose & Valero, 2010; Steen, 2001a).

> In our work with elementary and middle grade teachers, we have identified four mathematical activities that underlie both arithmetic and algebra and, therefore, provide a bridge between the two. These are: •understanding the behavior of the operations, •generalizing and justifying, •extending the number system, and •using notation with meaning.
> …. Computational fluency with the four basic arithmetic operations is a core of the elementary curriculum. In these years, students move from counting to computation. It is an expectation that students enter middle school with a firm grasp of addition, subtraction, multiplication, and division of, at least, whole numbers. Most students come into the secondary grades with procedures for solving basic arithmetic problems. Yet, even among students who carry out these procedures correctly, there are persistent problems as they make the transition from arithmetic to algebra. Many of these problems can be traced to lack of knowledge about the properties and behaviors of the operations…

> A second mathematical activity that connects arithmetic to algebra is articulating, representing, and justifying generalizations about the operations.......general ideas arise frequently in the course of students' study of arithmetic.... There are two aspects of engaging with general claims that we see teachers developing in the elementary grades:•articulating particular general claims based on the regularities students notice in the behavior of numbers and operations •developing a mathematical argument to justify a general claim for a class of numbers....
> .. as students get older, discussions about generalizations provide openings for consideration of new kinds of numbers. Does a property they have justified for whole numbers, and perhaps now take for granted, still hold when expanding the number system to include fractions, decimals, or negative numbers? As they consider new classes of numbers, students sort out which behaviors of the operations must remain consistent as the number system expands and which only appear to be general when considering certain classes of numbers. ...
> .... Students expressed general claims in symbolic notation. In the student curriculum we have developed, we introduce some use of algebraic notation in the elementary grades. However, we have been careful not to move too quickly. In order to support students 'use of algebraic notation with meaning, they first need to spend a good deal of time articulating general claims clearly in words and then connecting those statements to arguments based on representations. (Russell et al., 2011, p. 44–45, 53–54, 59, 63)

Research findings

We spoke with an Australian and a New Zealand primary teacher. Each offered wonderful, and rather atypical, approaches to supporting students in terms of learning any school subjects.

Context: I started off in high schools and then moved on to other settings. The primary school where I worked is a small regional school with fewer than 200 students and just 12 classroom teachers. More than 30% of the students are children with refugee backgrounds.

> Visualizing math is beautiful because it taught me how I can do it. The way that you count across your knuckles and in the gaps between knuckles. The ways that other cultures navigate number sense is really sophisticated. So, there's no real issues there. But it was the capacity to be able to draw and represent visually some of what they were trying to do. And for me to label that with the English in order to help them to draw on what they already know. Because many of them come with some significant strengths and life experiences that they could draw on. It is connecting the non-concepts that they already know and helping them to translate that through the English which takes a little bit of time.

One of the other projects that were involved in was one from the local university PE department. What it allowed was quite a few of those students who were very physical to really excel in some of the physical activities whilst exploring the maths and number related to the sport science and how to improve their performance. It was that real peer working with each other. You saw some really beautiful conversations that occurred. I had Afghani students that picked up some of the Swahili. I had some Congolese students that picked up some Farsi words and it was a whole range of things. They also learned those English words that they picked up all their languages that are the same across all of them. So, there was a really eclectic conversations because kids find a way to talk and communicate. Even if they are not verbal, they still find a way of working together, playing, doing nice things and a lot of what we learn is through play. So, the other part was strategic grouping students. I'm not talking about ability grouping, I'm talking about strategic grouping where students could support each other, could scaffold each other, could just help them navigate things in a different way.

Context: Our school has under 500 students from Years one to eight. I've been there for quite some time and taught in lots of different classes. I've had more years in the juniors and currently teach a Year 3 class. We've recently started to get former refugees. We also have a migrant population of Pacific Islanders and Asians. So, we have different cultures in our school. I think it's a real snapshot of our society. I do have a firm belief in communication with families and the importance of knowing the child, and their culture and religions. Knowing what they can or can't eat, how to greet the family in their home language and what communication works best for them.

We actually don't do as much testing as we used to do. We're sort of looking closely at what the child is doing all the time. What they're doing when they're reading, and what do they need to do next. What are they doing when they're problem solving and numeracy, and what do they need to do next? That's the kind of assessments we're doing really. For example, there are three four areas in our school that we've got the writing books of all 130 children and line them up in terms of finding out what are they doing. Then we decide who needs to be pulled out and who needs extension. And we go from there, but certainly not a formal testing situation. I don't actually think any people in our school does formal testing anymore. It's pretty much looking at the child, what they're doing and what they need next. Earlier, we had national standards and they've gone, which is great because they put a whole lot of pressure on parents. There were some good things out of it. But overall, we kept the good things and national standards have gone.

Unique contexts, global principles

Educating newly arrived students for whom English is not their first language brings a host of challenges for teachers. Our Australian teacher spoke extensively about the importance of introducing mathematics in multiple ways. He used drawings to help students grasp mathematical concepts and display their understandings. This teacher also tapped into research being conducted by the local university that blended mathematics and physical movement. This teacher was very purposeful in his approach to grouping students engaged in mathematics lessons. He was not concerned with matching students based on level but rather grouping students to provide scaffolding for learning. He was particularly pleased that such experiences developed relationships and sparked verbal and non-verbal dialogue between his students. Our New Zealand primary teacher offered insights into a school that has reinvented how it monitors students. This school has dropped formal testing and replaced it with an intensive observation and portfolio review process. In terms of mathematics, teachers monitor and engage with students as they problem-solve and analyse their work to identify growing capacities and areas for improvement. Further, by regularly looking at the work of all students in the grade, teachers can spot issues as they arise and modify their teaching as needed. According to this teacher, the removal of national standards in New Zealand primary schools has aided this approach and reduced the stress felt by parents, students and educators.

Building on students' prior knowledge and introducing new concepts requires teachers to adeptly employ a diverse set of approaches in a classroom of native English speakers. When classrooms begin to reflect the diverse reality of the global diaspora, teachers may need to take additional steps to ensure their approaches are effective. As our Australian teacher demonstrated, educators need to experiment with alternative mathematics' approaches and programmes to meet the needs of children with refugee and asylum-seeker backgrounds. Within those new programmes and approaches, teaches must find ways to foster student relationships through collaboration. As our NZ teacher highlighted, embedding yourself in the work of students and carefully monitoring their progress in mathematics is an effective way to support their education. By monitoring progress and comparing students across an entire grade, teachers have an opportunity to see individual issues, learning gaps with groups of students and areas where the curriculum and teaching may have been ineffective. It is noteworthy that in 2017 New Zealand effectively ended national education standards at the primary level, freeing up teachers from testing demands and enabling them, as evidenced by our research participant, to more intensively monitor student progress. By doing the hard work of understanding what newly arrived students know and can already do, and by delivering creative and differentiated lessons, teachers have an opportunity to help each of their students feel valued and become engaged learners.

Supporting mathematical thinking

The difficulty experienced by learners who have English as a second or additional language can be exacerbated by the ways in which language is used in mathematics (Schleppegrell, 2007; Setati, 2008). Whilst some vocabulary is clearly understood to be mathematical metalanguage with precise meaning and characteristics, many other terms used in mathematical learning are commonly in use in other contexts. Many of these expressions that are found in diverse contexts adopt a totally different meaning when used mathematically. This may lead to misunderstandings of the terms in this context or inappropriate use in both everyday communication and mathematical situations. Illustrated dictionaries can provide invaluable support both as online tools and as hard copy resources for consultation (Bray & Tangney, 2015). Mathematical visuals (Siemon et al., 2013) present many mathematical concepts in ways that require very little metalanguage and allow students with diverse cultural backgrounds and mathematics competence to present their understandings in a mode that is mathematically correct and culturally appropriate (Bishop, 1988; Boaler, 1993; Rodriguez & Kitchen, 2005; Skovsmose, 1994; Steen, 2001b; Sullivan & Australian Council for Educational Research, 2011). Boaler (1993) advocates learning mathematical concepts by using visual imagery, design and construction for planning, exploring and recording mathematical learning. Included in these mathematical visuals are charts, maps, plans, diagrams and graphs, amongst others. These mathematical visuals are not confined to mathematics classrooms and frequently are indicative of the multiple ways in which mathematical concepts are foundational to all the other disciplines in the school curricula in much the same way as literacy (Fox & Surtees, 2010; Geiger et al., 2015; Sellars, 2018).

While teachers of younger students are cognisant of the multiple roles they fulfil in terms of teaching various discipline content, many secondary teachers remain discipline focused, and, whilst accepting they are teachers of literacy in addition to their discipline area, many seem unaware of the roles they play as teachers of numeracy (Geiger et al., 2015; Sellars, 2018). Traditionally, literacy and numeracy have often been polarised as opposites, with students believing they may be good at one but not the others. However, numeracy skills are the foundation of language in both its construction and comprehension (Geiger et al., 2013; Marston, 2010; Sellars, 2017a, 2017b; Watson, 2012). Similarly, studies in geography cannot progress without knowledge of position, scale and other measurements, history without advanced understanding of time, elapsed time and duration, in addition to the multiple ways in which logic is presented in mathematical thinking. Participating in sport, games, dance and all the creative and performing arts are rich opportunities for these specialist teachers to stress the mathematical components of time, averages, strategy, patterning, proportion and perspective amongst other mathematical calculations. The sciences are equally demanding of mathematical content and process for success. Multiple tasks require data compilations as charts, graphs and diagrams and other representations founded in mathematical thinking and learning. Across the school day there are as many opportunities for utilising mathematical and numeracy knowledge and skills as there are prospects for language and literacy development, assuring constant engagement with at least two of the three skills required for success in the twenty-first-century world (Rosa & Orey, 2015).

> The application of number in visual art/design learning involves observing, analysing, measuring, counting and considering relationships between numbers, shapes, forms and rhythms in order to gain spatial harmony and balance when making design works. The very beauty of our constructed world has evolved from the investigation of the rules of number underpinning nature

and most design endeavours (Hemenway, 2008; Pickover, 2009). The journey to this understanding for all students involves observing the macro or the micro worlds of the earth and the universe. It involves discovering their numerical secrets and then applying them to one's own design problems and problem-solving processes that emerge from a social, cultural or personal need.....

To introduce the world of graphic design (surface design), architectural design, or spatial reasoning using models or surfaces, we simply have to look to the shapes, proportions and patterns in organic structures in nature such as the snow flake and soap bubble, or the constructed forms of the spider web, bee hive or bird's nests to see how they have been mathematically interrogated, rules discovered and principles applied. Take the time to consider the works of Chris Bosse (Bosse, 2013), who designed the Water Cube for the Beijing Olympic Games based on bubbles, or the work of Buckminster Fuller on geodesic dome structures (Fuller, 2008, 2013). You may also consider looking at the umbrellas, domes and tents created by the architect Frie Otto, who works with structural mathematics (Otto, 2013). Or study the ancient cultural legacy of the structures of the yurt or ger (Kernery, 2006), the Japanese art of origami (Lang, 2011) and its geometric three-dimensional shapes and forms, or examine the cultural complexity of textile art and design, the 3-D dimensional world of weaving that crosses both the construction of forms (baskets) to tapestry or rug design, and moves into the mathematical and structural world of Jacquard (loom) weaving in industry.

So let's now consider how the world of spaces, shapes, structures and patterns co-exist with the world of numbers, counting sequencing, measuring, calculating spaces and applying the rules of ratio and proportion. We can do this by observing, analysing, recording and applying the natural patterns or organisational structures found in nature or in manmade cultural and contemporary visual design objects. Thinking in numbers penetrates into our unconscious everyday life and lies at the heart of art/design works. (Grushka & Curtis, 2019, pp. 424–425)

Research findings

We interviewed an Australian primary teacher in a rural setting and an Australian primary teacher in a regional city. Each of these teachers focused on the need to deliver content in an engaging manner across academic disciplines.

Context: The first schools that I worked at had mostly high proportion of non-English-speaking student backgrounds and a lot of refugee students. That was how I began teaching. Then I taught students with similar backgrounds at different schools. For teaching newly arrived refugees, it quickly became obvious that the emotional wellbeing of the student had to be the first priority. So, any so-called academic experiences needed to take second place. It's based in play and making sure their emotional and social needs are met.

In maths, I think language is often something that makes it inaccessible for them. It's about teaching the language through hands on experience or pre-loading them with the language before they go into a math session, so they feel more confident. And just in general, making sure that the pedagogy is hands on. If they don't feel confident in talking, they can have more experiential types of learning that they can transfer into other types of learning. So, I guess a range of pedagogy that are inviting for them is very broad.

Context: I've now been teaching for almost 20 years. I've had a lot of experience in communities with high populations of Aboriginal students. I've been a teacher and an instructional leader. I've worked at multiple schools in the region. I've also taken on an assistant principal role.

I do lots of repetitive tasks, especially in mathematics learning different skills. It's all games-based, and they learn skills repeatedly and then in different situations, so we can get that generalized learning happening in whatever situation. I know this skill and I can apply it in this game and that game. It doesn't matter what it looks like. So yeah, lots of games-based lots of hands-on learning and yeah, I don't rely a lot on visuals as such, I make it more real life.

Unique contexts, global principles

When we asked our research participants about their approaches in various academic disciplines, we repeatedly heard the same two cautions. First, all learning comes after students' wellbeing is addressed; and second, classroom pedagogy must be as engaging as possible. Our regional Australian teacher stressed the need for hands-on learning with as many mathematics concepts as possible. She is concerned with not allowing language to be a barrier for her non-English speakers, and she spends time equipping students with key vocabulary prior to new learning experiences. A veteran educator and a keen observer, this teacher does not expect her newly arrived students to be active participants in classroom dialogue, as she knows they are taking away insights to apply in other situations. Our second Australian teacher is an advocate of games-based learning in mathematics. She focuses on developing key skills in a hands-on manner, and she is purposeful in providing opportunities for learning to transfer from one experience to another. This teacher provides her students' opportunities to develop their self-efficacy by providing repetitive tasks but embedding them in engaging activities. Both teachers see learning as far more than a didactic process. For them, effective instruction is multi-modal, activity-based and engaging.

For many teachers, having students with refugee and asylum-seeking backgrounds in their classes forces them to be both innovative and foundational in their pedagogy. The challenge of educating students dealing with trauma and displacement coupled with academic, cultural and language differences exhort teachers to develop remarkable lessons that engage students. Yet, these same realities ground teachers in the foundations of teaching – clearly teaching concepts, providing opportunities for repeated practice and helping students generalise learning across topics. Each of our Australian teachers worked to make mathematics instruction as engaging as possible, yet they were each clear in their purpose. By incorporating games and hands-on activities, our participants have found ways to make mathematics accessible for their students. It may prove helpful for teachers who find themselves serving non-English-speaking students to mentally go back to their first year of teaching and recall the purposeful planning, the scaffolding, the focus on student engagement and collaboration and differentiation.

Conclusion

This chapter has interrogated the possibilities and potential of investing the mathematics discipline in novel ways to support language, thinking and conceptual readiness for learning in other disciplines and for thinking creatively about the ways in which mathematics is the foundational structure upon which all learning can be based and on which the development of multiple skills and cognitive schema can be achieved by students. Whilst only small snapshots of the criticality of mathematical and numerical concept work to the development of success across the curriculum can be demonstrated here, even a cursory glance at the disciplines regularly included as school subjects will reveal their potential for mathematical knowledge to be introduced, identified in specific learning concepts and actioned in contexts other than the mathematics classroom. Just as all teachers are teachers of literacy, all teachers need to recognise themselves as teachers of mathematics, most especially for groups of students with refugee and asylum-seeker backgrounds whose access to knowledge, skills and ideas may otherwise be compromised.

References

Alsina, C. (2009). *Too Much Is Not Enough Teaching Maths through Useful Applications with Local and Global Perspectives.* Kluwer Academic Publishers. http://0-www.jstor.org.library.newcastle.edu.au/stable/pdfplus/3483300.pdf

Angier, C., & Povey, H. (1999). One teacher and a class of school students: Their perception of the culture of their mathematics classroom and its construction. *Educational Review, 51*(2), 147–160. https://doi.org/10.1080/00131919997588

Atweh, B., & Brady, K. (2009). Socially response-able mathematics education: Implications of an ethical approach. *Eurasia Journal of Mathematics, Science & Technology Education, 5*(3), 267–276. http://ezproxy.newcastle.edu.au/login?url=http://search.ebscohost.com/login.aspx?direct=true&db=ehh&AN=43972788&site=eds-live

Atweh, B., & Clarkson, P. (2010). Internationalisation and globalisation of mathematics education: Towards an adenda for research/action. In B. Atweh, H. Forgasz, & B. Nebrers (Eds.), *Sociocultural Research on Mathematics Educxation: An International Prespective* (pp. 77–94). Routledge.

Baker, D., Street, B., & Tomlin, A. (2003). Mathematics as social: Understanding relationships between home and school numeracy practices. *For the Learning of Mathematics, 23*(3 (Nov)), 11–15.

Bal, A. P. (2016). The effect of the differentiated teaching approach in the algebraic learning field on students' academic achievements. *Eurasian Journal of Educational Research, 16*(63), 185–204. https://doi.org/10.14689/ejer.2016.63.11

Barton, B. (1996). Making sense of ethnomathematics: Ethnomathematics is making sense. *Educational Studies in Mathematics, 31*(1), 201–233. https://doi.org/10.1007/bf00143932

Bishop, A. J. (1988, June 1). The interactions of mathematics education with culture. *Cultural Dynamics, 1*(2), 145–157. https://doi.org/10.1177/092137408800100202

Blair, R., & Getz, A. (2011). A brief history of the quantitative literacy movement. *Background Information for Faculty Arithmetic and Algebra Skills Aren't Enough Any More!* https://www.carnegiefoundation.org/blog/a-brief-history-of-the-quantitative-literacy-movement/

Boaler, J. (1993). Encouraging the transfer of 'school' mathematics to the 'real world' through the integration of process and content, context and culture. *Educational Studies in Mathematics, 25*(4), 341–373. https://doi.org/10.1007/bf01273906

Boaler, J. (2016). *How you can be good at math, and other surprising facts about learning*, YouTube. https://www.youtube.com/watch?v=3icoSeGqQtY&t=9s

Booker, G. (2011). *Building numeracy: Moving from diagnosis to intervention*. Oxford University Press.

Bosse, C. (2013). Chris Bosse: Water cube. http://www.flickr.com/search/?s=int&q=watercube+bosse&m=text

Bray, A., & Tangney, B. (2015). Enhancing student engagement through the affordances of mobile technology: A 21st century learning perspective on Realistic Mathematics Education. *Mathematics Education Research Journal, 28*(1), 173–197. https://doi.org/10.1007/s13394-015-0158-7

D'Ambrosio, U. (1985). Ethnomathematics and its place in the history and pedagogy of mathematics. *For the Learning of Mathematics, 5*(1), 44–48. http://www.jstor.org/stable/40247876

Filloy, E., & Rojano, R. (1989). The transition from arithmetic to algebra. *For the Learning of Mathematics, 9*(2 (June)), 1925.

Fox, S., & Surtees, L. (2010). *Mathematics across the Curriculum*. Continuum.

Fuller, R. B. (2008). *Buckminster Fuller: Starting with the Universe*. Whitney Museum of American Art in association with Yale University Press.

Fuller, R. B. (2013). *R. Buckminster Fuller: World Man*. Princton Architectural Press.

Geiger, V., Forgasz, H., & Goos, M. (2015). A critical orientation to numeracy across the curriculum. *ZDM—International Journal on Mathematics Education, 47*, 611–648.

Geiger, V., Goos, M., & Bennison, A. (2013). Exploring the demands and opportunities for numeracy in the Australian curriculum: English. *36th Annual Conference of the Mathematics Education Research Group of Australasia*, Melbourne, Vic.

Grushka, K., & Curtis, N. (2019). Visual design and numeracy. In M. Sellars (Ed.), *Numeracy in Authentic Contexts*. Springer

Gutstein, E., & Peterson, B. (2005). *Rethinking Schools*.

Hemenway, P. (2008). *The Secret Code: The Mysterious Formula that Rules Art, Nature and Science*. Evergreen, Springwood.

Ingram, D., Seashore, L., & Schroeder, R. (2004). Accountability policies and teacher decision making: Barriers to the use of data to improve practice. *Teachers College Record, 106*(6), 1258–1287.

Kernery, B. (2006). *Yurts: Living in the round*. Gibbs Smith

Lang, R. (2011). *Origami Design Secrets: Mathematical Methods for an Ancient Art*. A K Peters/CRC Press

Marston, J. (2010). Developing a framework for the selection of picture books to promote early mathematical development. In *33rd Annual Conference of the Mathematics Education Research Group of Australiasia*. Freemantle.

Mesquita, M., Restivo, S., & D'Ambrosio, U. (2011). Some mathematical "images and actions". In *Asphalt Children and City Streets: A Life, a City and a Case Study of History, Culture, and Ethnomathematics in Sao Paulo*. Sense Publishers.

Nogueira de Lima, R., & Healy, L. (2010). The didactic cut in equation solving or a gap between the embodied and the symbolic mathematical worlds? In *Proceedings of the 34th Conference of the International Group for the Psychology of Mathematics Education*, Belo Horizonte, Brazil: PME.

Otto, F. (2013). Frie Otto. http://www.freiotto.com/

Pais, A. (2011). Criticisms and contradictions of ethnomathematics. *Educational Studies in Mathematics, 76*(2), 209–230. https://doi.org/10.1007/s10649-010-9289-7

Pickover, C. (2009). *The Math Book: From Pythagoras to the 57th Dimension. 250 Milestones in the History of Mathematics*. Sterling.

Pinxten, R., & François, K. (2011). Politics in an Indian canyon? Some thoughts on the implications of ethnomathematics. *Educational Studies in Mathematics, 78*(2), 261. https://doi.org/10.1007/s10649-011-9328-z

Pournara, C. (2020). Grade 9 learners' algebra performance: Comparisons across quintiles, insights from errors and curriculum implications. *South African Journal of Science, 116*(9/10). https://doi.org/10.17159/sajs.2020/8125

Powell, A., & Frankenstein, M. (1997). *Ethnomathematics*. State University of New York Press. http://site.ebrary.com/lib/newcastle/docDetail.action?docID=10064652

Rodriguez, A., & Kitchen, R. (2005). *Preparing Mathematics and Science Teachers for Diverse Classrooms: Preomising Strategies for Transformatiuve Pedagogy* (A. Rodriguez & R. Kitchen, Eds.). Lawrence Erlbaum Associates, Inc.

Rosa, M., & Orey, D. C. (2015). A trivium curriculum for mathematics based on literacy, matheracy, and technoracy: An ethnomathematics perspective. *Zdm, 47*(4), 587–598. https://doi.org/10.1007/s11858-015-0688-1

Rowlands, S., & Carson, R. (2002). Where would formal, academic mathematics stand in a curriculum informed by ethnomathematics? A critical review of ethnomathematics. *Educational Studies in Mathematics, 50*, 79–102.

Russell, S. J., Schifter, D., & Bastable, V. (2011). *Developing Algebraic Thinking in the Context of Arithmetic*. (pp. 43–69). Springer Berlin Heidelberg. https://doi.org/10.1007/978-3-642-17735-4_4

Schleppegrell, M. J. (2007). The Linguistic challenges of mathematics teaching and learning: A research review. *Reading & Writing Quarterly, 23*(2), 139–159. https://doi.org/10.1080/10573560601158461

Sellars, M. (2017a). Numeracy across the curriculum: A pathway to critical thinking. *International Journal Innovation Creativity and Change*, (3), 75–83.

Sellars, M. (2017b). Reconciling the terrible twins: Investigating the relationship of literacy and numeracy in primary education. *TOJET—Turkish Online Journal of Educational Technology*, (Special Issue), 825–829.

Sellars, M. (Ed.). (2018). *Authentic Contexts of Numeracy: Making Meaning across the Curriculum*. Springer.

Sellars, M., & Imig, S. (2020). The real cost of neoliberalism for educators and students. *International Journal of Leadership in Education*, 1–13. https://doi.org/10.1080/13603124.2020.1823488

Setati, M. (2008). Access to mathematics versus access to the language of power: The struggle in multilingual mathematics classrooms. *South African Journal of Education, 28*, 103–116.

Siemon, D., Beswick, K., Brady, K., Clark, J., Faragher, R., & Warren, E. (2013). *Teaching Mathematics: Foundations to Middle Years*. Oxford University Press.

Skovsmose, O. (1994). Towards a critical mathematics education. *Educational Studies in Mathematics, 27*(1), 35–57. http://www.jstor.org/stable/3482665

Skovsmose, O. (2012). Symbolic power, robotting, and surveilling. *Educational Studies in Mathematics, 80*(1/2), 119–132. https://doi.org/10.1007/s10649-012-9388-8

Skovsmose, O., & Valero, P. (2010). Breaking politicxal neutrality: The critical engagement of mathematics education with democracy. In B. Atweh, H. Forgasz, & B. Nebrers (Eds.), *Sociocultural Research on Mathematics Education* (pp. 37–56). Routledge.

Steen, L. (2001a). *Data, Shapes, Symbols: Achieving Balance in School Mathematics Second Discussion Draft,*. http://www.asclegg.co.uk/downloads/maths/pisa/Data%20Steen.pdf

Steen, L. (Ed.). (2001b). *Mathematics and Democracy. The Case for Quantitative Literacy.* National Council on Education and the Disciplines (NCED). http://www.woodrow.org/nced/mathematics___democracy.html

Stillman, G., & Balatti, J. (2010). Contribution of ethnomathematics to mainstream mathematics classroom practices. In B. Atweh, H. Fogasz, & B. Nebrers (Eds.), *Sociocultural Research on Mathemathics Education: An International Perspective* (pp. 313–328). Routledge.

Sullivan, P., & Australian Council for Educational Research. (2011). *Teaching Mathematics : Using Research-Informed Strategies.* ACER Press.

Tall, D., Lima, R., & Healy, L. (2014). Evolving a three-world framework for solving algebraic equations in the light of what a student has met before. *Journal of Mathematical Behavior, 34*, 1–13. https://doi.org/10.1016/j.jmathb.2013.12.003

Watson, J. (2012). History and statistics: Connections across the curriculum. *Agora, 47*(3), 58–64. http://ezproxy.newcastle.edu.au/login?url=http://search.ebscohost.com/login.aspx?direct=true&db=ehh&AN=95394551&site=eds-live

Zevenbergen, R. (2010). Mathematics, social class and linguistic capital: An analysis of mathematics classroom inteaction. In B. Atweh, H. Fogasz, & B. Nebres (Eds.), *Sociocultural Ressearch on Mathematics Education: An Intenational Perspective* (pp. 201–216). Routledge.

6 Personal development

Introduction

The participants interviewed were all teachers in co-educational contexts. For some students and their families, this was an initial concern but as schooling was mandatory, there was very little choice in the schools that their children and young people attended. This chapter on personal development and Chapter 7 on physical education and exercise serve to highlight many of the cultural differences that may be problematic in western educational contexts. Both areas of discipline focus on the students as individuals and as members of society and the ways in which they develop their principles, attitudes and values in addition to managing their relationships, developing autonomy and making personal decisions. Western societies are notably different in many of these areas of thinking and behaving with multiple perspectives and accommodations that challenge groups with refugee and asylum-seeker experiences from other parts of the world. Many adults in societies everywhere find the ways in which children and young people are parented, the messages in the ways they dress and their sexual and provocative behaviours extremely confronting; it is certainly not confined to those who are newcomers to the countries. Some religious groups, especially Muslim groups whose homelands were originally Middle Eastern countries, may be particularly affronted as these societies have cultural dimensions which oppose many world views of western countries (Hofstede, 1986, 2001, 2011; Hofstede et al., 2010; Hofstede & Bond, 1988). In the school context, the diversity of perspectives becomes particularly difficult to negotiate when culturally prohibited or heavily sanctioned topics are part of a mandatory curriculum area such as personal development. Many of the difficulties arise from views on 'appropriate' interaction between males and females, especially in the context of participation in the classroom instruction and collaborative communication during lessons in this specific discipline.

Decision-making and having choices

The capacity to make life decisions is one that is constantly developed and mediated by experiences simply because all decisions have consequences. The irony of having this aspect of self-development as an aspect of a mandatory curriculum in schools is that, for many students of all ages, this may be the context in which there

DOI: 10.4324/9781003207900-7

are few opportunities to have choice and make decisions. However, in the teaching and learning around reflection, the pros and cons of decision-making and the possible consequences of their choices, teachers may easily overlook the fact that, in some circumstances, there are students who will not have any opportunities to make their own decisions and, even more neglected, may be the situations where the students have no expectations of making their own decisions, such are their cultural values and principles. In western culture, young people have certain expectations regarding the right to make their own decisions. These expectations differ vastly from one group in society to another and may be influenced by multiple considerations, based predominantly on the cultural norms, standards and values in which they were raised. The same type of cultural socialisation impacts on the expectations of many students with refugee and asylum-seeker experiences leading them to have different world views on autonomy and the potential for them to develop decision-making skills. The ecological systems model of development developed by Bronfenbrenner (1979) has the potential to support teacher understanding of the diversity of perspectives and values that students may bring to the classroom (Bronfenbrenner, 1979, 1986, 1988; Bronfenbrenner & Morris, 2006; Yok-Fong, 2013).

Bronfenbrenner posits that children are impacted, from birth, by the influence of increasingly broad, interrelated contexts in which they are growing. He theorises that the ways in which these interrelated systems influence each other has a considerable impact on the development of the individual. His model allows a glimpse into the ways in which incompatible influences are brought to bear on the development of students with refugee and asylum-seeker experiences. The microsystem is the immediate world of the young child. Originating in the home context, it expands to other contexts of childcare such as day care centres and to family and peers in the common contexts of playgrounds and sport, religious celebrations and worship and, eventually, school. The ways in which the components of this system influence each other is important, as this system is foundational to the child's development and is considered to be bidirectional. This mean that the child can influence the attitudes and behaviours of others, in addition to the individuals influencing the child, who at this stage is considered highly dependent. The interrelationship of the components of the micro system is termed the 'mesosystem'. Ideally, each of the child's microsystems should be characterised by positive impacts one upon another. Even at this early stage, it is not difficult to envisage that there may easily be a lack of coherence within the components of this system in terms of values, principles and acceptable practices between home environments that espouse traditional, non-western cultural and religious values and western school contexts.

The exosystem introduces the interplay of a wider influence in the community, including individuals with whom the child may have no direct relationship but is influenced indirectly. These may be neighbours, the people with whom parents work or whose influences and attitudes impact on the parents and therefore on the child indirectly. It may also include people who represent systems such as social services personnel or school officials with whom parents may interact and the consequences of the interface or communication influences the child's development. As the world of the child becomes gradually wider and more complex, the influences of already-established cultural perspectives and values play a role in the development of the child and young person. These may include the perceptions of social class, socio-economic status, ethnicity, gender and other matters. The child is born into and immersed into this macrosystem, irrespective of the individual differences and impressions of their specific microsystem. This is despite the assertion that the positive, nurturing quality of the microsystem is the most powerful system in determining the nature and direction of the developmental pathways. The final system is one that has a lifelong impact, the chronosystem, which acknowledges the power of events that change the environment over a lifespan. In this case, it would include the experiences of displacement, loss, journeying and resettlement of each student with refugee and asylum-seeker experiences.

Consequently, students who are developing as young people in two different environments because of their refugee and asylum-seeker experiences cannot readily dispense with one of the intricate ecologies into which they are enculturated, however much they may desire to do so. Developing autonomy in school situations may be contradictory to the norms and expectations of their microsystems and create significant concern and conflict between various players in the mesosystem, especially in the case of female students who may be subjected to restrictive social practices in their microsystems, whilst simultaneously having the responsibility of being more outspoken and definitive in their opinions in school interactions. Students with refugee and asylum-seeker experiences may frequently find themselves trying to live in two cultures (Das, 2019), juggling attitudes and behaviours which are considered inappropriate, unreasonable and disrespectful in one world and applauded, congratulated and rewarded in another. While many teachers of refugee and asylum-seeker students are aware of the social and cultural differences in relation to volition and choice in childhood, adolescence and young adulthood, they are also sensitive to the need to educate these cohorts of students to thrive, not just survive, in their new homelands. That may necessitate focusing on teaching and developing skills of decision-making and developing autonomy whilst respectfully acknowledging the complications and conflicts this may create in some communities.

> Hall (1976) likens culture and its impact on human interactions and expression of feelings to an iceberg. Indicating that only the top 10% of any iceberg shows above the waterline, Hall proposed that aspects of culture that can be publicly observed such as costume, dance, food, music, festivals, flags and other cultural artefacts are surface culture and represented by the tiny part of the iceberg that is visible. Hall considers this to be relatively low emotional intensity. In comparison, the two levels he identified below the surface are of increasing emotional intensity the deeper the level of the submersion. Shallow culture, directly below the surface of the water level is identified as unspoken culture and includes appropriate communicative

behaviours such as those considered in Chapter Four Communicating Effectively. This level also includes notions of childrearing, adolescence, hygiene and cleanliness and is considered to be of high emotional intensity. The deepest cultural level is unconscious culture which has an intense emotional level. The cultural influences at this level include beliefs about obscenity, gendered roles and their associated implications for compliance or dominance, concepts of competition and self and understandings of hardship and pain tolerance. This level also encompasses beliefs about social status, the past and the present (Sellars, 2017a, p. 196). Many of the difficulties and issues presented by the content of personal development programs of any type can be explained by understanding the implications of Hall's theory.

Research findings

We interviewed an Australian primary school teacher who shared insights about the challenge of helping students find their voice. We also spoke with a New Zealand primary teacher who was keenly aware of the varied learning styles of her newly arrived students.

Context: The messages that we create in our classroom is around identity and hierarchy. I think, students are constantly aware of hierarchy inside a classroom. If I can dissipate the power in the room by helping someone to become visible, they'd feel less anxious. In every classroom, if it's got refugees students in it or not, there's always children that wanted to be invisible. We need to help them become visible but making sure they know that you care and that they're not invisible to you. We can build up their position and help them learn to become visible by sharing their thoughts and their ideas in the classroom so that they begin to become comfortable with being visible eventually.

> One student that I had for two years, she would be in the area of invisibility. She just wanted to be invisible. We did work on her confidence through mainly project-based learning where she investigated aspects of Afghani culture. She felt more validated in the room and began to really find her voice by bringing in food and sharing, bringing in clothing and doing presentations and talking about her culture. Also, we did talk about male and female. I knew she wasn't able to speak up because it wasn't something that was encouraged in her home life. There was a lot of boys in that family, and she didn't have a strong voice at home. So, the way I talked about that might be a bit controversial, but I just wanted to give her a sense that she could speak up about things. She looked at a lot of female role models and sports people.

Context: The school I am working in is ethnically and linguistically diverse. We are a large primary school catering for children from Year 1 to Year 6. We enrol children from 5 years of age, and they leave at around 11 years of age for their intermediate schooling. We celebrate diversity in many ways in our school. We have flags up around the school so that children can identify with. We have a lot of books, art and opportunities to help people identify with their culture. When they come into the school, we try to make the entrance way welcoming and take time to take the families on a tour of the school.

> We are finding that good pedagogy will help all of our students. That is an example of the process we have underway at the moment. Another aspect we are looking at is how different cultures learn. For example, we know that Pacifica children learn best in group situations and that many of our Asian students prefer more formal seating situations. We are finding that in a whole class situation, many refugee students avoid speaking in class and participating in class activities that involve play and games.

Unique contexts, global principles

As students with refugee or asylum-seeker backgrounds enter a new classroom, they bring a world view grounded in their home country. Coming from places where schooling and the role of students looks very different, the desire to remain 'invisible' is understandable. As our Australian primary teacher observed, these students are attuned to classroom hierarchies at play, and they are often hesitant to verbally engage. This teacher was able to engage and develop the confidence of her Afghan student by bridging the gap between school and home through having the student research and share aspects of her culture with her classmates. This teacher also exposed her Afghan student to powerful female role models to counter the male-dominated reality at play in her home, an act she recognised could be seen as controversial. Our New Zealand teacher and her colleagues intentionally work to link the home and school lives of her students. By placing flags and signs in home languages around the building, this teacher's school is helping students and families feel connected and recognised in this new context. This teacher is also expanding her understanding of the cultures of her students by engaging in research about learning styles and educational structures in their home countries. The information she has about how groups of students may feel about pedagogical approaches, classroom participation and even seating arrangements influences the way she organises and runs her class.

Over time, one might expect newly arrived students to progressively embrace the classroom behaviours and practices of their host country peers. But this progression is not a given, nor should it be expected. Students with refugee or asylum-seeker backgrounds bring strong cultural beliefs and practices that may have defined their worldview for 5, 10 or even 15 years prior to arriving in a host country. These students may also return home each night to families who firmly embody the cultural values and practices of their home country and may expect their children to remain loyal to those practices. As both our New Zealand and Australian teachers confirm, helping students find a congruence between their home and school environments takes an effort on the part of educators. Teachers should endeavour to make students' home countries more visible in school; they should research their students' cultures and encourage students to share with their peers. While our Australian teacher provided opportunities to help her Afghan student connect with her peers, she also pushed a western view on the role of women. The fact that she recognised this as controversial implies a sensitivity and ability to reflect that all teachers must possess.

Sex education

There are few areas of the curriculum which cause as much consternation and trepidation as the mandatory units that focus on the human reproduction systems, intimacy and sexual behaviours and the associated cognitive, moral and emotional impacts (Khan et al., 2020). The difficulty of providing a culturally inclusive curriculum in this area has multiple challenges (Haggis & Mulholland, 2014; Zain Al-Dien, 2010). It may be common to assume that students of the Islamic faith may face the most home/school conflict in what is being taught in each context about sexuality and appropriate behaviours as it is countercultural to their religious beliefs (Nagi, 2018; Roudsari et al., 2013). However, proponents of the world views of each of the three major world religions (Christianity, Judaism, Islam) have voiced their concerns about what and how the knowledge is interpreted and taught in western secular school contexts (Muhammad, 2020). In making similar comments, Khan et al. (2020, p. 3) describe the various terms and content that is treated in differently focused programmes which fall into the following categories: Comprehensive Sexuality Education (CSE), Holistic Sexuality Education, Life and Living Skills, Relationships and Sex Education (RSE), Sex Education, Sexuality Education, Sexuality and following Reproductive Health (SRH). The Comprehensive Sexuality Education model is the programme most implemented in secular western schools as it not only deals with the physical aspects of sexual relationships and reproduction but also includes education about safe sexual practices, sexual health, the impact of individuals' choices for themselves and others and the importance of knowledge and values in their decision-making and behaviours.

WHO Regional Office for Europe and BZgA (2010 para. 6) view holistic sexuality education as follows:

> Learning about the cognitive, emotional, social, interactive and physical aspects of sexuality. Sexuality education starts early in childhood and progresses through adolescence and adulthood. It aims at supporting and protecting sexual development. It gradually equips and empowers children and young people with information, skills and positive values to understand and enjoy their sexuality, have safe and fulfilling relationships and take responsibility for their own and other people's sexual health and wellbeing.

For many religious groups, the major problems with this type of education are lack of emphasis on the ways in which the body itself is seen as sacred and the sexual act as an agreement between two people who are in a relationship that is permanent, exclusive and blessed by the appropriate religious authorities. However, challenges may be more widespread than anticipated as a study conducted with Muslim youth in the Netherlands revealed an unexpected disrespect for Islamic religious leaders who disagreed with the young participants' views and interpretations of the Qur'an (Smerecnik et al., 2010). It is not appropriate to establish exactly the content and implementation of the programmes that were interpreted and implemented by the participants' schools and approved by their state and local education authorities, but in religious schools, it is highly likely that the interpretation was heavily focused on the theme of abstinence before marriage, in keeping with their respective values and beliefs with regards to morality, ethics and principles. However, the importance of abstinence before marriage, critical as it may be, especially for females, is not the only issue that challenges religious leaders and communities. When considering the value and importance of sexuality education, there are multiple other issues that are recognised as contrary to the teaching and practices that are prescribed by faith-based communities, and which may serve to cause personal conflict and self-depreciation for students. All major churches provide marriage preparation courses to their young people, and, for many, this is the time when sex education is most appropriate as it is provided by relevant clergy or others who present the faith-based information.

One of the most common challenges or difficulties for students and their families to cope with outside of the abstinence perspective may be the major traditional churches' lack of acceptance of lesbian, gay, bisexual, transgender, queer, intersex and asexual individuals (Masci & Lipka, 2015). Some reformed Christian and Jewish communities permit gay marriage, but the teachings of the Roman Catholic and other major Christian churches, the Orthodox Jewish Church and Islam forbid any sexual relationships other than those between a man and a woman who are married to each other. Although there appears to be an appeal for acceptance of these groups into Islam on the basis that there is no evidence in the Qur'an that condemns these practices (Kugle, 2003), most Islamic groups appear to remain with traditional values. The penalty for transgressing these religious rules are contextually based as western countries where these students find new homelands do not have civil laws which criminalise sexual activity outside these religious parameters. However, although communities with refugee and asylum-seeker experiences have been resettled in these new cultures, many hold fast to the principles and laws of their homelands, which can be readily understood under the theory proposed by Bronfenbrenner (1979). This may the case with Islamic communities whose former homelands embraced religious law as a total way of life and did not distinguish it from civil law, making them one and the same for all citizens. Frequently, the law and potential punishments of the new homelands would not deter the infliction of traditional punishments for forbidden sexual activities, especially for females as the countries so described are currently predominantly Islamic and patriarchal (Hofstede, 2001, 2011; Hofstede et al., 2010).

Other information that may be presented in these curricula are matters of sexual health and circumcision. Early infant male circumcision has been common practice in many countries for centuries and has been identified as being influential in maintaining male sexual health. Morris et al. (2017, p. 90), whilst noting a slight decline in male circumcision in anglicised countries, including the United States, found that early male circumcision was a 'desirable public health intervention' as it

> ...confers immediate and lifelong benefits by protecting against urinary tract infections having potential adverse long-term renal effects, phimosis that causes difficult and painful erections and "ballooning" during urination, inflammatory skin conditions, inferior penile hygiene, candidiasis, various sexually transmissible infections in both sexes, genital ulcers, and penile, prostate and cervical cancer.

However, this is not the case for female circumcision, which, while practised in some parts of the world by Christian, Jewish and Muslim communities, has no health, hygiene, religious or social benefits (Kouba & Muasher, 1985) and is performed solely to increase male sexual pleasure and minimise that of the female (Dilbaz et al., 2019). World Health Organization (2006 para 1–3) figures indicate that 200 million women and girls have been subjected to one of the four procedures identified as female genital mutilation in countries where this is a widely practised custom. Another 3 million are at risk every year in areas of Africa, the Middle East, Asia and parts of South America. There are no estimates of the numbers of girls who are living outside of these areas as migrants, refugee or asylum seekers but it is acknowledged that many will be at risk of suffering the procedure, by being sent to their original homeland to have it done traditionally either by older women with knives, or by members of their communities who are also living in western countries. Female genital mutilation generally takes place before the girls are 15 years old. This mutilation has significant negative health implications for these individuals. In identifying the different types of procedures, they detail the invasive nature of this barbaric practice, and the sites where they are most likely to happen,

> Current estimates (from surveys of women older than 15 years old) indicate that around 90% of female genital mutilation cases include either Types I (mainly clitoridectomy), II (excision) or IV ("nicking" without flesh removed), and about 10% (over 8 million women) are Type III (infibulation). Infibulation, which is the most severe form of FGM, is mostly practiced in the northeastern region of Africa: Djibouti, Eritrea, Ethiopia, Somalia, and Sudan. In West-Africa (Guinea, Mali, Burkina Faso, etc.), the tendency is to remove flesh (clitoridectomy and/or excision) without sewing the labia minora and/or majora together.

In addition to the damage done to the girls physically and emotionally, their general and sexual health is considerably compromised. World Health Organization Africa (2021) indicates, 'Procedures can cause severe bleeding and problems urinating, and later cysts, infections, as well as complications in childbirth and increased risk of newborn deaths.' This is in addition to records of the multiple broken bones that are experienced as the girls try to escape from those forcibly holding them down throughout their ordeal. Despite female genital mutilation carrying heavy monetary and incarceration penalties for those performing the procedures, facilitating the procedure or enabling girls to leave the country to have the mutilation performed on them, thousands of girls are still at risk in in their resettlement in western countries.

The situation for young people from cultural backgrounds that have different beliefs and practices around sexuality and sexual relationships can be very difficult because of the multiple degrees of difference in the ways that sexuality is explored by their peers in their new homelands. The influence of the media, the availability of suggestive sexual material, and the dress and behaviours of some young people of similar ages may contrast markedly with the expectations and values that are espoused by their parents and religious communities. Kumar et al. (2021) investigated the sexual health knowledge and understandings of girls with refugee experiences from diverse backgrounds. It was established that many had misunderstandings about sexual activity itself, about US law relating to sexual matters, about contraception and about sexually transmitted diseases. It also became apparent that their home contexts presented them with unique challenges in accessing knowledge about sexuality, rendering them more likely to have negative sexual health outcomes than their peers who were native to the US. The study highlighted the importance of considering contextual influences when supporting girls' education in sexual health, as did Sanjakdar (2005) speaking about the need for an appropriately Islamic sexual health curriculum for Australian schools.

Mengesha et al. (2017) found that in Australia there were several major themes that impacted on migrant and refugee women's sexual and reproductive health. These themes may be useful to teachers implementing programmes that include information on sexual and reproductive health for students with refugee and asylum-seeker backgrounds. The themes that were identified included that, as migrant and refugee women, they considered issues if sexual and reproductive health unimportant as they had not been provided for in their homelands. They had very little knowledge of sexual and reproductive matters, which appeared to be a theme in other, related research findings (see, for example, Botfield et al., 2018; Metusela et al., 2017; Ortiz-Echevarria et al., 2017). These women were also sensitive to their gendered roles in the decisions that they made about their own sexual and reproductive health, indicating that they needed to discuss matters of care with their husbands, which in turn impacted on the provision of women-centred care. In addition to all these pressures, girls and young women may be educated by their cultural peers to see childbearing as a mandatory aspect of their identity as women and to perceive contraception as a negative option for them (Hawkey et al., 2018).

> Botfield et al. (2018) found that many young refugee and immigrant young people in Sydney, Australia were not utilising the sexual health services that were available for them. All participants indicated that discussions about sex were 'taboo' in their households and that generational differences around the topic would make them feel uncomfortable to see their family doctor or one from their own culture as they felt that the 'older' generation judged people and their choices.

Research findings

We spoke with a teacher in New Zealand who recognises the importance of communication and developing strong relations between her school and the region's newly arrived families.

Context: We are one of the most culturally diverse primary schools in our country. We have many multilingual students, not just bilingual. In our school, we're not assimilating the children. We're just helping them integrate into our school environment and understand our school vision and values. We talk through things with parents. We encourage our students to value their culture and their language. We also encourage children to inquire and ask questions about aspects of each other's cultures. We have so many different faiths, and we can learn about the different worldviews.

> Yeah, especially when you have Muslim children coming into your school. When they are used to praying five times a day. Ramadan comes with certain things that the parents will say what the children can and can't do. We do the best we can to be culturally responsive and there's always things that come up that we were not expecting. I guess that's just what happens when you have an ethnically diverse school like ours.
>
> Another example of a positive change we have made occurred last year prior to teaching the health education programme called 'Keeping Ourselves Safe (KOS)'. It is a programme run by the police that addresses different aspects of abuse and safety. Many people from refugee families are scared of or don't trust police or community officers. In the past, they tended to withdraw their children from this programme as well as other health education programmes like sexuality education. Prior to teaching certain health education programmes, it is a requirement to run an information evening. In the past we would get one or two parents turning up to the information evenings and they were usually from our European families. Last year, 52 parents attended in our KOS programme, and I think about 45 of them were from refugee and migrant families. So, that was really down to the work of my English language bilingual learning assistants; they are my greatest resource. They communicate and break down all the barriers. That's our way of addressing some of the challenges. It's not perfect, but we've made a big breakthrough with that. Also, it's a way of getting children involved in our school sport and things like that. We just try to make sure that they get the information. Sometimes we do have the hands over the ears going on. When that happens, we try to find out why and what we can do about it?

Unique contexts, global principles

This New Zealand educator is clear that her school is not concerned with assimilating newly arrived students; rather, they are focused on integration. She promotes integration through meaningful dialogue with parents and by encouraging her students to ask each other about their homelands. While she is culturally sensitive, she is also reflective and understands that there is no way to be prepared for all the unknown challenges that can arise when different cultures collide. Her anecdote about families being fearful of the police is important as it helps to explain their world view and unwillingness to allow their children to participate in certain programmes. This teacher recognises that communicating directly with newly arrived families is vital, and she credits her bilingual learning assistants for making inroads with these communities. While many of her families may hold very traditional views on sex and sexual education, she knows that having in-person conversations about the curriculum and its intent is a way to help foster understanding. Her observation that some students place their hands over their ears in class is a powerful illustration of a clash of cultures. Her response to this behaviour, seeking understanding and puzzling over next steps, is indicative of this teacher's thoughtful approach.

Introducing sexual education can be a lightning rod in any classroom as religious and personal beliefs come up against classroom curricula. For children with refugee or asylum-seeker experiences, the contrast between the cultural norms in their home country and those of their host country can magnify this challenge. Engaging in conversation and holding face-to-face sessions with families can be helpful in conveying the purpose and content of sexual education programmes. As our New Zealand teacher demonstrated, encouraging and empowering families to show up and engage in such sessions may require an invitation from individuals who are seen as equals and worthy of trust. A further way to bolster cultural understanding in the classroom is also to take on a very proactive approach towards cultural differences. Creating a classroom where students openly discuss the norms of their home countries, raise questions in a caring manner and share their perspectives without the stigma that usually follows such differences is a powerful step for teachers. Teachers will never get the balance between home and school totally right, and families will continue to have concerns and fears, but sensitivity and dialogue are ways to help mitigate the effects of disconnects between home and school.

Collaborative learning

The capacity to collaborate effectively with others in a team-based project is one of the cornerstones of twenty-first-century components for success in any workplace. In school contexts, it is of substantial benefit to all those who engage with it (see, for example, Hue & Kennedy, 2013; Moss, 1990; Pastoor, 2017; Sellars, 2021a; Tschannen-Moran & Hoy, 2000). However, encouraging students to work together in schools may challenge their cultural and personal beliefs and those of their parents. As it has been noted, mixed-gender classrooms are not the cultural norm in gender referenced societies, especially as the students get older and become adolescents. Dimensions of culture (Hofstede, 2001, 2011) may also prove problematic. In determining the ways in which societies are characterised, Hofstede identified themes from participant opinions in many countries of the world to determine the major trends on several important social issues. He theorised these as cultural 'dimensions'. Amongst those that may directly impact on effective collaborative or cooperative efforts for students in schools are beliefs and expectations identified in the dimension relating to Individualist versus Collectivist societies. This dimension is indicative of the types of relationships people have with others in close groups. In Individualist societies, there are less expectations of loyalty to a group and to the overall wellbeing and success of the group. Many western countries, including the United States, Australia and the United Kingdom, for example, are identified as Individualist countries. In Collectivist countries, group loyalties and shared responsibility are expectations of the members of the group, who, in turn, will defend and protect the interests of the others in the group. This cultural dimension indicates that some communities of students could be confronted by non-harmonious group structures as they may feel uncomfortable with non-consensual opinions, with speaking individually in such a group and with concerns about 'losing face', which is the ultimate humiliation in many cultures. Individualistic cultural norms have low 'face consciousness' for the main part and are more comfortable to bring difficulties, different ideas, confronting perceptions and diverse perspectives to the fore for discussion without experiencing an essential need to express a shared opinion or perspective and demonstrate group loyalty.

Collaborative work in classrooms may also suffer in the absence of racial tolerance, understandings of difference and blatant discrimination (see, for example, Anderson, 2001; Edgeworth, 2014b; Campbell, 2017; Keddie, 2012a, 2012b; Liebe et al., 2018; McBrien, 2005; Nwosu & Barnes, 2014; Oikonomidoy, 2009; Pinson & Arnot, 2010; Schroeter & James, 2015). While education systems can frequently demonstrate and foster inequality and breed discriminatory attitudes even amongst homeland native students (Hughes, 2021), schools are institutions and have the potential to permeate these values and attitudes in the culture and ethos or challenge them to work humanely within the system (see, for example, Chiu et al., 2015; Edgeworth, 2014a; Faircloth & Hamm, 2005; Sellars, 2017b, 2021b). School communities play a critical part in educating students about difference, acceptance and tolerance even though it may mean restructuring their pedagogical strategies and critically apprising their approach to collaborative teamwork projects.

> The attitude adopted by their teachers in class is equally important for the young refugee children. The children revealed very sensitive antennae as regards the teachers' behaviour toward them, especially at the beginning. It was important that teachers showed themselves to be welcoming, but without drawing too much attention to the children's difference from their fellow pupils. The opportunity to say something about their home area was appreciated if the context was appropriate (e.g. a project on different cultures and countries of origin). Demonstrative 'refugee-friendly' statements on the part of teachers were, however, seen as being superfluous or embarrassing. (Anderson, 2001, p. 191)

Research findings

We interviewed a high school teacher in the United States who was fiercely proud of her school's willingness to accept and teach all students within a society that doesn't always accept all students.

Context: I taught elementary physical education for 15 years, and now I teach high school health and physical education. Our school is a breath of fresh air. It's cutting edge. We do everything that the world doesn't want to do. We serve all students and don't care where they come from. We don't care what documents they have, the colour of their skin and who they are. We meet them where they are and hold them as close as we possibly can to get them to graduation. We still continue to build relationships, when we let them go.

Well, the first setting in my classroom is 'Ohana'. Ohana means no one is left behind or forgotten. We use the collaboration protocol. So, we put them in a team. And then in those teams, they have roles. Those roles might be a leader, a communicator, a referee, etc. It depends because I teach health and physical education. It gives them an opportunity to be comfortable to lead or also to follow. So, they can practice and learn just in a smaller setting so that we can continue to build a foundation for courage. Because sometimes when we're a newcomer, we're scared to speak. We're in the quiet phase. So, it helps them with their peers to start opening up.

My classroom is almost fully student led. It is not led by me. I call my students my co-teachers. Especially in the world of physical education and health education and through a health lens, it's about 'what do you want to learn? What's relevant for you? How do we make this a healthy learning environment?' I do a passion project and ask them 'where their passions are? What needs do they see in their community?' The kids do this work in a small group. I rotate them and then we have what we call draft day. They know what they need for their teams to be successful. So, they might not have a friend that they're really close to in their group but now they know they have another friend in another team. So, they just start building more confidence with the bigger community.

I truly believe in social emotional learning and constant check-ins. And not just being able to name it an emotion like 'why am I here or why am I feeling it?'. I really enjoy restorative justice and the fact that we can create a circle and talk about it. It doesn't have to be restored like something was harmed or broken but just constantly community building. What are you thinking about this? How does this impact our thinking? For example, around Christmas time a lot of time we have ICE [Immigration and Customs Enforcement] raids, and we notice that a classmate is gone. They got picked up for deportation to go to the detention centre. So, having those feelings and those conversations of 'what should we do?', 'how should we go about to resolve this?', 'how does it make you feel comfortable in this moment?', and 'what will make you feel better?' gives us opportunities to write and address them.

Advocacy is one of my health standards. It's taking a firm stance on something that you truly believe in. Teaching the kids that they have a voice no matter what their documentation is. We as a school, not just in my classroom or in my advisory, truly believe in 'tell your story. You have your own narrative to share and to give the world. Don't let that hold you back'. So, we practice it in the classroom. We practice it on a different scale within the school. We put them into the school community and give them opportunities like speaking at 'Kids in Need of Defence (KIND)'. We just give those opportunities to advocate in a real-world setting.

Unique contexts, global principles

This American high school teacher has a very structured approach for empowering her students through collaboration learning experiences. Keenly aware that newly arrived students are often quiet and unwilling to contribute to the whole group, she has created a progressive system of group work that sees students first assigned to small groups with prescribed roles. These roles and groups change as students band together based on shared interests to pursue passion projects. As this teacher asserts, these rotating groups provide a 'foundation for courage' until students feel comfortable engaging in whole class discussions. She uses discussion circles to process events, including the arrest and possible deportation of classmates, and this strategy helps students to both process trauma and engage with their peers. This teacher has also put her students in decision-making roles in terms of instruction. She relies heavily on her 'co-teachers' to shape content, instruction and promote the classroom culture. By empowering her students to work together to make curricular decisions, she is fostering collaboration and building student autonomy. She has also made advocacy a cornerstone of her instruction which again offers her students meaningful ways to connect with each other around topics that affect their lives.

For many students with refugee or asylum-seeker backgrounds, collaboration in the classroom is foreign to the practices they may have experienced in their home country. As illustrated by our American teacher, collaborative learning opportunities need to be purposefully developed and scaffolded so that roles and expectations are clear. For students who may not understand the dynamics or benefits of working in groups, teachers need to model and illustrate appropriate and positive practices. Placing newly arrived students into small groups with empathetic classmates is a helpful first step, and it is also vital that group work is meaningful for students. Empowering groups to pursue an area of passion, perhaps addressing a community challenge or advocating on behalf of marginalised individuals, is a way of pulling in reticent students. A common refrain among business leaders in western countries is they are desperate for employees with soft skills, including the ability to collaborate. For this capacity to be in such short supply in nations where educational standards promote group work is telling about the challenge and effort it takes to develop true collaborative skills. Within schools that serve students with refugee or asylum-seeker backgrounds, teachers need to work together to create, pilot and share effective processes for developing collaborative skills across classrooms.

Conclusion

This chapter highlights the importance of supporting growth and development across the range of human capacities. There are numerous cultural challenges and societal practices to negotiate with regards to the very personal capacities embedded in the diversity of this discipline and the ways it may be presented as school subjects. This may be an area where parents and caregivers, including extended family members, may wish to be involved in conversations that sensitively unpack the curriculum content, the values and aims that underpin it and the ways in which they might engage in dialogue with their children and young people about these areas of cultural and personal sensitivity. These students are their children. Refugee and asylum-seeker communities have lost so much that it is important that the individuals to whom they are entrusted at school appreciate how precious they are, most especially in the ways they develop and learn to live in communities.

References

Anderson, P. (2001). 'You don't belong here in Germany....' On the social situation of refugee children in Germany. *Journal of Refugee Studies, 14*(2), 187–199.

Botfield, J. R., Newman, C. E., & Zwi, A. B. (2018). Engaging migrant and refugee young people with sexual health care: Does generation matter more than culture? *Sexuality Research and Social Policy, 15*(4), 398–408. https://doi.org/10.1007/s13178-018-0320-6

Bronfenbrenner, U. (1979). *The Ecology of Human Development: Experiments by Nature and Design.* Harvard University Press.

Bronfenbrenner, U. (1986). Ecology of the family as a context for human development: Research perspectives. *Developmental Psychology, 22*(6), 723.

Bronfenbrenner, U. (1988). Interacting systems in human development. Research paradigms: Present and future. In N. Bolger, A. Caspi, G. Downey, & M. Moore-House (Eds.), *Person in context: Developmental processes* (pp. 25–50). Cambridge University Press.

Bronfenbrenner, U., & Morris, P. (2006). The bioecological model of human development. In W. Damon & R. Lerner (Eds.), *Handbook of child psychology: Theoretical models of human development* (pp. 793–828). Wiley.

Campbell III, James Adam (2017). Attitudes towards refugee education and its link to xenophobia in the United States. *Intercultural Education, 28*(5), 474–479. https://doi.org/10.1080/14675986.2017.1336374

Chiu, M. M., Chow, B. W.-Y., McBride, C., & Mol, S. T. (2015). Students' sense of belonging at school in 41 countries. *Journal of Cross-Cultural Psychology, 47*(2), 175–196. https://doi.org/10.1177/0022022115617031

Das, M. (2019). Between two worlds: An immigrant story. *Humanity & Society, 43*(3), 327–345. https://doi.org/10.1177/0160597618784732

Dilbaz, B., İflazoğlu, N., & Tanın, S. A. (2019). An overview of female genital mutilation. *Journal of Turkish Society of Obstetric and Gynecology, 16*(2), 129–132. https://doi.org/10.4274/tjod.galenos.2019.77854

Edgeworth, K. (2014a). Black bodies, white rural spaces: Disturbing practices of unbelonging fo 'refugee' students. *Critical Studies in Education.* https://doi.org/10.1080/17508487.2014.956133

Edgeworth, K. (2014b). Black bodies, white rural spaces: Disturbing practices of unbelonging for 'refugee' students. *Critical Studies in Education.*

Faircloth, B. S., & Hamm, J. V. (2005). Sense of belonging among high school students representing 4 ethnic groups. *Journal of Youth and Adolescence, 34*(4), 293–309. https://doi.org/10.1007/s10964-005-5752-7

Haggis, J., & Mulholland, M. (2014). Rethinking difference and sex education: From cultural inclusivity to normative diversity. *Sex Education: Sexuality, Society and Learning, 14*(1), 57–66. http://ezproxy.newcastle.edu.au/login?url=http://search.ebscohost.com/login.aspx?direct=true&db=eric&AN=EJ1028191&site=eds-live http://dx.doi.org/10.1080/14681811.2013.824873

Hall, E. (1976). *Beyond Culture*. Knopf Doubleday Publishing Group.

Hawkey, A. J., Ussher, J. M., & Perz, J. (2018). "If You Don't Have a Baby, You Can't Be in Our Culture": Migrant and refugee women's experiences and constructions of fertility and fertility control. *Women's Reproductive Health, 5*(2), 75–98. https://doi.org/10.1080/23293691.2018.1463728

Hofstede, G. (1986). Cultural differences in teaching and learning. *International Journal of Intercultural Relations, 10*(3), 301–320.

Hofstede, G. (2001). *Culture's Consequences: Comparing Values, Behaviors, Institutions and Organizations Across Nations* (2nd ed.). Sage.

Hofstede, G. (2011). Dimensionalizing cultures: The hofstede model in context. *Online Readings in Psychology and Culture, 2*, 1–26.

Hofstede, G., & Bond, M. (1988). The confucius connection: From cultural roots to economic growth. *Organizational Dynamics, 16*(4), 5–21.

Hofstede, G., Hofstede, G. J., & Minkov, M. (2010). *Cultures and Organisations: Software of the Mind*. McGraw-Hill.

Hue, M.-T., & Kennedy, K. J. (2013). Building a connected classroom: Teachers' narratives about managing the cultural diversity of ethnic minority students in Hong Kong secondary schools. *Pastoral Care in Education, 31*(4), 292–308. https://doi.org/10.1080/02643944.2013.811697

Hughes, A. (2021). Positioning Indigenous knowledge systems within the Australian mathematics curriculum: Investigating transformative paradigms with Foucault. *Discourse: Studies in the Cultural Politics of Education, 42*(4), 487–498. https://doi.org/10.1080/01596306.2020.1715345

Keddie, A. (2012a). Pursuing justice for refugee students: Addressing issues of cultural (mis)recognition. *International Journal of Inclusive Education, 16*(12), 1295–1310. https://doi.org/10.1080/13603116.2011.560687

Keddie, A. (2012b). Refugee education and justice issues of representation, redistribution and recognition. *Cambridge Journal of Education, 42*(2), 197–212. https://doi.org/10.1080/0305764x.2012.676624

Khan, M., Rassool, G., Mabud, S., & Ahsan, M. (2020). *Sexuality Education from an Islamic Perspective*. Cambridge Scholars Press.

Kouba, L. J., & Muasher, J. (1985). Female Circumcision in Africa: An Overview. *African Studies Review, 28*(1), 95–110. https://doi.org/10.2307/524569

Kugle, S. (2003). Sexual diversity in Islam: Is there room in islam for lesbian, gay, bisexual and transgender muslims? Retrieved March 14, 2022, from https://www.mpvusa.org/sexual-diversity

Kumar, J. L., Chan, W. Y., & Spitz, A. (2021). Pathways to sexual health among refugee young women: A contextual approach. *Sexuality & Culture*. https://doi.org/10.1007/s12119-021-09850-9

Liebe, U., Meyerhoff, J., Kroesen, M., Chorus, C., & Glenk, K. (2018). From welcome culture to welcome limits? Uncovering preference changes over time for sheltering refugees in Germany. *PLoS One, 13*(8), e0199923. https://doi.org/10.1371/journal.pone.0199923

Masci, D., & Lipka, M. (2015). Where Christian churches, other religions stand on gay marriage. Retrieved March 14, 2022, from https://www.pewresearch.org/fact-tank/2015/12/21/where-christian-churches-stand-on-gay-marriage/

McBrien, J. L. (2005). Educational needs and barriers for refugee students in the US: A review of the literature. *Review of Educational Research, 75*(3), 329–364.

Mengesha, Z. B., Perz, J., Dune, T., & Ussher, J. (2017). Refugee and migrant women's engagement with sexual and reproductive health care in Australia: A socio-ecological analysis of health care professional perspectives. *PLoS One, 12*(7), e0181421. https://doi.org/10.1371/journal.pone.0181421

Metusela, C., Ussher, J., Perz, J., Hawkey, A., Morrow, M., Narchal, R., Estoesta, J., & Monteiro, M. (2017). "In My Culture, We Don't Know Anything About That": Sexual and reproductive health of migrant and refugee women. *International Journal of Behavioral Medicine, 24*(6), 836–845. https://doi.org/10.1007/s12529-017-9662-3

Morris, B. J., Kennedy, S. E., Wodak, A. D., Mindel, A., Golovsky, D., Schrieber, L., Lumbers, E. R., Handelsman, D. J., & Ziegler, J. B. (2017). Early infant male circumcision: Systematic review, risk-benefit analysis, and progress in policy. *World Journal of Clinical Pediatrics, 6*(1), 89. https://doi.org/10.5409/wjcp.v6.i1.89

Moss, E. (1990, Winter). Social interaction and metacognitive development in gifted preschoolers. *Gifted Child Quarterly, 34*(1), 16–20. https://doi.org/10.1177/001698629003400104

Muhammad, H. (2020). Islam, sexuality and culture. *Rahima*. Retrieved March 14, 2022, from https://swararahima.com/en/2020/10/05/islam-sexuality-and-culture/

Nagi, M. (2018). Islam, sexualities, and education. In H. Daun & R. Arjmand (Eds.), *Handbook of Islamic Education* (pp. 263–287). Springer International Publishing. https://doi.org/10.1007/978-3-319-64683-1_11

Nwosu, O., & Barnes, S. (2014). Where 'difference is the norm': Exploring refugee student ethnic identity development, acculturation, and agency at Shaw Academy. *Journal of Refugee Studies, 27*(3), 434–456. https://doi.org/10.1093/jrs/fet050

Oikonomidoy, E. (2009). The multilayered character of newcomers' academic identities: Somali female high-school students in a US school. *Globalisation, Societies and Education, 7*(1), 23–39. https://doi.org/10.1080/14767720802677358

Ortiz-Echevarria, L., Greeley, M., Bawoke, T., Zimmerman, L., Robinson, C., & Schlecht, J. (2017). Understanding the unique experiences, perspectives and sexual and reproductive health needs of very young adolescents: Somali refugees in Ethiopia. *Conflict and Health, 11*(Suppl 1), 26. https://doi.org/10.1186/s13031-017-0129-6

Pastoor, L. D. W. (2017, 03/04). Reconceptualising refugee education: Exploring the diverse learning contexts of unaccompanied young refugees upon resettlement. *Intercultural Education, 28*(2), 143–164. https://doi.org/10.1080/14675986.2017.1295572

Pinson, H., & Arnot, M. (2010). Local conceptualisations of the education of asylum-seeking and refugee students: From hostile to holistic models. *International Journal of Inclusive Education, 14*(3), 247–267. https://doi.org/10.1080/13603110802504523

Roudsari, R., Javadnoori, M., Hasanpour, M., Hazavehei, S., & Taghipour, D. (2013). Socio-cultural challenges to sexual health education for female adolescents in Iran. *Iranian Journal of Reproductive Medicine, 11*(2), 101–110.

Sanjakdar, F. (2005). *Teachers' struggle for an Islamically appropriate sexual health education curriculum at their school*. Australian Association of Research in Education Conference, Parramatta.

Schroeter, S., & James, C. E. (2015). "We're here because we're Black": The schooling experiences of French-speaking African-Canadian students with refugee backgrounds. *Race Ethnicity and Education, 18* (1), 20–39. https://doi.org/10.1080/13613324.2014.885419

Sellars, M. (2017a). *Reflective Practce for Teachers* (2nd ed.). Sage.

Sellars, M. (2017b). Schools as institutes of acculturation: A question of belonging. *Turkish Online Journal of Educational Technology*, (Special Issue), 843–846. http://www.tojet.net/special/2017_12_2.pdf

Sellars, M. (2021a). Belonging and being: Developing inclusive ethos. *International Journal of Leadership in Education*, 1–24. https://doi.org/10.1080/13603124.2021.1942994

Sellars, M. (2021b). Belonging and being: Developing inclusive ethos. *International Journal of Leadership in Education Theory and Practice*. https://doi.org/10.1080/13603124.2021.1942994

Smerecnik, C., Schaalma, H., Gerjo, K., Meijer, S., & Poelman, J. (2010). An exploratory study of Muslim adolescents' views on sexuality: Implications for sex education and prevention. *BMC Public Health*, *10*(1), 533. https://doi.org/10.1186/1471-2458-10-533

Tschannen-Moran, M., & Hoy, W. K. (2000, Winter). A multidisciplinary analysis of the nature, meaning, and measurement of trust. *Review of Educational Research*, *70*(4), 547–593. https://doi.org/10.3102/00346543070004547

WHO Regional Office for Europe and BZgA. (2010). *Standards for Sexuality Education in Europe: A Framework for Policy Makers, Education and Health Authorities and Specialists.*

World Health Organization. (2006). *Female Genital Mutilation*. Retrieved March 14, 2022, from https://www.who.int/teams/sexual-and-reproductive-health-and-research-(srh)/areas-of-work/female-genital-mutilation/prevalence-of-female-genital-mutilation

World Health Organization Africa. (2021). *Female Genital Mutilation*. Retrieved March 14, 2022, from https://www.afro.who.int/health-topics/female-genital-mutilation

Yok-Fong, P. (2013). Working with immigrant children and their families: An application of bronfenbrenner's ecological systems theory. *Journal of Human Behavior in the Social Environment*, *23*, 954–966. https://doi.org/10.1080/10911359.2013.800007

Zain Al-Dien, M. M. (2010). Perceptions of sex education among muslim adolescents in Canada. *Journal of Muslim Minority Affairs*, *30*(3), 391–407. https://doi.org/10.1080/13602004.2010.515823

7 Exercise and sport

Introduction

For many students, the school experience is characterised by many hours of sitting. This may be true for even the youngest students. The importance of learning opportunities that are well planned and involve various types of bodily kinaesthetic activity not only provides students with opportunities for whole body learning, but also indicates an awareness of the need for these learning activities to contribute to cognitive, physical, emotional and social development (Dalziell et al., 2015; Karagiannidis et al., 2015). This is important for all students but has particular relevance for students with refugee and asylum-seeker experiences who can find enjoyment in this area of learning without the stresses of having to demonstrate English language and literacy competencies, or an understanding of Hindu-Arabic mathematical concepts. Ironically, the benefits of participating in various exercise and sports activities, which can be made available to non-English-speaking students readily as they can be modelled or demonstrated, actually include many occasions to develop literacy and numeracy competencies in addition to the opportunities to improve inclusion and belonging (Block & Gibbs, 2017; HA & LYRAS, 2013). While these additional benefits may remain unexplored by many teachers, they may be critical to the overall success of these students. The limitations on participation of this element of mandatory school learning or undesirable impacts perceived by some parents and caregivers may be as the result of cultural-, religious-, social- or health-related concerns but these need to be understood and negotiated by teachers in order to ensure that the benefits of participation in these subjects are understood and appreciated as part of the new society into which they have been resettled.

Learning to play

In refugee and asylum-seeker communities, the notion of play may be seen as frivolous or non-productive. In many cases, this is because the children and young people play an important role in the maintenance of the household and the production of food for the family. In other circumstances, it is because the environments in which they lived were unsafe and so children at play were at risk. Macmillan et al. (2015), in their analysis of the drawings of children depicting their

DOI: 10.4324/9781003207900-8

pre-migration play, found that the majority of the drawing did not depict any play activity at all. The post-migration pictures and explanations provided evidence of the children physically at play in a variety of contexts. The importance of play, in both formal settings of school curricula and sports teams and the less -formal contexts of playgrounds and out-of-school play are considered critical to the development of children and young people who have suffered traumatic experiences and losses of multiple kinds. Kirova (2010) found that even the youngest children could engage with play as a medium through which to express their cultural identity and create a common culture amongst the multicultural group to which they belonged. Marsh (2017) (Marsh & Dieckmann, 2017) also discovered that informal musical play afforded refugee and asylum-seeking young students opportunities to create social bonds and to engage with aspects of their first culture. These findings highlight the need for resettlement of these families in places with adequate play facilities, both as indoor and outdoor venues and the criticality of these environments providing safe places for children to play (Lau et al., 2018).

The more formal setting of organised exercise programmes and sporting activities have also provided many opportunities for students with refugee and asylum-seeker backgrounds to participate in activities with others which highlighted their skills and talents and afforded new social and collaborative activities. Community groups, recognising the mental and physical health benefits of participation and opportunities for increased inclusion, have also developed strategies and allocated funding to support the inclusion of refugee and asylum-seeker children and youth in sport (see for example, 'Grant to boost migrant and refugee participation in sport', 2020; 'Promoting sports participation for refugee-background young people Sports Participation Progress Report', 2015). Other communities focused on inclusion of the whole refugee community in physical exercise and sporting activities (Abur, 2016; Amara et al., 2004; Valentine et al., 2009; Wieland et al., 2015) and encouraging midlife refugee women to participate (Zou et al., 2021). All these approaches are beneficial for school students as they offer possible encouragement from their families and communities.

Students with refugee and asylum-seeker backgrounds have also shared their perspectives of sport participation in schools. Harwood (2019) investigated the importance of school sport to these groups of students. Encouraged by the school guidance counsellor, who advised, 'I'll write your thesis for you – sport means everything to most of these kids!!!' (p. 94), Harwood discovered that the counsellor was right. She discussed a student with a refugee background attending a cross-country meet despite being suspended, a girl whose place in the school community was not established until she started playing in an all-girls soccer team, a senior boy whose love of basketball was challenged when he started playing in representative teams, an orphaned Libyan girl who played sport to avoid her unhappy home life and a Tanzanian boy who realised a lifelong dream of becoming a leader in the only sport he knew – soccer. Despite their successes, these students did not only play sport to enjoy. They played to escape the tensions and stresses of conflicting social and cultural expectations both at school and at home. Cseplö et al. (2021), studying the perspectives of students from a perspective of salutogenesis (Braun-Lewensohn & Sagy, 2011), reported that three major themes captured the perceptions of sport and the experiences of school sport amongst their participants, a group of diverse 16–18-year-old students with refugee and asylum experiences. They reported that students observed that sport was more important in their resettlement contexts than in their original homelands for two reasons: firstly, the short-term enjoyment benefits and, secondly, the long-term health advantages and the learning opportunities. They acknowledge the social advantages of playing sport and the inclusive nature of playing in addition to the feelings of wellbeing and health outcomes. Secondly, they realised that understanding the purpose of activities and the attendant rules and regulations helped them to become better communicators. Thirdly, and most insightfully, they commented that learning and achieving in sport-related activity required constructive, collaborative relationships with both teacher's and peers. From the play of the earliest years to the structured, competitive team sports played in the senior years of schooling, physical activity in school contexts was recognised as a powerful tool in promoting wellbeing and inclusion for these diverse cohorts of students and their communities.

> This child commented, 'In Iran there was no play. ... I did not play in Iran' and went on to describe her drawing.. 'Play, in Iran. We lived with six family members in one room too afraid to play outside, I am holding a doll. We only had one or two dolls and I have 2 sisters and a brother. I was not happy'. By contrast, she described her post-migration drawing.... 'In Australia I am very happy. We play at the park with my sisters and brother. It is very good here'.
> (Macmillan et al., 2015, p. 773)

Research findings

We spoke with a high school teacher in the United States who recognised the power of sport to help ease the transition to a new school setting.

Context: I teach English to a heterogeneous, like-combined class of nine to ten students together in the same room. These are students who are totally across the spectrum and language level. Some are newcomers, some have interrupted education and some are just about what we call exit the ESL system and everything in between. Our school is almost 100% free and offers reduced lunch. Most kids are from Central America, and then the ones that are not are from the Middle East or Africa. We are fortunate enough to have a really helpful staff and students' support team at our school. I don't know how we'd function without them.

> There's much more like sports and stuff going on and new kids as much as kids who've been in the country for a few years are both just as likely to be fighting over who gets on the soccer team. I know when we do intake one of the questions, we asked kids is like what sports do you like, and we give them some sports information like right off the bat so they can start building a community and get like invested in school. Which to some of them is a totally

new thing as they've been out of school for years. But you know soccer is their thing, and that will help them build a closer relationship to school and with their peers and things. Clubs, it's been tricky to get clubs going in our school we've really tried, as a school. I ran like a movie club like a cinema club which was pretty cool actually. I like showed popular American movies that they probably never heard of or seen before, which was fun. But transportation-wise, that has been slightly challenging to pull off.

Unique contexts, global principles

Our American high school teacher works in a community that serves large numbers of students from Central and South America, as well as the Middle East and Africa. For many of these students, the school's sports and activities help them to find a sense of enjoyment and community and bolster their connection with the school. It's notable that the school's intake process includes questions about students' interest in sports and provides students with information about available activities. The teacher's observation that some of her students may have been out of school for years is a stark reminder about the life-altering journeys many students make to western classrooms. In this school, soccer is a popular sport that helps newly arrived students put aside some of the anxiety that comes with being a new student, speaking a foreign language, in a new land. In fact, as illustrated in this school, sports enable newly arrived students to immediately engage with peers and compete on a level-playing field. This teacher has also attempted to create other activities and clubs for students to find enjoyment and connection but the ability of interested students to get transportation to these has proven difficult.

In much of our research, there has been a consistent message from global educators about prioritising the wellbeing of newly arrived students before diving into content. In the case of physical education and sport, the content itself can do much to support wellbeing. Sport helps to build immediate connections with students who may not speak English or know any other students. While some children with refugee or asylum-seeker backgrounds may have little experience with organised sport or physical activity, others possess a depth of sporting knowledge and skill. As our American high school teacher shared, building rich orientation sessions and welcome events that introduce students to all that school communities have to offer is important. For newly arrived students who are unfamiliar with the language and the conventions of western schools, discovering that education systems also promote playing soccer might be seen as a reason to come back the next day. Another reality illustrated by our American high school is that many students don't have the opportunity to engage in extracurricular activities because their families lack transportation, or resources, or the language skills needed to understand the opportunities available. Schools should place an equal emphasis on helping newly arrived students access extracurricular activities as they place on making classroom learning accessible.

Literacy and numeracy in learning to play

Cseplö et al. (2021), in their study about students, insightfully observed that participating in sport facilitated better communication, indicating that, as a two-way process, the teachers had to give clear, unambiguous instruction and the students had to listen carefully as the directions were given. Playing sport, engaging with exercise drills and perfecting skills are a wonderful means by which students can improve both their oral language skills and their own sporting expertise. It is impossible to play any game, formal or informal, without some concepts of space. This could easily bring into play the language of directionality, laterality, position and personal space. All team games have positions which determine the direction of play, as well as the areas that are available for access and those which are offside. Skill may include determining dominant and non-dominant hands or feet, striking or aiming for goals from different angles and distances, which invariably involves the language of measurement in many different expressions of quantity. Some may be formal and others not so.

Sporting activities are fertile ground for the language of two-dimensional space and three-dimensional objects as the equipment used to play various games and activities are distinguished from one another by their characteristics or properties. Discussions may be generated around the differences in the properties of the balls used to play different football codes, the size and materials of the equipment, and why they are suited to specific sporting contexts. The learning to play the games may involve multiplicative thinking (Downton & Sullivan, 2017; Hurst, 2017), proportional reasoning, and estimates of chance and probability, which is a much underrated life skill that requires accurate knowledge and understanding of all the possibilities that exist in their new contexts. Using the regular Hindu-Arabic number system in calculating scores, averages and personal best times contributes significantly to the numeracy experiences of those students who may have only previously engaged with concepts in ethnomathematical systems (Sellars, 2018; Stillman & Balatti, 2010). The context of sporting and physical activity provides an opportunity for much of the vocabulary used in mathematical constructs to be explored, demonstrated and practised in a real, non-conceptual manner allowing for the basics of many of the diverse strands of mathematical learning and language to be accessed as whole body learning (Sousa, 2012), or embodied cognition (Osgood-Campbell, 2015). While the implications for literacy and numeracy learning in sports and exercise contexts may seem not within the realm of specialist teachers in this learning domain, there are many programmes that offer opportunities to 'overlay' physical activities with explicit mathematical content based on the overall benefits of physical activity for general wellbeing and for effective cognition as the result of increased oxygen flow to the brain (Lloyd et al., 2018) and the degree to which the positive experiences impact on thinking (Fredrickson, 2000, 2001).

> As the lecturer climbed the stairs to exit the lecture theatre, she noticed a boy with his mother in the undergraduate audience. The lecture had focussed on the foundational importance of numeracy concepts across all school subjects. As they were leaving their seats, they all met in the aisle and the lecturer asked the boy, 'How was that lecture for you?' He replied, 'I enjoyed that, it was really interesting, especially the numeracy in sport. I know all about angles. I play cricket'.

Research findings

We spoke with a high school teacher in the United States who uses her physical education classroom to support learning in all academic disciplines.

Context: Currently, we're co-located with another high school. When we first started, we were three high schools. We were actually nine trailers and a small high school when we first started. Now we share the building with another high school. The surrounding community where we currently are is in a food desert. It's a walkable community. Most of our kids commute because they're not in a neighbourhood school. It's approximately almost a two-hour bus ride for our students to have access or their parents or families to our school. I taught elementary physical education for 15 years; now, I teach high school health and physical education.

> I'm on team essentials, we are essential to life, we cannot be the best self without the essentials, music our health and peace. The school try to name us electives but we're not elective. As you can imagine a lot of physical educators are isolated. We're so far different from other people and people think we're gym teachers and we roll out the ball and we read newspaper, and that is not true. Some people do, but there are math teachers who do that too, they just give you a worksheet and go about the business. I got to see myself outside of my content, because we sit down and introduce the disciplinary teams, and we get to have these discussions and digging in each other's curriculum and asking questions about the social justice lens. Is this multiculturally?, Are we being receptive?, What might it look like?, What another educator might bring to the table to enhance your curriculum area? So yes, we sit down with the math team and, yes, we sit down with social studies and science and see where we can cross-school wise help each other. For example, a writing formula so we're all teaching writing, teaching English language learners and we use, everybody uses RTQ as in 'restate the question' and that is school wide.

Unique contexts, global principles

Situated an hour outside of a major US city, the high school where our teacher works is highly regarded by advocates for refugees and by families with refugee and asylum-seeker backgrounds. This is evidenced by the fact students spend up to two hours commuting to attend the school. Though it may be respected by a slice of the population, the school also sits in an impoverished community that is a food desert. Our teacher offers a powerful statement about the importance of physical education, drama, art, music and other electives in her school by stating she is on 'team essentials'. She understands that for many students these are subjects that make school worth attending and life interesting. As a physical education teacher, she admits she feels a bit isolated and believes people have negative perceptions about her profession. Yet, her school has created a collaborative structure where she meets with teachers across disciplines to identify ways to support teaching and learning. She incorporates math lessons and English concepts and key points from social studies and science into her teaching and helps to reinforce and expand on student understandings. The collaborative structure also enables her to support and challenge her colleagues to focus on being respectful and responsive to the cultural backgrounds of their students.

Creating schools where teachers collaborate and communicate often is a powerful way to ensure students feel consistent support and reduced anxiety as they move from classroom to classroom. This is particularly important for children with refugee or asylum-seeker experiences who may find a large high school very intimidating or triggering. Collaborative schools also offer teachers the rare gift of having colleagues reinforce and expand on the lessons they teach. As our veteran educator in the United States demonstrated, courses such as physical education offer ways to make key vocabulary and concepts visible. A consistent theme that has emerged across our research is the importance of teacher collaboration to promote shared practices, values and content. While a school's principal can develop an organisational structure that promotes cross-grade and cross-subject collaboration, in many schools teachers must take the lead on developing teams with a clear purpose or they simply will not form.

Barriers to participation

'Promoting sports participation for refugee-background young people Sports Participation Progress Report' (2015, p. 1) has published a significant statement about the participation of migrant youth (predominantly youth with refugee and asylum-seeker backgrounds). They state that

> refugee and migrant youth have low participation rates in sport however, and identified barriers include costs, discrimination and a lack of cultural sensitivity in sporting environments, a lack of knowledge of mainstream sports services on the part of refugee background settlers, lack of access to transport, culturally determined gender norms and family attitudes.

Whilst some of these considerations are not concerns for those teachers providing sporting instruction at school as part of the curriculum, some of the most salient and most challenging reasons need consideration. Hopefully, school leaders are sufficiently sensitive to the financial situations of the refugee and asylum-seeker communities to offer free school uniforms, sports kit and equipment to the students. This appeared to be a common trend in the research conducted with school leaders in five countries who were participants in a leadership project that recorded strategies of safety and welcome for diverse cohorts of refugee and asylum-seeker students in their schools (Imig et al., 2021; Sellars, 2021; Sellars & Imig, 2021). The matter of discrimination and lack of cultural sensitivity is more complex and may originate with a group of teachers or a single teacher, or with a subgroup of students who are not accepting of the differences and diversity that these students bring to the teams or activities (Brooks & Watson, 2019). Female students in a study conducted by Farello et al. (2019) revealed that their feelings of incompetence in sport were the major barriers to enjoyment, inclusion and a sense of belonging. These feelings were exacerbated by the reaction of the more skilled teammates at school who were intolerant and ungracious when mistakes were made by these less skilled girls. One girl noted:

> For physical [PE class], there are a lot of skillful people, not a lot of nice people when it comes to game. I make mistakes sometimes, and they say something that makes me want to be out of the team so I don't—so I feel like I don't fit in.
> (Farello et al., 2019, p. 66)

In search of culturally appropriate sports pedagogies, Luguetti et al. (2020) investigated the interactions of African-Australian sports coaches with refugee backgrounds and their African-Australian players with refugee and asylum-seeker backgrounds. Their successes were attributed to three components of their collaboration. The coaches felt that they could support the players to achieve on the playing fields and in life generally because of their capacities to navigate the complex cross-cultural barriers and help the players make contact to services and agencies that could support them. They also felt that there was a shared perception of power. The coaches and the players interacted as 'family' and created a similar sense of belonging to that recorded by Cseplö et al. (2021). Finally, the coaches provided an environment where the players could openly discuss and critique the ways in which certain practices discriminated against them. Certainly, having an opportunity in any aspect of school life to have contact with individuals in 'authority' who have come from the same cultural background or similar refugee or asylum-seeker background appears to have multiple benefits for these groups of students. It may be critically beneficial in negotiating culturally orientated gender norms and the attitudes of parents towards their children and young people participating in sporting activities.

The culturally orientated gender norms are frequently problematic in sporting and physical activities where Muslim girls and young women are required to participate. The ways in which the sport outfits can be negotiated and adapted to fit religious and cultural identities is especially important in Islamic culture as the Qur'an dictates that, although both genders are to be modest in their dress, females are subjected to additional restrictions to maintain an Islamic perspective of modesty. Palmer (2009, pp. 29–30) describes how the all-female Muslim soccer team who were the participants in her research took to the field for training. The detail with which she describes the problems of being a Muslim female playing sport is an indication of the challenges that face teachers in the school physical exercise and games activities. She describes many of the complications that they must face regularly and with more complexity as the participants in the study were all from one part of the world who had been resettled in Australia. The requirement for modesty was the first consideration, as it would be for any culturally sensitive pedagogical approach. She notes:

> The interview and field observation data suggested that there was great diversity in the ways in which the Muslim women in the soccer team interpreted Islam, and this manifested itself as a constantly shifting tension in which the young

women parleyed their multiple, often conflicting, cultural identities as members of a sporting team, as members of the Somali community and as young women growing up in contemporary Australian society. Some of the players, for example, were relatively unconcerned about the religious import of engaging in sport and physical activity. Others, by contrast who adhered to a more traditional interpretation of Islam, followed much more closely the religious requirements of concealing their bodies from male view, particularly when engaging in exercise or physical movement. As such, there was a need to accommodate flexible uniform requirements which could both respect these religious beliefs and also preserve the collective identity of the soccer team which wearing a uniform affords. Some of the team elected to wear the shorts and short-sleeved tops of the customary soccer strip, while others chose to wear long sleeved T-shirts and tracksuit pants under their uniform. Some young women wore a bandana in place of their hijab (headscarf which covers the hair and neck area). Others wore the krimar (which covers the hair and front of the body) during training and competition, while a small number who normally wore the niqab (face veil, often worn with the krimar), removed it when in the female-only training environment. Still others elected to play entirely bare headed.

This diversity of uniform and bodily coverage was a concession to the diversity that existed in the girls' perceptions of what was morally acceptable attire in an all-female environment. However, if males were to be amongst the spectators at competition games, the adaptations of uniform could change substantially to cover the entire body, including the head. One impact of these dress requirements was that they were hot and heavy to play in, and they restricted movement. The range of strategic movement and skills that could be learned to support success were already limited by the players' interpretations of what was known as 'moral safety' (Palmer, 2009, p. 31). Due to their diverse interpretations of Islam and, frequently, the disapproval of family, some of the exercises and strategies were considered to be too sexually explicit for modest players, such as the trusting needed to execute a chest pass. The complications of heading the ball whilst wearing head coverings also detracted from the efficacy of team play. This study serves to illustrate the complexity of trying to bring Muslim females together as a coherent team in any context as the ways in which the religious teachings were interpreted by the players themselves and their parents and families impacted on every aspect of the game, leading to within-team tensions and frustrations.

Other studies also indicate that gendered roles and beliefs such as those indicated at the deepest level of consciousness and greatest emotional intensity in the Hall (1976) iceberg model were instrumental in female participation in sport. Robinson et al. (2019, p. 6) found that female members of the youth club who participated in their study recorded the following comments relating to gender-based restrictions on activity participation:

> I am a girl and it is better to only have girls in gym class
> I can't swim with boys because of my culture
> Sometimes parents don't allow you to have permission [to participate]

Whilst it may appear that Muslim girls have the most difficulty in engaging in sporting activities for various reasons related to religious beliefs and expectations, this is not an exclusive group. In many cultural groups, girls are forbidden to participate in sporting activities and exercise because of the critical need to preserve their hymen. Because of the belief that any strenuous activity would have the potential to break the hymen, girls are frequently allocated indoor activities in their homelands and are not encouraged to participate in sporting activities at school in their new homelands. In these cultures, sex before marriage is forbidden for girls. A broken hymen may suggest that, upon marriage, when it would be most likely to be discovered, the girl had engaged in premarital sexual activity (Matswetu & Bhana, 2018; Mishori et al., 2019; Moussaoui et al., 2022). Situations such as these may necessitate that the groom returns his bride to her family in disgrace. This would cause the girl and her family to lose their honour in their societies at the very least. At worst, the girl may be subjected to severe or fatal beatings from her husband's family or from her own. These cultural traditions are, like female genital mutilation, found in cultures with diverse religious beliefs and may be covertly continued in the countries in which the families with refugee and asylum-seeker experiences are resettled. Engaging female students whose cultural backgrounds subscribe to these notions of the hymen's fragility and importance may remain a challenge for teachers of physical exercise in resettlement countries for some time to come, despite the positive benefits of wellbeing, literacy, numeracy and life skills, a healthy lifestyle and inclusion.

Virginity testing is not an African issue, it is a component of harmful practices aimed at subjugating the bodily integrity of women (Cele, 2016).

We parents have been marginalised: I am not renting children owned by the government. If my ancestors tell me to do this [virginity testing], I can't argue with them (Mrs. Luthuli, IRIN 2005).

In January 2016 a row over virginity testing was reignited when the mayor of uThukela district in Kwazulu-Natal, Dudu Mazibuko, instituted a Maiden's Bursary program. Sixteen scholarships for tertiary study were awarded to virgin females. These girls had undergone virginity testing previously. Their scholarships would be renewed as long as they maintained their virginity during their studies and to prove this they would need again to periodically undergo the test.

The mayor's awards sparked off another intense discussion around the issue of virginity testing. The issue has been a fraught one in recent years, particularly in the Kwazulu-Natal region, where the test is associated with the traditional Zulu Reed Dance ceremony. The mayor's intent was practical: she felt that far too many girls ruin their education by falling pregnant and so the award would incentivize them to focus on their studies. (Rafudeen & Mkasi, 2016, p. 118)

Research findings

We interviewed a primary teacher from the United States and an educator in England. Both teachers talked about the importance of helping students with refugee or asylum-seeker experiences overcome barriers to engage in sport.

Context: I've been teaching for 30 years now. I am currently the chair of ESOL department of our school and also teach the fifth grade. We do have a total population of close to 1000 kids, but our ESL students are like 65% of that. Our ESL students come from 30 different countries all throughout Asia, America, Central America, Latin America, Africa and the Middle East. The students are represented by 26 different languages that they speak. We do have ESOL students from kindergarten to fifth grade. What makes our school special is the newcomer classroom.

> We do have swimming classes. I'm not really hundred percent sure but I'm not seeing those Afghani kids participating in the swimming classes. Also, a lot of those that are staying behind from field trips are Afghani kids too because their parents won't allow them to go. They're very sensitive with their culture, but once you can get their trust, they start talking and sharing everything about their lives. Especially during Ramadan when they're not eating lunch with the other kids, we support them. We separate them and give them an option like play games instead of eating lunch with the other kids and the other kids also respect their option. This year in Ramadan during lunchtime, my fifth graders started sharing things with me like 'you know, Miss, you need to do the sacrifice because you need that for your body, so you'll be healthy'. So, they were opening things like that and telling me about the big party they're going to have after Ramadan. It's nice talking with them.

Context: Part of my job was to work in a sports capacity, and kind of an aspect of that was working with refugee young people in the community. I did a lot of sports, and it's been part of my work really thinking about how I do this with the local guys as well. That was really great.

> I tried to bring different guys in to meet the boys, guys from Eritrea guys from Sudan, Ethiopia. And then, I really just get to know everyone, have a good relationship. When I was doing community work, we had a ramp going up to the football, it was indoor football, you have to go up the ramp. And then there was a table with people that sat there and let them in. And I realized that sometimes when these guys will climb up the stairs, they got to the table and most times they turned back. Because actually the people at the table were not recognizing that these guys, they can be sometimes intimidated by [being asked] 'so what do you want?', 'where do you need to go?' And it can be quite overwhelming, and I decided to really have a word with those people and said, 'look, we have refugee people come in here, can you please be a bit more. Just take your time when they come in, try to recognize, that the language might not be there and just really allow them, enable them, be a bit more welcoming.

Unique contexts, global principles

Each of our teachers offered anecdotes about easing the way for students with refugee or asylum-seeker experiences to respect their own cultures and still participate in activities. Our primary teacher is aware that her Afghan students are seldom allowed by their parents to engage in swimming lessons or field trips. This teacher makes an effort to talk with her students and their families to understand the rationale behind their decisions. Her communication has helped to develop trust between parents and school and fostered greater student participation in activities. During Ramadan, she separates her class and allows her Islamic students to play games instead of sitting with their peers for lunch. This sensitivity has helped her to build a healthy rapport with her students. Our English high school teacher uses the aura of sport to help his students feel connected to the community. He brings accomplished local athletes into his classroom to inspire and engage his students. When his soccer-mad students sought to play on the local sports ground, they were turned away by gruff individuals who were staffing the registration table. This teacher took a very proactive approach and addressed the staff members directly. He explained their language and cultural differences and asked them to be more patient, more welcoming and more helpful.

For children with refugee or asylum-seeker experiences, there are a host of obstacles that can prevent them from taking part in sports and activities. As our American example illustrates, teachers need to recognise that students must navigate between two worlds and adhering to cultural and family expectations means that they sometimes choose not to participate in extracurricular activities. When newly arrived students elect not to participate in activities, teachers need to engage in respectful dialogue to develop understanding of what is underpinning such choices. Teachers also need to modify classroom routines where possible to reduce the additional scrutiny students feel from making decisions rooted in cultural and family expectations. In the case of our English example, participation was hindered by individuals acting without sensitivity, and it required our teacher to educate the community. The challenges newly arrived students face do not start and end at the school gate. It's worth remembering that the depth of knowledge and empathy many educators possess from their years of learning about and supporting newly arrived students is rare in society. Therefore, when possible, teachers need to educate community members and policymakers who intentionally, or unintentionally, erect barriers in front of individuals who have already faced years of barriers, disruption and trauma.

Conclusion

Play is often associated with small children, but in this chapter it applies to all school-aged students. Participation in playing and exercising is considered to be a mandatory school subject not only because it promotes healthy outcomes, but because it engages the brain in different ways of knowing and learning. Great athletes, team players and all those who excel in this discipline are excellent strategists, 'game players', and have an increased awareness of themselves and others in close proximity. This is especially so in team games where spatial concepts are critical to success, safety and skilful play. It is unfortunate that cultural restrictions related to gender-based roles and concerns may disrupt the opportunities for female participation in some of these activities. It disadvantages them considerably as the benefits for females are more substantial than those for males. Current research indicates that physical activity is a positive component in avoiding breast cancer due to the ways in which the hormones are balanced during fitness regimes (Ennour-Idrissi et al., 2015). All play is purposeful and has many benefits for all participants, not just those who have refugee and asylum-seeker experiences. The benefits are not simply in terms of physical health and fitness, but in terms of emotional, cognitive and brain health. This is because the endorphins released by the brain when engaging in physical activities of exercise and sport not only are stress relieving but also have the potential to relieve depression and anxiety (Heijnen et al., 2016), making this a priority for those recovering from trauma.

References

Abur, W. (2016). Benefits of participation in sport for people from refugee backgrounds: A study of the South Sudanese community in Melbourne, Australia. *Issues in Scientific Research*, *1*(2), 10–26. Retrieved March 27, 2022, from https://journalissues.org/isr/wp-content/uploads/sites/9/2020/01/Abur.pdf

Amara, M., Coalter, F., Aquilina, D., Taylor, J., Argent, E., Betzer-Tayar, M., Green, M., & Henry, I. (2004). The roles of sport and education in the social inclusion of Asylum seekers and refugees: An evaluation of policy and practice in the UK. 1–118. Retrieved March 27, 2022, from https://www.sportanddev.org/sites/default/files/downloads/the_roles_of_sport_and_education_in_the_social_inclusion_of_asylum_seekers_and_refuge.pdf

Block, K., & Gibbs, L. (2017). Promoting social inclusion through sport for refugee-background youth in Australia: Analysing different participation models. *Social Inclusion*, *5*(2), 91–100. https://doi.org/10.17645/si.v5i2.903

Braun-Lewensohn, O., & Sagy, S. (2011). Salutogenesis and culture: Personal and community sense of coherence among adolescents belonging to three different cultural groups. *International Review of Psychiatry*, *23*(6), 533–541. https://doi.org/10.3109/09540261.2011.637905

Brooks, J., & Watson, T. (2019). School leadership and racism: An ecological perspective. *Urban Education*, *54*(5), 631–655. https://doi.org/10.1177/0042085918783821

Cele, S'. (2016). *Bathabile Dlamini blasts virginity testing and 'oppressive' cultural practices*. https://www.news24.com/citypress/News/bathabile-dlamini-blasts-virginity-testing-and-oppressive-cultural-practices-20160203

Cseplö, E., Wagnsson, S., Luguetti, C., & Spaaij, R. (2021). 'The teacher makes us feel like we are a family': Students from refugee backgrounds' perceptions of physical education in Swedish schools. *Physical Education and Sport Pedagogy*, 1–14. https://doi.org/10.1080/17408989.2021.1911980

Dalziell, A., Boyle, J., & Mutrie, N. (2015, Nov). Better Movers and Thinkers (BMT): An exploratory study of an innovative approach to physical education. *European Journal of Psychology*, *11*(4), 722–741. https://doi.org/10.5964/ejop.v11i4.950

Downton, A., & Sullivan, P. (2017). Posing complex problems requiring multiplicative thinking prompts students to use sophisticated strategies and build mathematical connections. *Educational Studies in Mathematics, 95*(3), 303–328. https://doi.org/10.1007/s10649-017-9751-x

Ennour-Idrissi, K., Maunsell, E., & Diorio, C. (2015). Effect of physical activity on sex hormones in women: A systematic review and meta-analysis of randomized controlled trials. *Breast Cancer Research, 17*(1). https://doi.org/10.1186/s13058-015-0647-3

Farello, A., Blom, L., Mulvihill, T., & Erickson, J. (2019). Understanding female youth refugees' experiences in sport and physical education through the self-determination theory. *Journal of Sport for Development, 7*(13), 55–72. Retrieved March 27, 2022, from https://jsfd.org/2019/11/01/understanding-female-youth-refugees-experiences-in-sport-and-physical-education-through-the-self-determination-theory

Fredrickson, B. (2000). Cultivating positive emotions to optimize health and well being. *Prevention and Treatment, 3*. Retrieved September 3, 2013, from http://www.unc.edu/peplab/publications/Fredrickson_2000_Prev&Trmt.pdf

Fredrickson, B. (2001). The role of positive emotions in positive psychology. *American Psychologist*, March(56, 3), 218–226.

Grant to boost migrant and refugee participation in sport. (2020). *Connect*. https://www.une.edu.au/connect/news/2020/07/grant-to-boost-migrant-and-refugee-participation-in-sport

Ha, J.-P., & Lyras, A. (2013). Sport for refugee youth in a new society: The role of acculturation in sport for development and peace programming. *South African Journal for Research in Sport, Physical Education and Recreation, 35*(2), 121–140.

Hall, E. (1976). *Beyond Culture*. Knopf Doubleday Publishing Group.

Harwood, G. (2019). *What Is the Meaning of Sport for Young People From Refugee Backgrounds? A Case Study of a State High School in Brisbane, Queensland*. Queensland University of Technology https://eprints.qut.edu.au/132321/4/Georgie%20Harwood%20Thesis.pdf

Heijnen, S., Hommel, B., Kibele, A., & Colzato, L. S. (2016, January 7). Neuromodulation of aerobic exercise—A review [Mini Review]. *Frontiers in Psychology, 6*. https://doi.org/10.3389/fpsyg.2015.01890

Hurst, C. (2017). Children have the capacity to think multiplicatively, as long as. *European Journal of STEM Education, 2*(3), 1–14.

Imig, S., Sellars, M., & Fischetti, J. (2021). *Creating Spaces of Wellbeing and Safety for Students with Refugee and Asylum Seeker Experiences: Lessons from School Leaders*. Routledge.

Karagiannidis, Y., Barkoukis, V., Gourgoulis, V., Kosta, G., & Antoniou, P. (2015). The role of motivation and metacognition on the development of cognitive and affective responses in physical education lessons: A self-determination approach. *Motricidade, 11*(1), 135–150. http://ezproxy.newcastle.edu.au/login?url=http://search.ebscohost.com/login.aspx?direct=true&db=s3h&AN=103179329&site=eds-live

Kirova, A. (2010). Children's representations of cultural scripts in play: Facilitating transition from home to preschool in an intercultural early learning program for refugee children. *Diaspora, Indigenous, and Minority Education, 4*(2), 74–91. https://doi.org/10.1080/15595691003635765

Lau, W., Silove, D., Edwards, B., Forbes, D., Bryant, R., McFarlane, A., Hadzi-Pavlovic, D., Steel, Z., Nickerson, A., Van Hooff, M., Felmingham, K., Cowlishaw, S., Alkemade, N., Kartal, D., & O'Donnell, M. (2018, Sep 4). Adjustment of refugee children and adolescents in Australia: Outcomes from wave three of the Building a New Life in Australia study. *BMC Medicine, 16*(1), 157. https://doi.org/10.1186/s12916-018-1124-5

Lloyd, A., Eather, N., & Riley, N. (2018). Physical education and numeracy. In M. Sellars (Ed.), *Numeracy in Authentic Contexts: Making Maening across the Curriculum* (pp. 341–372). Springer.

Luguetti, C., Singehebhuye, L., & Spaaij, R. (2020). Towards a culturally relevant sport pedagogy: Lessons learned from African Australian refugee-background coaches in grassroots football. *Sport, Education and Society*, 1–13. https://doi.org/10.1080/13573322.2020.1865905

Macmillan, K. K., Ohan, J., Cherian, S., & Mutch, R. C. (2015). Refugee children's play: Before and after migration to Australia. *Journal of Paediatrics and Child Health*, *51*(8), 771–777. https://doi.org/10.1111/jpc.12849

Marsh, K. (2017). Creating bridges: Music, play and well-being in the lives of refugee and immigrant children and young people. *Music Education Research*, *19*(1), 60–73. https://doi.org/10.1080/14613808.2016.1189525

Marsh, K., & Dieckmann, S. (2017). Contributions of playground singing games to the social inclusion of refugee and newly arrived immigrant children in Australia. *Education 3–13*, *45*(6), 710–719. https://doi.org/10.1080/03004279.2017.1347128

Matswetu, V. S., & Bhana, D. (2018). Humhandara and hujaya: Virginity, culture, and gender inequalities among adolescents in Zimbabwe. *SAGE Open*, *8*(2), 215824401877910. https://doi.org/10.1177/2158244018779107

Mishori, R., Ferdowsian, H., Naimer, K., Volpellier, M., & McHale, T. (2019). The little tissue that couldn't – dispelling myths about the Hymen's role in determining sexual history and assault. *Reproductive Health*, *16*(1), 1–9. https://doi.org/10.1186/s12978-019-0731-8

Mkasi, L., & Rafudeen, A. (2016). Debating virginity-testing cultural practices in South Africa: A taylorian reflection. *Journal for the Study of Religion: JSR; KwaZulu-Natal*, *29*(2), 118–133, 161–162.

Moussaoui, D., Abdulcadir, J., & Yaron, M. (2022). Hymen and virginity: What every paediatrician should know. *Journal of Paediatrics and Child Health*, *58*(3), 382–387. https://doi.org/10.1111/jpc.15887

Osgood-Campbell, E. (2015). Investigating the educational implications of embodied cognition: A model interdisciplinary inquiry in mind, brain, and education curricula [Article]. *Mind, Brain & Education*, *9*(1), 3–9. https://doi.org/10.1111/mbe.12063

Palmer, C. (2009). Soccer and the politics of identity for young Muslim refugee women in South Australia. *Soccer & Society*, *10*(1), 27–38. https://doi.org/10.1080/14660970802472643

Promoting sports participation for refugee-background young people Sports Participation Progress Report. (2015). 2. Retrieved March 27, 2022, from https://mspgh.unimelb.edu.au/__data/assets/pdf_file/0020/2077031/SportsParticipationProgressReport_Aug2015.pdf

Rafudeen, A., & Mkasi, L. P. (2016). Debating virginity-testing cultural practices in South Africa: A Taylorian reflection. *Journal for the Study of Religion*, *29*, 118–133. http://www.scielo.org.za/scielo.php?script=sci_arttext&pid=S1011-76012016000200007&nrm=iso

Robinson, D. B., Robinson, I. M., Currie, V., & Hall, N. (2019). The Syrian Canadian Sports Club: A community-based participatory action research project with/for Syrian Youth Refugees. *Social Sciences*, *8*(6), 163. https://doi.org/10.3390/socsci8060163

Sellars, M. (2018). Mathematics and numeracy in a global society. In M. Sellars (Ed.), *Authentic Contexts of Numeracy: Making Maening across the Curriculum* (pp. 5–21). Springer.

Sellars, M. (2021). Belonging and being: Developing inclusive ethos. *International Journal of Leadership in Education*, 1–24. https://doi.org/10.1080/13603124.2021.1942994

Sellars, M., & Imig, S. (2021). School leadership, reflective practice, and education for students with refugee backgrounds: A pathway to radical empathy. *Intercultural Education*, 1–13. https://doi.org/10.1080/14675986.2021.1889988

Sousa, D. (2012). *Mind, Brain and Education: Neuroscience Implications for the Classroom*. Solution Tree Press.

Stillman, G., & Balatti, J. (2010). Contribution of ethnomathematics to mainstream mathematics classroom practices. In B. Atweh, H. Fogasz, & B. Nebrers (Eds.), *Sociocultural Research on Mathemathics Education: An International Perspective* (pp. 313–328). Routledge.

Valentine, G., Sporton, D., & Nielsen, K. B. (2009). Identities and belonging: A study of somali refugee and Asylum seekers living in the UK and Denmark. *Environment and Planning D: Society and Space, 27*(2), 234–250. https://doi.org/10.1068/d3407

Wieland, M. L., Tiedje, K., Meiers, S. J., Mohamed, A. A., Formea, C. M., Ridgeway, J. L., Asiedu, G. B., Boyum, G., Weis, J. A., Nigon, J. A., Patten, C. A., & Sia, I. G. (2015). Perspectives on physical activity among immigrants and refugees to a small urban community in Minnesota. *Journal of Immigrant and Minority Health, 17*(1), 263–275. https://doi.org/10.1007/s10903-013-9917-2

Zou, P., Kadri, Z., Shao, J., Wang, X., Luo, Y., Zhang, H., & Banerjee, A. (2021, May 24). Factors influencing physical activity participation among midlife immigrant women: A systematic review. *International Journal of Environmental Research, 18*(11), 1–25. https://doi.org/10.3390/ijerph18115590

8 Science and technology

Introduction

In addition to the many social and cultural changes that communities with refugees and asylum seekers may experience in their new homelands are the multiple ways in which scientific advances impact on their lives as technological ways of being and doing. The degree to which technology challenges or is a familiar part of everyday life depends on the geographical position, the family background and income and the availability of infrastructures that support technological resources in their homelands. Many communities who have lived in the large cities of their homelands would be aware of the implementation of scientific and technological tools in everyday life, even if they are not familiar with engaging with it personally. However, in remote, isolated and impoverished communities, there may be little evidence of modern scientific approaches to communication, health or other aspects of everyday living, despite the advantages they offered student learning (Drolia et al., 2020; Fitzgerald & Smith, 2016; Kim et al., 2011).

This places students from refugee and asylum-seeker backgrounds at varying degrees of disadvantage when attending schools in their new homelands. For some, the technological components that are embedded in every school discipline are hugely challenging (Koehler et al., 2007; Mishra & Koehler, 2006), and, despite the attraction of computers, mobile phones, social media, and teaching and learning media, they represent a world that may be totally alien to that of their homelands and find the highly technological access routes to many of the resources available to them impossible to navigate (Sabie & Ahmed, 2019). As with the acquisition of language and literacy skills, parents and older community members may rely on students to support their learning in technology. Whilst this may be a common situation, even in some communities in the countries of resettlement, the financial commitment that underpins participation in the technological world is frequently beyond the means of many refugee and asylum-seeker families. This limits access, not simply to the learning support tools that are provided by technology but also to the school and wider community of users who rely on these devices to convey their culture, expectations and identity formation to others (Hussain et al., 2020). It also limits interaction with those who communicate the information required about the institutional structures of the school systems in which these students participate. In common with the requirements of school

DOI: 10.4324/9781003207900-9

science in laboratories or other practical contexts, it is the constant practice and engagement with equipment, technologies and their potential to introduce and support new learning that can support effective integration and acculturation (Ager & Strang, 2008; Berry, 1997, 2005; Berry et al., 2006; Doná & Berry, 1994; Sam & Berry, 2010). Teaching and learning in these complex, critical areas of learning for life may need teachers to consider revisiting the pedagogical notion of '*Experience before Explicit*' where possible in order to allow the full enthusiasm and potential that these combined disciplines offer to students with refugee and asylum-seeking backgrounds.

Science and technology: Linking to life

'Science' holds multiple opportunities for learning in different contexts. This umbrella term covers the fields of physics, chemistry, biology, environmental studies, agriculture and anatomy, which are just a few of the sub-disciplines that form part of many school curricula. Science and technology are frequently taught together as 'blended learning' (Bidarra & Rusman, 2017, p. 6). However, some other contexts of blended learning are not always as readily recognised as being learning in science and technology. The use of technology in the context of drama and digital storytelling may appear to be far from the science and technology curricula of many school districts, but it has proven to be an important aspect of student integration, therapy for mental health concerns and language development (see, for example, Bansel et al., 2016; Dunn et al., 2012; Emert, 2013, 2014; Karam, 2018; Kaukko, 2021; Vecchio et al., 2017; Watkins et al., 2019). The critical aspect from a science perspective is the learning that was the outcome of engaging with technology as users and directors, not simply as consumers. Learning to operate the various technologies of visual and audio tools designed with great precision and accuracy to capture the actions and storytelling of the students afforded multiple opportunities to learn the craft of podcasting, cutting and editing media products amongst other skills required to produce and present digital media outcomes effectively. It offered challenges to problem-solving, developing hypotheses and seeking proof when working within the boundaries of the apps and equipment that were specifically selected to support the activities designed, not as science learning, but for investigating multiple other outcomes. These 'incidental' learning outcomes may easily be overlooked in the studies that utilised these technologies, but they are, nevertheless, an important contribution to student experiences of technology as a meaningful component of science and technology learning.

Other school-based activities which have the potential to support science learning in the context of research into other benefits for students with refugee and asylum-seeker backgrounds are those associated with the development and maintenance of school gardens. Smith and Motsenboker (2005) linked their research explicitly to science outcomes, indicating that, although there were multiple benefits for the students, including those with refugee and asylum-seeker backgrounds, their findings were predominantly focused on the improvement of the students' scores in science testing. Cutter-Makenzie (2009) widened her research aims to examine the impact of participating in school garden projects to the language development, culture and environmental awareness demonstrated by the students with refugee and asylum-seeking backgrounds. Seeking to establish multicultural gardens in low socio-economic schools that were sensitive to the diversity of the school population, it was established that many schools did not have the financial or human resources to design, establish and maintain school gardens independently. Consequently, disadvantaged schools were supported by a programme that supplied teaching and learning activities, raw materials, expertise, volunteers and coaching for a school year. The aim was that the garden and all the potential for learning that it offered was incorporated into the school curriculum the following year. The participating schools were encouraged to,

> use a whole-school, multidisciplinary approach to the curriculum; model the garden on environmental sustainability practices; consider the project as a long term commitment and provide ongoing maintenance; empower schools by enabling students to plan and implement a real environmental project; stimulate creativity and celebrate diversity connect parents and local multicultural communities with the school contribute to student health and wellbeing build upon volunteer contributions to community well-being and encourage their ongoing support; and strengthen and build the social and educational capacity within the school.
>
> (Winters, 2008, pp. 7–8; Cutter-Makenzie, 2009, p. 125)

Allowing the students to design and research their own projects was a critical aspect of the project as it gave a voice to students with refugee and asylum-seeker experiences. The encouragement of inviting a 'gardening buddy' (Cutter-Makenzie, 2009, p. 125) to work with the students also contributed to the richness of the multiple experiences that the environmental garden projects provided. Many newly arrived family members and community members acted as these buddies, finding a place to share their expertise in a school context from the outset. Whilst strengthening students' knowledge of the characteristics of an unfamiliar, new environment, the climate and conditions for growth, it also allowed them to overcome their cultural differences by making them aware of similarities in their traditional ways of all things related to food. Gardening and cooking are perfect partners, and these activities allowed the students to further explore aspects of basic chemistry as produce was transformed into dishes with diverse traditions and backgrounds.

> I quietly sat with a group of children as they talked about the traditional way of eating in Afghanistan with the right hand and no cutlery. A child modeled a handwashing ceremony that typically takes place before a meal with a special bowl called a "haftawa-wa-lagan." He talked about how a young child will usually pour water over a guest's hands. He then proceeded to pour water over my hands. Immediately following this several children from

> a Sudanese background talked about how this is similar to the Arabic custom of pouring water over the hands of the guests using the Ebrig, a shiny copper ewer. They also talked about how all guests are offered a towel to wipe their hands and large cloths to cover the knees. During this conversation one of the Sudanese students quickly brought me a towel to wipe my hands and then placed another towel over my knees. While only brief it was apparent that this sort of everyday cultural exchange that the multicultural school gardens program facilitated appeared to take children's gardening to a new level where the focus isn't just on gardening, but the children's culture making it far more meaningful for new immigrants to Australia. (Cutter-Makenzie, 2009, p. 129)

Research findings

We spoke with an Australian primary school teacher working in a small regional school who recognised the power of science to engage all her learners equally.

Context: I have been a teacher for over 20 years now. I used to work in a primary school where we had the highest number of enrolments across the region from EAL/D backgrounds. In this school, close to 70% (200 students or so) speak a language other than English, which doesn't necessarily mean they require English as additional language support; out of those 70%, close to 30% to 35% are from refugee backgrounds. I am currently working as an EAL/D education leader. In this role, I'm delivering some professional learning communities with the staff and teachers that are newly appointed to the EAL/D role at the high school.

> But science is a wonderful KLA [Key Learning Area] for EAL/D learners because there's so much hands on. They love experiments and learning about the different factors involved in in science just as much as native speakers. The good thing with that EAL/D specialist is that you work shoulder to shoulder teachers. One of our teachers worked really closely with the head teacher and several other teachers to get students on the same page in understanding that second language acquisition is really hard. It takes a long time. If you're delivering content that is syllabus and curriculum based in the New South Wales curriculum for a student that's only been in the country for two years, they want to be doing the same thing but obviously can't access that language or they don't have maybe the understanding. It's up to the teacher to really pick what's the important part that they want them to learn. The EAL/D specialists and the faculty have done a really good job in modifying and varying the content for a variety of levels of learners, so that someone with a beginning English can access the same topic as someone who's extending in that same topic. So, there's maybe three or four different levels of work being given to cater for the varying learning needs of that classroom.

Unique contexts, global principles

This teacher's school is extremely diverse, including large numbers of students with refugee or asylum-seeker backgrounds who may have arrived in Australia weeks, months and years ago. Her school colleagues have embraced the challenge of educating students whose proficiency with English is extremely varied, and they see science as a fantastic tool to effect growth. The hands-on nature of science makes it as popular with this teacher's native students as it is with her new arrivals. The school has created an understanding among all staff and students that learning a second language is hard work and can take many years. This teacher works in a very standardised-based education context, and she knows there are system-level pressures for students to perform regardless of their English language proficiency. The school's EAL/D specialist works collaboratively with teachers, helping them break down curriculum to core concepts that need to be conveyed which results in multiple levels of differentiation in the classroom. For this teacher, science has become a wonderful opportunity to develop language, engage her students and still convey core curricular concepts.

Students with refugee or asylum-seeker backgrounds can easily find themselves lost in English-speaking classrooms. Finding content that has universal appeal and can break down language barriers is the goal of every teacher working with newly arrived students. By virtue of its hands-on nature, science offers opportunities for teachers to grab students' attention, chunk out content and focus on language development. This chunking of content into key concepts that need to be conveyed is a powerful idea. When teachers collaborate with each other, including the school's language support specialists, to analyse curriculum, this facilitates differentiated practice. Our Australian teacher reported that her school took the unique step of educating the entire community about the difficulty of learning a second language. The appeal of such an approach is that it builds collective understanding of the pressures on newly arrived students, it helps native speakers recognise why their teacher may be repeating key learning concepts, and it may help to relieve some of the anxiety non-native speakers feel wrestling with a new language. As our research findings illustrate, by working collaboratively teachers can create environments where newly arrived students feel supported and understood and where learning is exciting and hands-on. In most cases, science classes offer an opportunity to create this reality.

The school science context

The importance of supporting students with refugee and asylum-seeker experiences in ways that enable and empower them to become successful in the same ways that their non-migrant peers aspire to requires not only increased financial support for schools but also the avoidance of ad hoc measures which become standard policies and procedures for these diverse groups of students (Bešić et al., 2020; Koehler & Schneider, 2019). Science per se is one of the most desirable subject domains in schools at the present time (Alberts, 2022; Fitzgerald & Smith, 2016; Stuckey et al., 2013) and is described a lifelong process in an ever-changing world (Falk & Dierking, 2019). The importance of learning in science disciplines is increasingly important for the lifelong success of students with refugee and asylum-seeker backgrounds but may be increasingly challenging for their teachers. Teacher understanding of the subject and the pedagogical strategies best suited to support aspects of learning in science laboratories and classrooms are increasingly critical for the success of their students (see, for example, Abell et al., 1998; Akerson et al., 2000; Appleton, 2003; Barnhart & van Es, 2015; Cowie & Bell, 1999; de Laat & Watters, 1995; Demir & Abell, 2010; Fitzgerald & Smith, 2016; Houseal et al., 2014). However, this may be challenging for both student and teacher. Miller (2009) discusses the difficulties of the science content language for students with interrupted schooling and how the difficulties were exacerbated by teacher assumptions about their language understanding. Language was also found to be the major difficulty in the study of students with refugee experiences and their failure in sciences courses. Coupled with the lack of capacity that their parents had to support them, Idin (2018) concluded that these students required additional after-school science lessons to succeed. This is not the only strategy that may support student learning in science.

In a more innovative intervention, Harper (2017) describes the process by which students with refugee experiences were able to use their own knowledge and first language skills combined with their English language proficiencies to engage meaningfully with scientific knowledge and investigative processes in the context for their cross-cultural classroom and whilst using voice technology to record their thinking and findings. This is one study of how accommodating the language and cultural difficulties required to engage with the meta language, decision-making and problem-solving associated with science and its processes may be overcome. Rethinking traditional science pedagogies and becoming more sensitive to the limitations of English language science textbooks that have little meaning for these students (Miller, 2009) may offer another way forward for success in this learning domain.

> Issues of equity in education for refugee students in resettlement have become more pressing in the United States over the past decade. According to the U.S. State Department, an average of 61,452 refugees per year has been admitted to the U.S. since 2005. Yet the national learning paradigm in the U.S. has not shifted to accommodate the needs of refugee students, many of whom have had interrupted, little, or no formal education. Standardised testing in schools assumes a conceptual command of the English language that refugee students in resettlement struggle to achieve in their first five years of living in the United States (Cummins, 2008). Similarly, the Next Generation Science Standards (NGSS) (Achieve, 2014) emphasis on performance through the use of science and engineering language and practices calls for students to adopt the mindset of scientists and engage in critical practices such as argumentation and constructing scientific explanations based on evidence. Refugee students may not have the academic or

> social confidence to engage in these practices in a meaningful way. Many refugee families resettling in the U.S. have escaped the trauma of war and have cultivated a climate of invisibility for survival. Consequently, the confidence required for open debate and critical thinking might be difficult for refugee students to acquire. Research on the compatibility of scientific inquiry and the cultural patterns of discourse of students emerging from non-dominant learning paradigms has indicated that often the confidence to position themselves as agents in science learning is missing (Lee, 2002). Within science education literature, little work has been done on how to integrate refugee students into science learning in a way that allows them to engage with scientific practices as agents with decision-making power (Martin, Wassell, & Scantlebury, 2013). (Harper, 2017, pp. 358–359)

Research findings

We spoke with a New Zealand primary teacher and an Australian educator who works across primary and high school. Both educators focused on the importance of learning key words and phrases in science.
Context: I've worked in education my whole life. Currently, I'm working at a multicultural school. We have about 70 different ethnicities. The school has three partial immersion classes learning te reo Māori. About 40% of the students at our school are Māori, more than 40%t are from other ethnicities and nearly 20% identify as being New Zealand European. We celebrate diversity, and that's what makes our school really special.

> We have frequent professional learning conversations with staff about the pedagogy for mainstream classes. This includes conversations about pedagogical content knowledge, scaffolding learning and teaching in meaningful authentic contexts for our English language learners. We have bilingual learning assistants working with English Language Learning Assistants (ELLAs) explaining the concepts and instructions in their first language. We do the same sorts of things with science but with more scaffolding for the children. So that they're not just learning the high frequency words, they will also learn the mid and low frequency words linked to the specific science concepts being taught. We try to base our teaching on students' needs and introduce the science language that the students will cope with and where possible try to have translators to explain concepts in their first language.

Context: I've taught students from EAL/D backgrounds for more than 30 years. I also worked as a refugee support leader in the past years. In that role, I worked with a range of schools (primary and high school) to support the teachers, schools, families and students from EAL/D background, and also helped in linking schools with agencies. In my current role as an EAL/D education leader, I have been working with network of schools to support them. Schools are very proactive.

They just want to do the best for these students and families from refugee and refugee-like backgrounds.

> I would ask the teachers to look at their program and identify the vocabulary, identify the academic language that they need to teach them. And of course, it's important to breaking things down. 'I need to get the children to here, but they're here. I've got to backward map. How can I get them to this point?' So, if you want to teach them the words to use like 'construct' rather than 'grow', you have to teach those words. So, if you want to use a special type of word like 'environment' or something like that, you would show them the word, explain the word and give them examples of what an environment is. And they can actually write the definitions of that word, but you will use that message abundancy where you would talk about it. You would play oral games like 'guess my word' where they guess your words and they use those words. You grow it like we introduced the word 'environment' and the following week we might do a guess my word or let's go back to these keywords because you've got to teach them the language. They won't use the language unless they understand they can use the language in different forms like reading and writing about the environment.

Unique contexts, global principles

Both educational veterans, our Australian and New Zealand teachers, focused on the importance of teaching key vocabulary in science and providing intensive support to drive home the meaning of words. Our New Zealand primary teacher begins with extensive planning with colleagues through professional learning conversations. In the school's mainstream classes, new words and concepts are introduced and explained in students' first language. This school places translators in the room when new topics are covered, thus ensuring children with refugee or asylum-seeker backgrounds are not at a disadvantage. Our Australian educator advocates backward mapping to envision what target concepts need to be conveyed and then identifying small steps that will help meet this target. She is mindful of the complexity of language, particularly in science, and is insistent that students gain the unique meaning of words. As she introduces new words in science, she is concerned with providing very clear definitions and visual illustrations. She is also focused on the concept of 'message abundancy' in which she returns to key words and phrases often and in varying academic contexts.

Carefully analysing the curriculum and identifying the key words and concepts in science was a point shared by numerous teachers in our research. While covering a year's worth of science standards, content and vocabulary may be expected, teachers of students with refugee or asylum-seeker backgrounds need to become adept at analysing and parsing curricula to its meaningful core. As our New Zealand educator advised, this is a process best done by the entire learning team as it ensures all educators share the same content knowledge and understanding of the pedagogical plan. Our Australian teacher raised a powerful point about the importance of language in science and the necessity of ensuring newly arrived students clearly understand vocabulary. Teachers need to explicitly introduce vocabulary, they need to illustrate it with multiple visuals, and they need to frequently revisit vocabulary in and out of the science context. Allowing students to understand the meaning of words incompletely or inaccurately in science builds a weak foundation for future learning. To support science instruction, schools need to organise their schedules to allow interpreters to be present, particularly when new concepts are being introduced. As the existing research has established, science is an area of the school curriculum that engages and empowers non-native speakers. It is impingent upon teachers to tap into this excitement and offer all students a rich and accurate science experience regardless of their background.

Pedagogies of science and literacy

The literacy skills that are required to understand scientific concepts and work with the processes and procedures of that subject domain may be perceived as the capacity to learn the new language associated with new equipment, methods and concepts. However, in order to engage with scientific thinking, like mathematical thinking, students need to develop a specific perspective and cognitive capacity to engage with the language, methods and concepts effectively and make meaningfully connections between them (Li & Guo, 2021). Pearson et al. (2010, p. 459), in their review of the literature about scientific literacy, indicated that there are two dominant schools of thought. One proposes it is knowledge of the natural world, its principles, key concepts and ways of thinking, and the other indicates it involves competences in making connections between the language of science, the various text forms in which it is couched and the knowledge that results from these connections. This involves being able to develop and write science texts, to understand the meaning of oral and written science texts and to understand and engage with the scientific enquiry. These notions of scientific literacy are conceptually more complex than the more simplistic practice of vocabulary recall and procedural knowledge (Schatzki, 2017). They require students to understand why scientists investigate, think, argue and write in the ways that they do. Proposing that no scientist instantly enters a laboratory and starts to manipulate equipment without having some hypotheses, they suggest a circular, multi-modal model of science in which students *Do* science, *Talk* science, *Read* science and *Write* science in no predesignated order. Additionally, they suggest literacy strategies that enable teachers to support both language proficiencies and scientist skills. Whilst not developed in the specific context of enabling and empowering students with refugee and asylum-seeker experiences, their work does offer pedagogical pathways which can easily be differentiated to support second language learners overcome the difficulties such as those described by Miller (2009) and Idin (2018). One of the salient features of this work is the acknowledgement that, for many science teachers, the pressure that high stakes testing and accountability places on them to cover a predetermined amount of content means that instead of students talking about science, it may be considered to be more economical and efficient if students listen to teachers reading about science. The consequence of this for students with refugee and asylum-seeker backgrounds is that it severely restricts their capacities to develop the multi-modal science skills that supports the development of science competencies.

Moje et al. (2001) discussed the role of discourse in science-based project learning, indicating that discourse is socially, cognitively and culturally determined as is the production of scientific knowledge, a notion not regularly discussed in traditional science pedagogies (Gobert & Buckley, 2000; Saribas & Ceyhan, 2015). Discourses in science teaching and learning, therefore, are epistemologically determined as they reflect specific ways of thinking, knowing and doing. Again, although the work is not developed with students of refugee and asylum-seeking backgrounds as a focus, the ways in which the three distinct classroom discourses interact and influence each other may be useful in determining the roles and discourses that these students bring to project-based teamwork in science and how these may complement, challenge or disrupt the discourses of others. The disciplinary discourses that are the teachers' disciplinary knowledge, explanations and means of assessing science skills are reflective of western ways of thinking, reasoning and knowing that are not universally acknowledged as being useful or preferable in many other cultures. The skills of hypothesising, predicting and explaining reasoning do not necessarily reflect the ways in which scientific inquiry is actioned in other cultures. This may provide a constantly discordant interactive classroom space for students with diverse ontological perspectives.

Any discordance with the disciplinary discourse naturally bleeds into the instructional and interactional classroom discourses. If the communicative patterns of diverse cultural groups are not reflected in the ways in which teachers action their pedagogical strategies, interact with students as science learners and seek to clarify the task requirements, the impact on the students from non-dominant groups is to effectively exclude them from gaining the benefits of their preferred learning contexts and expectations. Instructional discourses about textbook use, note taking and other procedures are often assumed to be understood by the students, when, in fact, they may be quite alien to them. This can be especially so if students originate from backgrounds of oracy. One of the greatest challenges for teachers, for example, is assuming the role of the dominant authoritarian who dispenses knowledge in the science classroom. As an inquiry-based discipline, these pedagogical approaches, which may be valued in many societies, would not support the cognitive skills required to develop science competencies as determined by mandatory curriculum expectations. Group projects, for example, may challenge everything that is culturally expected in an authentic learning context and leave students confused and anxious. The final discourse that is examined by Moje et al. (2001) as a critical component of the science teaching and learning space is that of the social/everyday discourses.

These discourses revolve around the prior knowledge, vocabulary and practices grounded in the home culture of the diverse student groups. Students may communicate less effectively to each other and to the teachers depending on the ways science is understood, described or discussed at home. Again, these challenges become more apparent in the group project pedagogical strategies teachers employ, and the students need to enter into everyday discourses as part of their collaboration, their understanding of their roles in a group and explaining their thinking and decision making. Again, different traditions of thinking, reasoning and actioning science skills may easily lead teachers to underestimate the capacities of students who do not use language and cognitive strategies in the ways of the students of the homeland cultures. The task of the science teachers becomes increasingly complex as the diversity of the student body widens. The challenge is to develop inclusive discipline, and instructional and interactional discourses, and to support the positive interpretation of multiple social/everyday discourses as a space in which debate and mediation enriches the learning. Western ontologies and epistemologies are not sacrosanct, and, whilst they may meet the legislative requirements, they may not always meet the student learning needs in this important disciplinary field, most especially in the critical component of scientific literacy, making connections.

Afghan students struggle to navigate U.S. Schools after fleeing Taliban

Mahdi Kabuli likes math. Sure, geometry eludes him sometimes, but overall he's really good at the subject. At 18, Kabuli is already thinking about college, where he wants to study economics or computer science. As of last year, nearing the end of his time at the top private school in Afghanistan, he was on track to do it. Then the Taliban took over his home, Kabul, in August, and he, his mother and his four younger brothers were forced to flee to the United States. They felt lucky to make it out: A day after they left Kabul, there was an explosion right where they had been hiding. Kabuli and his family came to the U.S. with only the clothes they were wearing and whatever papers they could grab. But those papers did not include their school transcripts.

When Kabuli and two of his brothers, ages 15 and 16, tried to enroll in their new public school in Prince George's County, Maryland, the school told them that without their transcripts, they would need to start over from the ninth grade. As the oldest son in the household, Kabuli felt responsible for supporting his family. His plan was to work part-time while he finished his final year of high school. Starting again as a freshman would make this more difficult. The two brothers decided to accept the school's terms and enter the system in the ninth grade. Kabuli felt he couldn't.

"Because they are younger, they have time," Kabuli said. "But I don't." Of the more than 50,000 Afghan refugees who'd come to the U.S. as of early November, nearly half are under 18...

Some school districts are taking steps to help Afghan refugee students resume their education without having to start anew. San Juan Unified School District in Sacramento County, California, serves more than 2,000 students who speak Dari or Pashto, Afghanistan's two primary languages. Its refugee specialists have been communicating with families in Afghanistan and asking them to bring their transcripts. But for students who already came without their transcripts, the specialists' hands are tied...

Burkhart said. "The Taliban has taken over, and there's no way for him to get his transcripts from his school." Many female students destroyed their transcripts as the Taliban advanced, afraid that the militants would target them as threats to the new regime. (Deng, 2022, p. 1)

Research findings

We spoke with a high school teacher in the United States and a high school teacher in Australia. Both teachers offered keen insights about opportunities and understandings newly arrived students bring to classroom.

Context: I am one of the ESL teachers, and I'm one of the [school's] founding teachers as well. The school opened its doors in 2015, and so I've been there since then to see it grow and to see several of our classes graduate at this point. Beforehand, I was an ESL teacher at a high school for, goodness, about seven or eight years in a neighbouring county. I had been an elementary school teacher and a regular education elementary school teacher, and I went back and got some coursework to become certified to be an ESL teacher because I had a number of ESL students in my class.

> A few years ago, we participated in an international competition, I had originally been the science teacher, the very first year that I was here. So, the second year I saw an opportunity for our students to do some STEM assignments with a school in Ghana. So, we were zooming with them even back then. And, we [entered a competition] and it was like environmental science and looking for ways to reduce pollution in the atmosphere. So our students, they maybe didn't have some of the, didn't have the traditional background I guess that you would need for this. But, we didn't stop, we just used our different ideas. Some of the students used things that they knew from just their own experiences of working and doing construction and working on farms and they used some of those [ideas] to help them. I think we came in of about 18 schools, we came in fourth place for this particular competition. But we did other competitions as well to try to get our kids in there. Maybe it's a poetry contest, but you know we're always looking for opportunities and providing them with, you know, a wide variety of classes. So, I used to work at a more traditional high school, and I know that very few of my students had those opportunities to take the classes. They were completely based on GPA and a lot of the students had taken honours level classes at the lower levels and 9th and 10th grade, whereas my students, because they had a special schedule, because they were taking a lot of ESL classes, so a lot of them were taking classes on testing because they didn't pass the state tests. So, instead of having these opportunities, they were just taking these remedial testing classes. So, I know that there's a lot more out there, that our students get at our school.

Context: I came to the school about three years ago. I came from a predominantly Anglo-Saxon school, and so coming here was a bit of a culture shock. I think when you first get into such a setting, you're not really sure what to expect, and then you get there, and you realise, I think I was teaching a poem and in the poem a pineapple came up. And after I had spent a few minutes talking about the part of the poem and the symbolism, I could start to read their blank faces. And then I asked the students if they knew what a pineapple was, and these were 17-year-olds, and I actually had a student in that class, who was 22. And, and he said no. He had never seen a pineapple, he'd never tasted a pineapple, and, you know, to try to explain to someone how a pineapple tastes is a big culture shock for a teacher.

> I think that this sort of testing [state standardised tests] doesn't take into consideration what our students know and what they can do. And it means that our students always on the back foot, a lot of my students don't end up finishing year 12. I've had students pull out of year 12 just recently like this past month because they can't face what is coming, it is too much for them. A lot of these students try and do a lot more of the practical subjects, but again in doing that, they cut themselves out of the ATAR for those courses that mom and dad think they're going to take afterwards, which is like medicine and law. So, I think that the testing doesn't have a place for the students, because it doesn't take into account what they can do, it only looks at what they can't do. Really it looks at what they can't do, and it creates a lot of barriers for them. Any test that needs to be typed is a barrier a test that needs something verbal is very much a barrier, so I mean that's how I feel about the testing. I know that they don't understand the importance of the testing. I think that it's not drummed into them, the way that perhaps like a student who is born in our country it's drummed into them because from very early on.

Unique contexts, global principles

Each of these teachers talked about the talents and intellect of their students with refugee and asylum-seeker backgrounds and the barriers that western schools put up in front of them. Our American teacher sought opportunities to highlight her students' knowledge, and she used her science course to connect her class with students in Ghana and then enter an environmental science competition. While she acknowledged that her students didn't have the western academic skills of their competitors, she pushed them forward towards success by tapping into the understandings they brought from their home cultures and life experiences. She replicated the success of this experience across the curriculum, entering her students in numerous competitions they embarked on together. Her reflections on the exclusionary test-focused practices in her prior school are heartbreaking. The policies that kept her students out of engaging upper-level courses and relegated them to remedial testing courses drove her to help create a school that honours all types of student knowledge. Our Australian teacher quickly discovered that the life experiences of her newly arrived students were quite different from her own. Her pineapple vignette illustrates the foundational disconnects that exist when cultures merge. This teacher is critical of the caustic effects standardised testing has on her students, many of whom come from cultures that have not built education on a foundation of testing. She observes that her students always feel behind, many drop out, and those who remain choose courses that do not allow them to aspire to the careers their parents envisage for them.

When you are immersed in a western education system that uses standardised test scores to value schools, rate and rank students and shape opportunities, it can be hard to recognise how constraining it is. For students with refugee or asylum-seeker backgrounds, formal and informal learning in their host country may have looked very different than their new classroom in Baltimore or Brisbane. As our American teacher demonstrated, offering novel opportunities for students to collaborate, to tap into their prior knowledge, and to achieve together is a powerful way to value what every child brings to the room. Finding opportunities that are unfamiliar to each student is also a way to keep the academic playing field level and ensure students feel a similar level of uncertainty. Our Australian teacher offered a powerful take on the effects of standardised testing regimens and the way they drive students out of school and away from their aspirations. While the testing conventions that shape many systems may not abate soon, teachers can provide learning opportunities daily that value students' prior learning and develop their sense of efficacy, potentially giving them the confidence to persist.

Conclusion

Science and technology are hallmarks of life in western countries. They are incorporated into school curricula and into everyday life. Whilst they are also part of everyday life in many other parts of the world, their access may be defined by financial considerations, availability, access and, in some areas, government and political boundaries. Supporting skilful use of scientific methodologies and technological competencies is considered a significant task in western education, despite the many disadvantages that may remain in the resettlement contexts of the students with refugee and asylum-seeker backgrounds. One of the many ways in which to encourage these students into science is to investigate related fields can be found in everyday life, the use of technology for social interactions where appropriate and the consistent use of scientific processes embedded in the laboratory component of school science. The everyday activities of cooking and gardening involve using scientific knowledge and skills, the integration of technology into the arts and media studies can supplement social communication on another level, and the school laboratory is where modelled practice can inform and support conceptual development without excessive use of unfamiliar language. All these contexts are important elements for integration into highly technologised societies.

References

Abell, S. K., Bryan, L. A., & Anderson, M. A. (1998, July). Investigating preservice elementary science teacher reflective thinking using integrated media case-based instruction in elementary science teacher preparation. *Science Education*, *82*(4), 491–510. https://doi.org/10.1002/(sici)1098-237x(199807)82:4<491::aid-sce5>3.0.co;2-6

Achieve, I. (2014). Next generation science standards. Retrieved December 28, 2014, from https://www.nextgenscience.org/

Ager, A., & Strang, A. (2008). Understanding integration: A conceptual framework. *Journal of Refugee Studies, 21*(2), 166–191. https://doi.org/10.1093/jrs/fen016

Akerson, V. L., Abd-El-Khalick, F., & Lederman, N. G. (2000, April). Influence of a reflective explicit activity-based approach on elementary teachers' conceptions of nature of science. *Journal of Research in Science Teaching, 37*(4), 295–317. https://doi.org/10.1002/(sici)1098-2736(200004)37:4<295::aid-tea2>3.0.co;2-2

Alberts, B. (2022). Why science education is more important than most scientists think. *FEBS Letters, 596*(2), 149–159. https://doi.org/10.1002/1873-3468.14272

Appleton, K. (2003). How do beginning primary school teachers cope with science? Toward an understanding of science teaching practice. *Research in Science Education, 33*(1), 1–25.

Bansel, P., Denson, N., Keltie, E., Moody, L., & Theakstone, G. (2016). *Young newly arrived migrants and refugees in Australia: Using digital storytelling practices to capture settlement experiences and social cohesion.* Young and Well Cooperative Research Centre, Melbourne. Retrieved 27/03/2022, from www.youngandwellcrc.org.au

Barnhart, T., & van Es, E. (2015). Studying teacher noticing: Examining the relationship among pre-service science teachers' ability to attend, analyze and respond to student thinking. *Teaching and Teacher Education, 45,* 83–93. https://doi.org/10.1016/j.tate.2014.09.005

Berry, J. W. (1997). Immigration, acculturation, and adaptation. *Applied Psychology, 46*(1), 5–34. https://doi.org/10.1111/j.1464-0597.1997.tb01087.x

Berry, J. W. (2005). Acculturation: Living successfully in two cultures. *International Journal of Intercultural Relations, 29*(6), 697–712. https://doi.org/10.1016/j.ijintrel.2005.07.013

Berry, J. W., Horenczyk, G., & Kwak, K. (2006). *Immigrant youth in cultural transition: Acculturation, identity, and adaptation across national contexts.* Lawrence Erlbaum Associates. http://newcastle.eblib.com/patron/FullRecord.aspx?p=331698

Bešić, E., Gasteiger-Klicpera, B., Buchart, C., Hafner, J., & Stefitz, E. (2020). Refugee students' perspectives on inclusive and exclusive school experiences in Austria. *International Journal of Psychology, 55*(5), 723–731. https://doi.org/10.1002/ijop.12662

Bidarra, J., & Rusman, E. (2017). Towards a pedagogical model for science education: Bridging educational contexts through a blended learning approach. *Open Learning: The Journal of Open, Distance and e-Learning, 32*(1), 6–20. https://doi.org/10.1080/02680513.2016.1265442

Cowie, B., & Bell, B. (1999). A model of formative assessment in science education. *Assessment in Education: Principles, Policy & Practice, 6*(1), 101–116. https://doi.org/10.1080/09695949993026

Cummins, J. (2008). Teaching for transfer: Challenging the two solitudes assumption in bilingual education. *Encyclopedia of Language and Education, 5,* 65–75.

Cutter-Makenzie, A. (2009). Multicultural school gardens: Creating engaging garden spaces in learning about language, culture, and environment. *Canadian Journal of Environmental Education, 14,* 122–135.

de Laat, J., & Watters, J. (1995). Science teaching self-efficacy in a primary school: A case study. *Research in Science Education, 25*(4), 453–464. https://doi.org/10.1007/bf02357387

Demir, A., & Abell, S. K. (2010). Views of inquiry: Mismatches between views of science education faculty and students of an alternative certification program. *Journal of Research in Science Teaching, 47*(6), 716–741. https://doi.org/10.1002/tea.20365

Deng, G. (2022). Afghan students struggle to navigate U.S. schools after fleeing Taliban. *HuffPost.* Retrieved March 27, 2022, from https://sg.news.yahoo.com/afghan-students-struggle-navigate-u-120009001.html?guccounter=1&guce_referrer=aHR0cHM6Ly93d3cuZ29vZ2xlLmNvbS8&guce_referrer_sig=AQAAALO-MRVWpg1gaVh4O0dvFhDcCI7QjrFKBSELxj-5Up65en7CwgQsjvTr606QBdFziybVHwyf5NLnccKlq3eNvqsU

L0yKywZma2CpOasx1XXsgUO5jYvhjvMuM7OhLmHiGVyEB1-s7W-rJZv3pIePWT32TDsFCdTU-Mm74E9CXOjA

Doná, G., & Berry, J. W. (1994). Acculturation attitues and acculturative stress of Central American refugees. *International Journal of Psychology, 29*(1), 57–70.

Drolia, M., Sifaki, E., Papadakis, S., & Kalogiannakis, M. (2020). An overview of mobile learning for refugee students: Juxtaposing refugee needs with mobile applications' characteristics. *Challenges, 11*(2). https://doi.org/10.3390/challe11020031

Dunn, J., Bundy, P., & Woodrow, N. (2012). Combining drama pedagogy with digital technologies to support the language learning needs of newly arrived refugee children: A classroom case study. *RIDE: The Journal of Applied Theatre and Performance, 17*(4), 477–499.

Emert, T. (2013). 'The Transpoemations Project': Digital storytelling, contemporary poetry, and refugee boys. *Intercultural Education, 24*(4), 355–365. https://doi.org/10.1080/14675986.2013.809245

Emert, T. (2014). "Hear a Story, Tell a Story, Teach a Story": Digital narratives and refugee middle schoolers. *Voices From the Middle, 21*(4), 33–39. http://search.proquest.com/docview/1519055930?accountid=10499

Falk, J. H., & Dierking, L. D. (2019). Reimagining public science education: The role of lifelong free-choice learning. *Disciplinary and Interdisciplinary Science Education Research, 1*(1). https://doi.org/10.1186/s43031-019-0013-x

Fitzgerald, A., & Smith, K. (2016). Science that Matters: Exploring Science Learning and Teaching in Primary Schools. *Australian Journal of Teacher Education, 41*(4), 64–78. https://doi.org/10.14221/ajte.2016v41n4.4

Gobert, J. D., & Buckley, B. C. (2000). Introduction to model-based teaching and learning in science education. *International Journal of Science Education, 22*(9), 891–894. https://doi.org/10.1080/095006900416839

Harper, S. G. (2017). Engaging Karen refugee students in science learning through a cross-cultural learning community. *International Journal of Science Education, 39*(3), 358–376. https://doi.org/10.1080/09500693.2017.1283547

Houseal, A. K., Abd-El-Khalick, F., & Destefano, L. (2014). Impact of a student-teacher-scientist partnership on students' and teachers' content knowledge, attitudes toward science, and pedagogical practices. *Journal of Research in Science Teaching, 51*(1), 84–115. https://doi.org/10.1002/tea.21126

Hussain, F., Safir, A. H., Sabie, D., Jahangir, Z., & Ahmed, S. I. (2020, Infrastructuring hope. *ICTD2020: International Conference on Information and Communication Technologies and Development, Guayaquil, Ecuador.*

Idin, S. (2018). The challenges of refugee students encountered in science courses: A phenomenological study. *Journal of Education and Future* (13), 79–94.

Karam, F. J. (2018). Language and identity construction: The case of a refugee digital bricoleur. *Journal of Adolescent & Adult Literacy, 61*(5), 511–521. https://doi.org/10.1002/jaal.719

Kaukko, M. (2021). Storycrafting refugee children's lives. Presenting Ali and the Long Journey to Australia. *International Journal of Qualitative Studies in Education*, 1–14. https://doi.org/10.1080/09518398.2021.1986645

Kim, P., Hagashi, T., Carillo, L., Gonzales, I., Makany, T., Lee, B., & Gàrate, A. (2011). Socioeconomic strata, mobile technology, and education: A comparative analysis. *Educational Technology Research and Development, 59*(4), 465–486. https://doi.org/10.1007/s11423-010-9172-3

Koehler, C., & Schneider, J. (2019). Young refugees in education: The particular challenges of school systems in Europe. *Comparative Migration Studies, 7*(1). https://doi.org/10.1186/s40878-019-0129-3

Koehler, M. J., Mishra, P., & Yahya, K. (2007). Tracing the development of teacher knowledge in a design seminar: Integrating content, pedagogy and technology. *Computers & Education*, *49*(3), 740–762. https://doi.org/10.1016/j.compedu.2005.11.012

Lee, J. D. (2002). More than ability: Gender and personal relationships influence science and technology involvement. *Sociology of Education*, 349–373.

Li, Y., & Guo, M. (2021). Scientific literacy in communicating science and socio-scientific issues: Prospects and challenges. *Frontiers in Psychology*, *12*, 758000–758000. https://doi.org/10.3389/fpsyg.2021.758000

Martin, S. N., Wassell, B., & Scantlebury, K. (2013). Frameworks for examining the intersections of race, ethnicity, class, and gender on English language learners in K-12 science education in the USA. In *Moving the equity agenda forward* (pp. 81–98). Springer, Dordrecht.

Miller, J. (2009). Teaching refugee learners with interrupted education in science: Vocabulary, literacy and pedagogy. *International Journal of Science Education*, *31*(4), 571–592. https://doi.org/10.1080/09500690701744611

Mishra, P., & Koehler, M. (2006). Technological pedagogical content knowledge: A framework for teacher knowledge. *Teachers College Record*, *108*(6), 1017–1054.

Moje, E., Collazo, T., Carrillo, R., & Marx, R. (2001). "Maestro, What is `Quality'?": Language, literacy, and discourse in project-based science. *Journal of Research in Science Teaching*, *38*(4), 469–498. https://deepblue.lib.umich.edu/bitstream/handle/2027.42/34514/1014_ftp.pdf?sequence=1

Pearson, P. D., Moje, E., & Greenleaf, C. (2010). Literacy and science: Each in the service of the other. *Science*, *328*(April), 459–462. www.sciencemag.org

Sabie, D., & Ahmed, S. I. (2019). Moving into a technology land. COMPASS '19. *Proceedings of the 2nd ACM SIGCAS Conference on Computing and Sustainable Societies*

Sam, D. L., & Berry, J. W. (2010). Acculturation. *Perspectives on Psychological Science*, *5*(4), 472–481. https://doi.org/10.1177/1745691610373075

Saribas, D., & Ceyhan, G. D. (2015). Learning to teach scientific practices: Pedagogical decisions and reflections during a course for pre-service science teachers. *International Journal of STEM Education*, *2*(1). https://doi.org/10.1186/s40594-015-0023-y

Schatzki, T. (2017). Practices and learning. In P. Grootenboer, C. Edwards-Groves, & S. Choy (Eds.), *Practice Theory Perspectives on Pedagogy and Education. Praxis, Diversity and Contestation*. Springer.

Smith, L., & Motsenboker, C. (2005). Impact of hands-on science through school gardening in Louisiana Public Elementary SchoolsS. *HortTechnology*, *15*(3), 439–443.

Stuckey, M., Hofstein, A., Mamlok-Naaman, R., & Eilks, I. (2013). The meaning of 'relevance' in science education and its implications for the science curriculum. *Studies in Science Education*, *49*(1), 1–34. https://doi.org/10.1080/03057267.2013.802463

Vecchio, L., Dhillon, K. K., & Ulmer, J. B. (2017). Visual methodologies for research with refugee youth. *Intercultural Education*, *28*(2), 131–142. https://doi.org/10.1080/14675986.2017.1294852

Watkins, M., Noble, G., & Wong, A. (2019). *IT'S COMPLEX! Working with Students of Refugee Backgrounds and their Families in New South Wales Public Schools*. NSW Teachers Federation, Surrey Hills NSW, Australia.

Winters, B. (2008). *Multicultural school gardens: linking schools to the community (Integrated unit of work)*. Gould Group, Victoria, Australia.

9 Social studies and diverse perspectives

Introduction

Discussions of history, culture and societies is an area of study in which students may have very different ideas to that of their teachers or textbooks. There are always multiple perspectives on how people were treated and why, how boundaries were determined, and how ethical and just the powerful regimes that rule is perceived to be. This is almost inevitable, whether the perspective reflects a collective world view or an individual, ethnographic experience (Grever & Adriaansen, 2019). The value and dignity given to these diverse views is indicative of the ways in which teachers are able to envisage and manage the educational richness of the ensuing conversation and debate and the balancing act of curriculum demands employing dialectic processes (Farjoun, 2019). The dialectic process is an apt perspective for a modern rapidly changing world in which new concepts are constantly emerging (Friedman, 2020) and for authentically engaging classrooms of students with diverse backgrounds and experiences. It provides opportunities for the students with refugee and asylum-seeker firsthand knowledge to share their understandings of a world and culture very different to that of the native homeland students and facilitates challenges to taken-for-granted beliefs and theories about the world, its history and its future.

It is in this discipline that contemporary cultural understandings and conditions for so-called good emotions such as compassion and empathy can be examined as multiple perspectives and world views, and others such as respect and dignity can be demonstrated. In order for this to happen, authentic cultural inclusion must be consistent, valued and openly acknowledged as part of the learning processes that comprise education in the resettlement contexts. Included in the duty of care of western schooling is the mandate not only to support learning and cognitive growth but also to address the wellbeing, emotional and physical safety and positive relationships that promote healthy, well-educated citizens. In many instances, teachers need to access more information about the characteristics of the diverse cultures and customs of their students' homelands, communicate effectively and strategically and seek opportunities to seamlessly weave aspects of these into their curriculum and everyday classroom interactions. It is particularly through the communication and collaborations in this area of learning that the culture of school can be realised and its commitment to inclusion evidenced. It has already

DOI: 10.4324/9781003207900-10

been noted in this writing that integration is the most positive psychological and social outcome for migrants (Berry et al., 2006; Sam & Berry, 2010), especially those with refugee and asylum-seeker experiences who may experience multiple degrees of difference in the cultural and social landscapes of their homeland and their resettlement contexts. The very notion of integration suggests two or more elements coming together, not one adapting to the other. It is only when all parties come together with the recognition that each has equal rights to opinions, world views and perspectives that a dialectical process can commence.

Educational integration

Like schools in many parts of the world, the English-speaking countries from which the participants of this study originated were institutionally organised. They were parts of larger systems with mandated documents such as policies and curricula and procedures that dictated the content and processes of their professional work (Sellars & Imig, 2020). Integral to these systemic institutions are the demands of governmentality (Christie & Sidhu, 2006; Foucault, 1991), which further restrict the ways in which new arrivals such as those with refugee and asylum-seeker experiences are enrolled and their learning needs accommodated (Sellars, 2020). The situation in which these students too find themselves is clearly articulated

> Those who travel are human beings', even though 'host' societies tend to see them as faceless people, whose previous experiences, values, emotions, families and cultures are usually disregarded.
> (Ayala, 2004, p. 181)

The teachers who participated in this study were not prepared to disregard the needs of their students. They were aware of the challenges they faced in their efforts to support these students and found that making small changes and taking small steps made them increasingly aware of the opportunities they had in their classrooms to interact with their diverse students respectfully, with cultural considerations and with respect for their capacity to both learn and contribute to the intellectual quality of the leaning context. This resonates with other studies (Alford, 2014; Banki, 2012; Block et al., 2014; Cassidy & Gow, 2005) which seek to challenge the notion of these students as academically deficit (Bal, 2014; Bešić et al., 2018; Campbell, 2017). Despite calls for new curriculum and school policies which would include peace education and other related subjects (Awada et al., 2017; Maadad & Yilmaz, 2021), very little has changed in western schooling. The huge leap that is required to educate diverse student populations would entail abandoning the solitary, economic purpose of neoliberal schooling and, in its place, developing educational aims which reflect humanistic values (Lovat et al., 2010; Sellars, 2020), pedagogical love (Arar et al., 2018; Darder, 2009; Noddings, 2005, 2012; Sellars & Imig, 2021; Vickers & McCarthy, 2010; Watson et al., 2021) and culturally sensitive leadership (Arar et al., 2019; Imig et al., 2021; Isik-Ercan, 2012; Sellars, 2021; Wilkinson & Kaukko, 2020).

Amongst the theoretical notions that have been recently proposed as educational reform are those by Gidley (2008, 2016, 2017), Darder (2009, 2017), Ladson-Billings and Tate (2009), Lipman (2009); Westerman (2009), Pugh et al. (2012) and Resnick (2010). Gidley (2016), using Steiner philosophy as a foundation, proposed a model whose characteristics have the potential to support diverse learners in developing the academic skills and knowledge, critical and creative thinking, and moral and ethical reasoning. Engaging with the critique that Kincheloe and Steinberg (1993) bring to the notions of developmentalism, most significantly the Piagetian model, and its associated notions of intelligence, Gidley (2016) employs this notion to highlight the ways in which schooling may exclude individuals from 'the community of intelligence' … based race (the non-white), class (the poor) and gender (the feminine) (Kincheloe & Steinberg, 1993, p. 298). Whilst not dismissing the idea of cognitive development, what is considered to be 'intelligence' in western schooling may have a considerable impact on the provision of educational opportunities and appreciation of relative strengths for students with refugee and asylum-seeker experiences and backgrounds. It provides multiple opportunities for dialectic process, anticipating problems and problem-solving. Moving past the five major characteristics of the factory model of neoliberal schooling (Sellars & Imig, 2020), Gidley (2016) suggests that schooling be shifted from its current, linear sequential model into a more organic, complex structure to facilitate education for 'Consciousness, Compassionate Spiritual development, Mobile, Life-Enhancing thinking, Complexification of Thinking and Culture and Linguistic and Paradigmatic Boundary Crossing' (Gidley, 2016, pp. 144–156). While this is conceptually distant from what is currently available in formal education systems which disadvantage many refugee and asylum-seeker students (Sellars, 2020), it offers ways forward for reflection and contemplation by those who seek to support learning for these diverse groups of students.

The shift from formal education to postformal education (Gidley, 2016, p. 145)

Formal Education	Postformal Education
Atomistic, reductionist	Holonic, holographic, holistic
Simple mechanical structure	Complex organic structure
Straight line, sequential	Helix, progressive recapitulation
Instrumentalism	Multilayered reflexivity
Formal logic, binary dualistic, excluded middle	Postformal logics: dialectical, fuzzy, included middle, paradox
Disciplinary segregation, specialisation, territorialism of knowledge	Transdisciplinary integration of knowledge and de-territorialism of knowledge
Cognitive orientation, privileging of the brain	Cognitive-affective participatory, balancing brain, heart and limbs
Knowledge as static, objective content, information based	Knowledge as process, subjective-objective capacity, wisdom orientated
Values neutral, secular	Values orientated, spiritual
Language as an objective tool, or pragmatic instrument of communication	Language as subjective-objective, imaginative, metaphoric medium

Methodological functionalism	Methodological pluralism
Analysis, data results, conclusion	Interpretation, patterns, context, coherence
Argument, debate, win-lose	Dialogue, understanding, win-win
Researcher outside (etic) the research, third-person language	Researcher outside (etic)/inside(emic) the research, third-person and first-person language
Universal, timeless	Universal and historical, and contextual

Research findings

We spoke with a primary teacher from New Zealand who shared insights about ways to support an extremely diverse group of students to learn about their own cultures and those of their classmates.

Context: In our school, we have children from across the Pacific. We have students from many other ethnicities, for example Middle Eastern areas, Southeast Asia, Asia, Latin American countries, African origins and European countries. Regarding our students from refugee backgrounds, they identify with a range of countries including Afghanistan, Pakistan, Syria, Kurdistan, Libya, Lebanon, Yemen, Indonesia, Nepal, Colombia, Ethiopia, Somalia, Eritrea, Rwanda, Democratic Republic of Congo, Myanmar, Cambodia and Bangladesh. Many have lived in more than one country and have incredible stories about their journeys. Some have moved from country to country, and it isn't always clear exactly which country they were originally from.

> We try to use an integrated approach in favour of teaching concepts rather than separate subjects. For history, for example, we're currently looking at critical histories of Aotearoa [Maori name for New Zealand]. We might have children from refugee countries who may say that they don't need to know that, and that they have their own history that they want to learn about, Māori history. And that's just the same as Europeans. It's not different. It's challenging thinking and learning more broadly, learning about different views, wider world views and expanding our vision. It's challenging looking at critical histories of our Aotearoa because it's about an indigenous world view of things. So, that's why we encourage our children to be critical thinkers and open minded and we ask them to share about their histories too.
>
> We really try to celebrate the diversity that we have. We encourage children to learn about other cultures by creating cultural villages. We also encourage children to inquire and ask questions about aspects of each other's cultures. For example, we have so many different faiths and we can learn about the different world views. We try to build a culture of care and concern. We aim to be culturally responsive and hope that the pedagogy permeates through the school, however we are realistic about the challenges.
>
> We do the best we can to be culturally responsive and there's always things that come up that we were not expecting, I guess that's just what happens when you have an ethnically diverse school like ours. When our Muslim children first arrive, the parents do not want the photos taken. They don't like photos being on the wall and things like that, so we're not assimilating the

children, we're just helping them integrate into our school environment and understand our school vision and values. We talk through things with parents. We encourage our students to value their culture and their language. We say, "please don't leave your language and culture at the gate". We celebrate diversity in lots of ways. We have flags up around schools that children can identify with. We have a lot of books, art, and opportunities to help people identify with their culture. When they come into the school, we try to make the entrance way welcoming and take time to take the families on a tour of the school.

Unique contexts, global principles

This teacher was able to quickly list the 18 countries from which her students with refugee or asylum-seeker backgrounds originated. She also made the interesting observation that many of her students took a long and circuitous journey to New Zealand, and she isn't entirely clear what they see as their home country. With such a diversity of students, she is purposeful about introducing a range of cultures and countries in her lessons, and she has filled her classroom with resources reflective of the range of backgrounds her students bring. The school is also filled with resources, signs and flags recognising other nations. Still, many of her students voice frustration that they must spend time learning about cultures with world views quite distant from their own as they are keen to learn about their own cultural backgrounds. She provides opportunities for students to develop cultural villages that bring their diverse cultures to life, and she encourages students to ask each other questions about their home country, their culture and even their religion. While this teacher and her colleagues are very proactive, she is also clear that unexpected events arise that push her thinking and require reflection. Honouring the wishes of Muslim families who do not want their children photographed is an obvious step for her. She is a believer in frequent communication with parents, and she encourages families to hold tight to their home culture and language.

Each child who sits in a classroom has a unique life experience of which they are quite proud, and for children with refugee or asylum-seeker backgrounds this experience can be quite complex but still just as affirming. It is important to keep in mind that while some students may have come directly to a western country with vivid memories of their home, others may have spent their formative years in refugee camps outside of their homeland. Our New Zealand teacher offers many insights about ways to honour the diverse cultures of a classroom full of unique students. Teachers need to make students' cultures visible in the classroom through art, flags, signs and books. Teachers also need to create a culture of respectful curiosity where students engage in dialogue about their experiences, their religion, their food, their dress and whatever else interests their peers. Modelling how to respectfully engage with others and making cultural conversation a normal part of the classroom build understanding and take the stigma off of differences. These respectful open conversations also need to extend to families. Teachers can build relations by encouraging families to hold tight to their cultural traditions and language.

Notions of empathy and compassion

It may not be a daily topic of conversation, but everyone has culture. This impacts on how emotions are expressed, regulated or interpreted. The discussions of how individuals develop their values and principles, perspectives and world views can be found in the thinking of Minkov et al. (2018), Hall (1976) and (Bronfenbrenner, 1979, 1988; Bronfenbrenner & Morris, 2006; Yok-Fong, 2013). The ways in which individuals understand empathy and compassion will depend on their cultural influences and their own experiences, as will the situations and circumstances which elicit these emotions. Empathy is considered to be a desirable emotion in the context of teaching and learning (see, for example, Peck et al., 2015; Sarraj et al., 2015). A critical perspective on empathy is offered by Mirra (2018), who differentiates between individual empathy and *Critical Civic Empathy*. Proposing that the former is desirable, she states that the latter should be the overarching purpose in all educators' work. Seeking to establish that civics education is focused on developing more socially aware, active citizenship as critical practice, she defines *Critical Civic Empathy* in terms of the following three characteristics:

> It begins from an analysis of social position, power and privilege of all parties involved.
> It focusses on the way that personal experiences matter in the context of public life.
> It fosters democratic dialogue and civic action committed to equity and justice.
>
> (Mirra, 2018, p. 7)

Building on the Freirean notion that in order to be fully human she then develops a four-square typography of empathy which captures the various perspectives of empathy in public life. These include the *imaginative refusal* which captures the anti-empathic rhetoric in which the press and media often engage with respect to individuals with refugee and asylum-seeker experiences and the anti-humanitarian policies developed by some politicians. It presents the *fake empathy* of those in public life seeking political kudos. These are heavily reliant on the term 'we' indicating solidarity with national values and like-minded people who support social unity, but under critical scrutiny these statements are frequently divisive and manipulative. Additionally, there are indications of how individual empathy may relate to a degree of civic empathy developed by students and others as the consequence of observing that some others are not as fortunate as themselves, but this empathy is not informed by the rules, policies and documents at all levels of political life which operate to create the inhumane, inequitable and punitive circumstances of refuge and asylum-seeker populations. This type of empathy has no critical perspective on the status quo. The final quadrant captures the nature of authentic *Critical Civic Empathy* and its mandated characteristics of criticality, democracy and social justice.

Ratcliffe (2012) offers another perspective in what he terms 'radical empathy'. This understanding requires individuals to position themselves outside of all their own cultural conditioning, knowledge and life experiences and place themselves into the everyday lives and circumstances of those with whom they are attempting to be empathic. Based in phenomenology, this approach is utilised by anthropologists and social science scholars who seek to gain a deep understanding of the lives of their study participants. Requiring substantial practice, it challenges these individuals to become the 'other' (Foucault, 1991; Said, 1978) and interrupts the 'taken for grantedness' that may be the common practice of many in professional educational practice. The assumed understanding of compassion as distinct from and separate to empathy is interrogated by Nussbaum (2001, p. 297) in terms of the three cognitive judgements that are made by individuals when considering compassionate emotion. She determines:

> Compassion, then, has three cognitive elements: the judgment of size (a serious bad event has befallen someone); the judgment of nondesert (this person did not bring the suffering on himself or herself); and the eudaimonistic judgment (this person, or creature, is a significant element in my scheme of goals and projects, an end whose good is to be promoted).

In the discussion of these three social and moral judgements about compassion, she echoes Freire's thinking about those who are the focus of the compassion, that they are not without agency and that the circumstances that are the cause of suffering are temporary and the result of very specific events. Relating this to the students with refugee and asylum-seeker backgrounds and their communities, it reaffirms their capacities to act positively on their own behalf and have agency. It also serves to engender hope that the marginalisation, dehumanising treatment and discriminative policies that disadvantage these groups are temporary and not ongoing in their new homelands. School culture and leadership can contribute significantly to mediating the impact of these practices.

In highly competitive, individualistic, academic environments the degree of self-interest is high and dominates what it means to be successful (Connell, 2013a, 2013b; Vickers & McCarthy, 2010). Additionally, in Rousseau's (Pinson et al., 2010) notion of compassion, it was predicated not only by the individual, but by the acknowledgement of community. In communities where students with refugee experiences are not included and are not considered to be part of the community, compassionate responses may be disparaged or not engaged with at all. Compassionate individuals need to have the capacity to remove the barriers of difference and identify themselves with those who are suffering. The impact of homogeneity, in addition to the standardization of pedagogies, assessment and standards itself, promotes self-interest at system, school and individual levels of participation and commitment to educational endeavours as part of the neoliberal notion of the rivalry required to support the 'free market' principle (Connell, 2013a; Gary, 2017; Steger & Roy, 2010).

> This, in turn, has the capacity to desensitize those involved in education to the point where individuals who are in any way different, or have diverse needs, do not have the attributes to authentically belong to that community and are therefore not regarded compassionately. (Sellars, 2020, p. 54)

Research findings

We spoke with two high school teachers in the United States who stressed the need for educators to empower newly arrived students to share and value who they are.

Context: I am a social worker for our school. I'm kind of the first point of contact for ninth and tenth graders. I've been at that position for a few years now. However, I've been involved with the school since its second year. I've worked with refugees and immigrants in the United States for many years. I provide individual and group therapy at school throughout the day. Our school is very multidisciplinary. We really rely heavily on everyone's different expertise. I work collaboratively with our advisory teams and create curriculum to incorporate into those spaces.

> We have kiddos from all over the world. We ask teachers in their interviews, 'Are you cognizant of the fact that you're not going to be able to just teach European history to these kiddos?' When we ask you to do world's history, we're talking about Central America, we're talking about the African nations, we're talking about Southeast Asia, we don't just want to hear about the US and England, and the European nations are colonized. We want our kids to be able to learn about their truth as well as world truth.
>
> The other piece is you needed to be educated is not only staying up to date on cultural events but staying up to date in cultural length, like different cultural linguistic terms. Just because I speak Spanish doesn't mean I speak the dialect in Guatemala or the dialect in Mexico or the dialect in Puerto Rico. So, just being really aware of like where did I learn my Spanish and how is that going to impact the conversation.

Context: I've been teaching for seven years now. I'm finishing my fourth year at this school. This year I'm in an ESL department, and I teach ninth and tenth grade. I teach three kind of ESL classes: ESL newcomer class and ESL beginner, and ESL lab, which is an elective. Our largest population in school is Guatemalan followed by Salvadorean and Honduran and, then, it kind of goes down from there. Our second largest group is refugee students. They represent, Afghanistan, Iraq and Syria, and we have a little bit of a smaller population that are some of the African countries from East and West Africa, Ethiopia, Congo, Cameroon, Haiti this year, and Dominican Republic and Atlantic Caribbean.

> This year, I've had more students from Afghanistan and Syria. With the pandemic this year, creating and designing assignments where students get to

share about them has been really successful. For example, we had them creating books where they were teaching us something. It was very open ended and that led to students...I had students teaching us how to edit a video. I had a student from El Salvador who knows how to play the trombone and she was in like a jazz band, but I would have never known that without an open-ended project like that. You're still able to cover the things. And now we're teaching about folk tales around the world. It starts with just a simple survey of kids like 'what's a folk?'. We teach about folk tales but it's like 'what's one from your culture?'. Then we developed this long list from every culture. The kids are just so excited if you have a list of tales from Afghanistan and they are like, 'that's my favourite story when I was a kid'. And then they feel more piped up to talk about it and tell their classmates about it. So, when you think about culturally responsive activities, like I didn't know anything about these Afghan folk tales, but once these kids gave me these names, I can provide that tool to them without being an expert in that student's culture.

Unique contexts, global principles

Each of our educators offered insights about the efforts teachers need to make to effectively support their newly arrived students. The social worker we interviewed in the United States runs multiple therapy sessions daily for students and works closely with teachers to ensure their teaching is culturally sensitive. This teacher recognises that curriculum in the United States, as is the case in many western countries, is heavily influenced by a colonial perspective. This school's staff make a point to let potential hires know that teaching a subject requires delving well beyond the stated curriculum to include the cultures of the students served. The school also encourages teachers to remain aware of current events and analyse their own biases and knowledge so that they understand how their world view may influence their teaching. Our high school teacher is an advocate of designing curriculums that enable students to present themselves to their peers. Her book project empowered her students by allowing them to shine a light on their own unique knowledge and talents. This teacher also presents a powerful way to connect content to students by giving them a pre-unit questionnaire about the upcoming topic. She was able to identify folk tales from a range of countries and then have the story in the room when her unit started. Though it undoubtedly took a rather sizable effort, this action excited her students and engaged them with the content.

Teaching is certainly among the most demanding professions in the world. This is in large part because being a good teacher means knowing each of your students and shaping an educational experience that values their unique journeys and abilities. As our social worker in the United States asserted, being an effective teacher also means understanding the unique perspectives we each bring to the classroom and working to continually expand our understandings. Teachers need to stay apprised of events in our students' home countries and events in our own countries that may be influencing their lives. But we need to recognise that our media, policymakers and curriculum present knowledge through a lens that may be discordant with the experiences of our students. Simply taking the time to ask questions about the sources of information, gathering more data and considering competing perspectives is a way to better connect with our students with refugee or asylum-seeker experiences. As our high school teacher posited, developing flexible opportunities for students to teach their peers is a purposeful way to empower students and help them present themselves as individuals. Additionally, making an effort with lesson planning to incorporate materials from students' home countries is a way to indicate that many cultures have a place in school and no one is preferred or more highly valued.

Dignity and inclusion

Teaching and learning in many subjects may be challenging for educators of students with refugee experiences, but this may be the most emotionally difficult to manage when homeland students may be expressing ill-informed opinions or perspectives of world issues in which their refuge and asylum-seeker classmates have first-hand experiences. Surprisingly, there appears to be little academic literature that informs about these challenges for students, teachers or students with refugee and asylum-seeker experiences and that stresses the value of the contributions of our participants in this work. Thombs et al. (2008) discuss culturally appropriate teaching in these areas using Webquests. Kilkan and Şimesk (2021) investigated the inclusion of the concepts of refugee and asylum-seeker students in Turkish schools, and found that there was little evidence of any inclusion, therefore disadvantaging all but homeland students. Some awareness of the difficulties of introducing sensitive areas of study in social studies was indicated by Christensen (2006), who advocated the use of graphic novels to study conflict in various parts of the world and the Holocaust. However, many of the questions for discussion that were included in the writing were not necessarily substantive enough to engage students in discussions of inclusion and social justice. Challenges may occur in studies of history, geography, politics, current affairs or civics. Many civic programmes, for example, use western logic and rationalisation to debate worldwide public issues, and few consider the very affective nature of personal opinion in relation to issues in the community or further afield. Recognising that the emotions that drive responses to civic matter are socially constructed, Keegan (2021, p. 15) proposes that the emotional attachment of both the teachers and the students be identified and considered in civic classroom discussions. He suggests a four-part strategy which requires students to become more informed about their emotions, suggesting that, with the inclusion of migrant students' perceptions, critical awareness of affect and its impact on political and social issues may inform student perceptions of social justice:

> (1) examining why we feel what we feel; (2) striving to enter a relation of affective equivalence; (3) interrogating the production and circulation of objects of emotion in everyday politics; and (4) focusing on the performativity of emotions to achieve social justice.

Authentic inclusion may be complex and elusive. The potential for creating school environments based on the principles of the SCARF model (discussed fully in Chapter 4) is largely determined by the school principals or head teachers, but, as in any intervention, if it is not authentically actioned in classrooms, it remains as a concept unexplored, another paragraph in a policy that is neither read nor implemented. The impact of such models as the SCARF model, when thoughtfully and reflectively employed with consistency, may have substantial consequences on the students and their families in many areas of out of school living. Many of the conceptual underpinnings of this model are recognised as contributing to the Sense of Coherence (SOC), which is the core of the Antonovsky (1993) theory of Salutogenesis. He described Salutogenesis as the capacity to have a positive disposition towards coping with the inevitable stresses of life in any context. In determining this, he identified the three constituent components of SOC as comprehensibility, manageability and meaningfulness. Therefore salutogenesis is the degree to which individuals feel they have an understanding of the relationships, conditions and circumstances in their lives, are able to manage these effectively to a certain degree and are able to relate to these aspects of their lives in meaningful ways. Enabling a deeper understanding of school structures and expectations can contribute to students' comprehensibility and how they may be able to work within the systemic and institutional frameworks. Developing a sense of *Meaningfulness* may be achieved by engaging all of the SCARF components but may contribute most especially to the means by which *Relatedness* is established and maintained in and by the school community. The trauma that is suffered by students with refugee and asylum-seeker backgrounds and their families may be frequently overlooked or minimised by others when they present as hopeful, supportive members of school communities. Pathologising these groups is not only negative but also unhelpful in multiple ways. However, a major contribution that can be made to improve the lives of these students and families is to foster genuine acceptance with respect and dignity. The notion of Salutogenesis and the components of SOC have been critically assessed as contributing to individuals' overall quality of life (Eriksson & Lindstrom, 2007; Griffiths et al., 2011). It is the responsibility of educators in every classroom to work towards ensuring the dispositions that will enable both the teachers themselves and the refugee and asylum-seeker communities with whom they interact to have the best possible quality of life.

The third important difference is found in the cross cultural and cross situational character of the SOC construct. Close consideration of the definition will show that the SOC contrasts to such concepts as self-efficacy, internal locus of control, problem oriented coping. the challenge component of hardiness, and mastery. These are strategies hallowed in particular cultures or subcultures, and may well be appropriate to particulate stressors. The SOC is. hopefully, a construct (and the items which constitute its operationalization) which is universally meaningful, one which cuts across lines of gender,

> social class, region and culture. It does not refer to a specific type of coping strategy, but to factors which. in all cultures, always are the basis for successful coping with stressors. This, of course, does not mean that different groups will have an equally strong average SOC. (Antonovsky, 1993, p. 726)

Research findings

We spoke with an Australian high school teacher who works in a language centre within his school. He is keenly aware of the learning preferences of many newly arrived students and the need to respect differences.

Context: I've been a class teacher for the majority of my career at the Intensive English Centre in our school. I've also been working as deputy principal in relieving capacity. We have refugee and refugee-like students in our school. Refugee-like students are those who might be on bridging visas, have difficulty with resources, obviously with the social contacts and perhaps with backgrounds that might not make it an easy transition to come into an Australian learning environment. The refugees we get have been from countries such as Afghanistan, Pakistan and Syria.

> I think one of the things that we can do is to make sure we give some understanding about cultural backgrounds, about how these kids learn. Some kids still learn to this day from their countries, at schools where rote learning is the way to go. A lot of the interactive aspects of learning that we do in Western countries, let's say for Australia, might be foreign to them. Pair work with people of the opposite gender might be a totally foreign concept. And also, some of them come from cultures where it's actually an expected thing when you could be in a class of 50 that you're just quiet and you do the book work. And in Australian context, of course, we encourage voice, we encourage individuality, and we encourage that kind of involvement. So, that's a massive thing as well. When I touched on the cultural thing, in some cultures it's not necessarily valued that you're outspoken or that you challenge concepts ideas. So, a lot of those kinds of things may seem obvious to a mainstream teacher. But you've got these kiddos who are quiet in class and you're not quite sure why you can't elicit the responses that you want. Well, that purely could be because they've been drilled a certain way. In the short term, we don't necessarily always modify their learning behaviours such that they can integrate at that level.

Unique contexts, global principles

That our Australian teacher describes his students as being 'refugees' or 'refugee-like' is revealing about the ongoing difficulties families face in their host countries, even after having suffered so much before and during their migration journeys. This teacher recognises that his students bring unique learning preferences that may run counter to the collaborative, participative students Australian schools seek to develop. Many of his newly arrived students are quiet, prefer rote learning, avoid group work and are uncomfortable partnering with students of the opposite gender. Some students, he observes, are keen to remain unnoticed in the classroom as they independently complete their work. He is cautious not to pressure his newly arrived students to modify their behaviours as he sees gradual integration as a cornerstone of his practice. As with many other teachers we interviewed, he contends that being aware of and understanding the lived experiences of students with refugee or asylum-seeker backgrounds is key to effectively supporting them.

As with any child who enters a new classroom in a new school, students with refugee or asylum-seeker backgrounds understand schooling based on their prior experiences. As discussed in Chapter 1, education looks and sounds quite different around the world, and the transition between regions and philosophies can be dramatic and painful for students. As our Australian educator demonstrated, understanding the educational experience of newly arrived students and the learning approaches they find comfortable are ways to ease the transition into a new setting. While classrooms have expected norms of participation and behaviour, it is impingent upon teachers to respect the life experiences that have shaped their newly arrived students and allow them space to approach school on their terms. Further, teachers need to help their native students and their colleagues understand why these newly enrolled students may be reticent to engage. Knowledge is a wonderful antidote to the ignorance that drives cruel behaviours towards newly arrived students. It is up to you, the reader of this text, to share your knowledge of the students with refugee or asylum-seeker experiences whom you educate. By sharing their background, their aspirations, their resilience and their uniquely human qualities with your students, your peers and your broader school community, you will undoubtedly improve the communities in which you live.

Conclusion

Social studies is essentially about the world, the people who inhabit it and the ways in which they live together, develop societies and establish customs and values. It is in this subject that the intensely diverse populations of students with refugee and asylum-seeker backgrounds can bring their wide and varied knowledge, experiences and cultural understandings to inform and educate their classmates, peers and wider school community. The entire notion of studying society and its environments should be the perfect vehicle through which cultural competencies are developed, not just by the students with refugee and asylum-seeker experiences, but by all members of the school community. Respectful and compassionate acknowledgement of the backgrounds of the students with refugee and asylum-seeker experiences depends on all students having accurate, specific knowledge of the traumatic events which were the cause of displacements in various parts of the world and using this knowledge to develop their sense of social justice and fairness. Their experiences of the narratives of their classmates which describe their lives in their homelands should be explored with sensitivity and caution, enabling the homeland students to know and accept that all societies do not work in similar ways and it does not necessarily make one culture better or worse than another, simply different. Being cognisant of diverse ways of knowing and doing can not only be enriching, but it can also be emancipating. It can help allow all students to challenge stereotyping, racial discrimination and prejudice. It can allow all students to critically examine the political agenda and systemic intolerance of the faceless individuals who propagate these and to see the face of humanity in their own classrooms, playgrounds and friendship groups. For many students, there are only a few people in their lives who can facilitate these types of awareness and reflective processes: their teachers. Teaching is *the* profession that can make a difference.

References

Alford, J. H. (2014). "Well, hang on, they're actually much better than that!": Disrupting dominant discourses of deficit about English language learners in senior high school English. *English Teaching: Practice & Critique (University of Waikato), 13*(3), 71–88. http://search.ebscohost.com/login.aspx?direct=true&db=ehh&AN=108368025&site=eds-live

Antonovsky, A. (1993). The structure and properties of the sense of coherence scale. *Social Science & Medicine, 36*(6), 725–733. https://doi.org/10.1016/0277-9536(93)90033-Z

Arar, K., Örücü, D., & Ak Küçükçayır, G. (2019). Culturally relevant school leadership for Syrian refugee students in challenging circumstances. *Educational Management Administration & Leadership, 47*(6), 960–979. https://doi.org/10.1177/1741143218775430

Arar, K., Orucu, D., & Kucukcayir, G. (2018). These students need love and affection: Experience of a female school leader with the challenges of syrian refugee education. *Leading and Managing, 24*(2), 28–43.

Awada, G., Diab, H., & Faour, K. (2017). A call for curriculum reform to combat refugees crisis: The case of Lebanon. *The Curriculum Journal, 29*(1), 43–59. https://doi.org/10.1080/09585176.2017.1400450

Ayala, E. (2004). Identidad y ciudadanía: Dos retos de la práctica educativa intercultural. [Identity and citizenship: Two challenges of the intercultural educational practice.]. In E. Ayala (Ed.), *La práctica educativa intercultural [The Intercultural Educational Practice]* (pp. 179–216). Editorial La Muralla, S. A.

Bal, A. (2014). Becoming in/competent learners in the United States: Refugee students' academic identities in the figured world of difference. *International Multilingual Research Journal, 8*(4), 271–290. https://doi.org/10.1080/19313152.2014.952056

Banki, S. (2012). Refugees as educators: The potential for positive impact on educational systems. In F. McCarthy & M. Vickers (Eds.), *Refugee and immigrant students: Achieving equity in education* (pp. 43–64). Information Age Publishing, Inc.

Berry, J. W., Horenczyk, G., & Kwak, K. (2006). *Immigrant youth in cultural transition: Acculturation, identity, and adaptation across national contexts.* Lawrence Erlbaum Associates. http://newcastle.eblib.com/patron/FullRecord.aspx?p=331698

Bešić, E., Paleczek, L., & Gasteiger-Klicpera, B. (2018). Don't forget about us: Attitudes towards the inclusion of refugee children with(out) disabilities. *International Journal of Inclusive Education*, 1–16. https://doi.org/10.1080/13603116.2018.1455113

Block, K., Cross, S., Riggs, E., & Gibbs, L. (2014). Supporting schools to create an inclusive environment for refugee students. *International Journal of Inclusive Education, 18*(12), 1337–1355. https://doi.org/10.1080/13603116.2014.899636

Bronfenbrenner, U. (1979). *The Ecology of Human Development: Experiments by Nature and Design.* Harvard University Press.

Bronfenbrenner, U. (1988). Interacting systems in human development. Research paradigms: Present and future. In N. Bolger, A. Caspi, G. Downey, & M. Moore-House (Eds.), *Person in Context: Developmental Processes* (pp. 25–50). Cambridge University Press.

Bronfenbrenner, U., & Morris, P. (2006). The bioecological model of human development. In W. Damon & R. Lerner (Eds.), *Handbook of Child Psychology: Theoretical Models of Human Development* (pp. 793–828). Wiley.

Campbell III, J. A. (2017, 09/03). Attitudes towards refugee education and its link to xenophobia in the United States. *Intercultural Education, 28*(5), 474–479. https://doi.org/10.1080/14675986.2017.1336374

Cassidy, E., & Gow, G. (2005). Making up for lost time : The experiences of Southern Sudanese young refugees in high schools. *Youth Studies Australia, 24*(3), 51–55.

Christensen, L. (2006). Graphic global conflict: Graphic novels in the high school social studies classroom. *The Social Studies* (November/December), 227–230.

Christie, P., & Sidhu, R. (2006). Governmentality and 'fearless speech': Framing the education of asylum seeker and refugee children in Australia. *Oxford Review of Education, 32*(4), 449–465. https://doi.org/10.1080/03054980600884177

Connell, R. (2013a). The neoliberal cascade and education: An essay on the market agenda and its consequences. *Critical Studies in Education, 54*(2), 99–112.

Connell, R. (2013b). Why do market 'reforms' persistently increase inequality? *Discourse: Studies in the Cultural Politics of Education, 34*(2), 279–285.

Darder, A. (2009). Teaching as an act of love: Reflections on Paulo Freire and his contributions to our lives and our work. In A. Darder, M. Baltodano, & R. Torres (Eds.), *The Critiacl Pedagogy Reader* (2nd ed.) (pp. 567–579). Routledge.

Darder, A. (2017). *Reinventing Paulo Freire: A Pedagogy of Love* (2nd ed.). Routledge.

Eriksson, M., & Lindstrom, B. (2007). Antonovsky's sense of coherence scale and its relation with quality of life: A systematic review. *Journal of Epidemiology & Community Health, 61*(11), 938–944. https://doi.org/10.1136/jech.2006.056028

Farjoun, M. (2019). Strategy and dialectics: Rejuvenating a long-standing relationship. *Strategic Organization, 17*(1), 133–144. https://doi.org/10.1177/1476127018803255

Foucault, M. (1991). Governmentality. In B. Burchell, G. Gordon, & B. Miller (Eds.), *The Foucault Effect: Studies in Governmentality* (pp. 1–307). Chicago University Press.

Friedman, T. L. (2020). *The Lexus and the Olive Tree: Understanding Globilisation*. Farrar, Straus and Giroux.

Gary, K. (2017). Neoliberal education for work versus liberal education for leisure. *Studies in Philosophy and Education, 36*(1), 83–94. https://doi.org/10.1007/s11217-016-9545-0

Gidley, J. (2008). Beyond homogenisation of global education: Do alternative pedagogies such as Steiner education have anything to offer an emergent globalising world? In S. Inayatullah, M. Bussey, & I. Milojevic (Eds.), *Alternative Educational Futures: Pedagogies for an Emergent World* (pp. 253–268). Sense Publications.

Gidley, J. (2016). *Postformal Education: A Philosophy for Complex Futures*. Springer.

Gidley, J. (2017). Contrasting futures for humanity: Technotopian or human-centred? *Paradign Explorer: The Journal of the Scientic and Mediacl Network*, September.

Grever, M., & Adriaansen, R.-J. (2019). Historical consciousness: The enigma of different paradigms. *Journal of Curriculum Studies, 51*(6), 814–830. https://doi.org/10.1080/00220272.2019.1652937

Griffiths, C. A., Ryan, P., & Foster, J. H. (2011). Thematic analysis of Antonovsky's sense of coherence theory. *Scandinavian Journal of Psychology, 52*(2), 168–173. https://doi.org/10.1111/j.1467-9450.2010.00838.x

Hall, E. (1976). *Beyond Culture*. Knopf Doubleday Publishing Group.

Imig, S., Sellars, M., & Fischetti, J. (2021). *Creating Spaces of Wellbeing and Safety for Students with Refugee and Asylum Seeker Experiences: Lessons from School Leaders*. Routledge.

Isik-Ercan, Z. (2012). In pursuit of a new perspective in the education of children of the refugees: Advocacy for the "family" [Article]. *Educational Sciences: Theory & Practice, 12*, 3025–3038. https://doi.org/10.1111/1475-3588.00286

Keegan, P. (2021). Critical affective civic literacy: A framework for attending to political emotion in the social studies classroom. *The Journal of Social Studies Research, 45*(1), 15–24. https://doi.org/10.1016/j.jssr.2020.06.003

Kilkan, B., & Şimesk, U. (2021). Investigation of Social Studies Curriculum in Regards to Migrant, Refugee, Asylum-Seekers Concepts. *Participatory Educational Research (PER), 8*(1), 395–408. Retrieved April 12, 2022, from http://www.perjournal.com

Kincheloe, J., & Steinberg, S. (1993). A tentative description of post-formal thinking: The critical confrontation with cognitive theory. *Harvard Educational Review, 63*(3), 296–322.

Ladson-Billings, G., & Tate, W. (2009). Towards a critical race theory of education. In A. Darder, M. Baltodamao, & R. Torres (Eds.), *The Critical Pedagogy Reader* (pp. 167–182). Routledge.

Lipman, P. (2009). Beyond accountability. In A. Darder, M. Baltodamao, & R. Torres (Eds.), *The Critical Pedagogy Reader* (2nd ed.) (pp. 364–383). Routledge.

Lovat, T., Clement, N., Dally, K., & Toomey, R. (2010). Values education as holistic development for all sectors: Researching for effective pedagogy. *Oxford Review of Education, 36*(6), 713–729. https://doi.org/10.1080/03054985.2010.501141

Maadad, N., & Yilmaz, M. (2021). Educational policies and schooling for Arabic speaking refugee children in Australia and Turkey. *Australian Journal of Teacher Education, 46*(11), 18–36. https://doi.org/10.14221/ajte.2021v46n11.2

Minkov, M., Bond, M., Dutt, P., Schachner, M., Morales, O., Sanchez, C., Jandosova, J., Khassenbekov, Y., & Mudd, B. (2018). A reconsideration of hofstede's fifth dimension: New flexibility versus monumentalism data from 54 countries. *Cross Cultural Research 53*(3), 309–333.

Mirra, N. (2018). *Educating for Empathy*. Teachers College Press.

Noddings, N. (2005). *The Challenge to Care in Schools; An Alternative Approach to Education* (2nd ed.). Teachers College Press.

Noddings, N. (2012). *The Philosophy of Education*. Westview Press.

Nussbaum, M. C. (2001). *Upheavals of Thought: The Intelligence of Emotions*. Cambridge University Press. https://doi.org/10.1017/CBO9780511840715

Peck, N. F., Maude, S. P., & Brotherson, M. J. (2015). Understanding preschool teachers' perspectives on empathy: A qualitative inquiry. *Early Childhood Education Journal, 43*(3), 169–179. https://doi.org/10.1007/s10643-014-0648-3

Pinson, H., Arnot, M., & Candappa, M. (2010). *Education, Asylum and the "Non-Citizen" Child: The Politics of Compassion and Belonging*. Palgrave Macmillan.

Pugh, K., Every, D., & Hattam, R. (2012). Inclusive education for students with refugee experience: Whole school reform in a South Australian primary school. *The Australian Educational Researcher, 39*(2), 125–141. https://doi.org/10.1007/s13384-011-0048-2

Ratcliffe, M. (2012). Phenomenology as a form of empathy. *Inquiry: An Interdisciplinary Journal of Philosophy, 55*(5), 474–495.

Resnick, L. B. (2010). Nested learning systems for the thinking curriculum. *Educational Researcher, 39*(3), 183–197. https://doi.org/10.3102/0013189x10364671

Said, E. (1978). Introduction. In *Orientalism* (8th ed.). Vintage Books.

Sam, D. L., & Berry, J. W. (2010). Acculturation. *Perspectives on Psychological Science, 5*(4), 472–481. https://doi.org/10.1177/1745691610373075

Sarraj, H., Bene, K., Li, J., & Burley, H. (2015). Raising cultural awareness of fifth-grade students through multicultural education: An action research study. *Multicultural Education*, 22(2), 39–45.

Sellars, M. (2020). *Educating Students with Refugee and Asylum Seeker Experiences: A Commitment to Humanity*. Verlag Barbara Budrich.

Sellars, M. (2021). Belonging and Being: Developing inclusive ethos. *International Journal of Leadership in Education*, 1–24. https://doi.org/10.1080/13603124.2021.1942994

Sellars, M., & Imig, D. (2021). Pestalozzi and pedagogies of love: Pathways to educational reform. *Early Child Development and Care*, 1–12. https://doi.org/10.1080/03004430.2020.1845667

Sellars, M., & Imig, S. (2020). The real cost of neoliberalism for educators and students. *International Journal of Leadership in Education*, 1–13. https://doi.org/10.1080/13603124.2020.1823488

Steger, M., & Roy, R. (2010). *Neoliberalism: A Very Short Introduction*. Oxford University Press.

Thombs, M. M., Gillis, M. M., & Canestrari, A. S. (2008). *Using WebQuests in the Social Studies Classroom : A Culturally Responsive Approach*. SAGE Publications. http://ebookcentral.proquest.com/lib/newcastle/detail.action?docID=1415876

Vickers, M. H., & McCarthy, F. E. (2010). Repositioning refugee students from the margins to the centre of teachers' work. *International Journal of Diversity in Organisations, Communities & Nations*, 10(2), 199–210. http://search.ebscohost.com/login.aspx?direct=true&db=sih&AN=65534342&site=eds-live

Watson, V. W. M., Reine Johnson, L. E., Peña-Pincheira, R. S., Berends, J. E., & Chen, S. (2021). Locating a pedagogy of love: (re)framing pedagogies of loss in popular-media narratives of African immigrant communities. *International Journal of Qualitative Studies in Education*, 1–21. https://doi.org/10.1080/09518398.2021.1982057

Westerman, W. (2009). Folk schools, popular education and a pedagogy of community action. In A. Darder, M. Baltodano, & R. Torres (Eds.), *The Critical Pedagogy Reader* (pp. 541–562). Taylor & Francis.

Wilkinson, J., & Kaukko, M. (2020, 01/02). Educational leading as pedagogical love: The case for refugee education. *International Journal of Leadership in Education*, 23(1), 70–85. https://doi.org/10.1080/13603124.2019.1629492

Yok-Fong, P. (2013). Working with immigrant children and their families: An application of bronfenbrenner's ecological systems theory. *Journal of Human Behavior in the Social Environment*, 23, 954–966. https://doi.org/10.1080/10911359.2013.800007

Index

acculturation 21–22, 114, *see also* belonging
Afghanistan 3–5, 9–10, 20–21, 27, 34, 38, 41, 50, 56, 70, 82–84, 107–108, 115–116, 123–124, 133, 137–138, 140
al Assad, Bashar 5
al Qaeda 4, 6
algebraic thinking 64, 67–71
Anderson, A. R. 54
Angola 6
Antonovsky, A. 140
anxiety 4, 13, 18, 21, 43, 50, 100, 103, 109, 117
Arab Spring 5
armed conflict 3–6, 10–11
art 38–39, 72–73
attentiveness 1, 18
autonomy 18, 54–55, 79–81, 92

Baker, F. 37
Bal, A. 36, 68
Bangladesh 7, 11, 133
Banks, C. 33
Banks, J. 33
barriers to participation 103–108, 125
Barton, B. 64–65
belonging 21–24
Berry, J. W. 22, 24
bilingual learning assistants 66–67, 88–89, 119
Boaler, J. 72
Botfield, J. R. 87
Bronfenbrenner, U. 80, 85, 135
Buddhism 7
Burundi 6

Cambodia 133
Cameroon 137
Catholicism 23, 85
child marriage 7, 9
child soldiers 6

Christensen, L. 139
Christianity 4–5, 10, 23, 48, 84–86
circumcision: female *see* female genital mutilation; male 85–86
climate change 6, 8
collaborative learning 89–92, 122–123
Collectivist societies 90
Colombia 3, 7, 12, 133
communication, effective 47–58, 100–101, *see also* language
compassions 135–139
counsellors 57–58, 98
Covid-19 7, 137–138
creative and performing arts 2, 36
critical thinking 41, 119
Cseplö, E. 98–101, 104
Csikszentmihalyi, M. 25
Cutter-Makenzie, A. 114–115

Danzak, R. L. 36, 39
Darder, A. 132
decision-making 79–84, 118
Democratic Republic of the Congo 6, 41, 70, 133, 137
dialectic processes 130
diaspora 1, 4–8, 13, 71
differentiation 32–35, 43
dignity 130, 139–143
disciplinary policy 12–13, 48
domestic violence 6
Dominican Republic 137
duty of care 12–13, 130

early marriage 7, 9
Egypt 5
El Salvador 7–8, 52, 137–138
Emert, T. 36
empathy 13, 51–52, 130, 135–139
employment 9
Ethiopia 41, 86, 107, 133, 137

ethnomathematics 64–65, 68, 101
Eurocentrism 33, 65
exercise and sport 70–72, 91, 97–109; barriers to participation 103–108; learning to play 97–103

Farello, A. 103
female genital mutilation 86–87, 106
fight or flight response 56
finger counting 65–66
fMRI scanning 25–26, 56, 65
Fonseca-Mora, M. C. 36
foodbank 23
Fowers, B. J. 54
Fredrickson, B. 24

gardening 115–116
gender 9–10, 79, 82, 89, 104, 109, 140, 142, see also LGBTQ communities; women and girls
genocide 6–7
Germany 3
Ghana 124
Gidley, J. 132–133
goal setting plans 39–43
Guatemala 7, 52, 137

Haiti 137
Hall, E. 81–82, 105, 135
Harmawati, D. 47
Harper, S. G. 118
Harwood, G. 98
Healy, L. 68
Hindu-Arabic system 64–65, 97, 101
Hofstede, G. 89
Honduras 7–8, 52, 137
hygiene 12
hypervigilance 1, 13, 18, 52

Idin, S. 118, 121
Individual Language or Learning Plans 39–40
Individualist societies 90
Indonesia 133
Ingram, D. 65
integration 3, 11–14, 22–25, 33, 47, 55, 58, 88, 114, 119, 126, 131–134, 141–142
intergenerational trauma 13, 17
interpreters 49, see also bilingual learning assistants
Iran 99
Iraq 4, 6, 41, 137
Islam 2, 9–10, 36, 48, 79, 84–88, 104–106, 133–134; Ramadan 107–108; Rohingya 6–7, 10–12; Shi'a 4–5, 50; Sunni 4–6, 50

Jones, C. 37
Judaism 84–86

Keegan, P. 139
Khan, M. 84
Kilkan, B. 139
Kincheloe, J. 132
Kirova, A. 98
Kumar, J. L. 87
Kurdistan 133

Ladson-Billings, G. 132
language 10–12, 22–24, 26, 32–43, 88, 134, 137; different pathways 35–39; differentiation 32–35, 43; effective communication 47–48, 52, 56–58; and exercise/sport 97, 99–101, 107–108; and numeracy 66–67, 70–71, 73–74; personalising language learning 39–43; research findings 34–35, 37–39, 41–43; and science/technology 113–114, 116–118, 120–126
Learning Poverty 9
Lebanon 133
LGBTQ communities 8, 85
Liberia 6
Libya 5, 98, 133
Lipman, P. 132
literacy 6, 9, 12, 34–35, 40, 64, 72, 97, 113, see also language; in learning to play 100–103; and science/technology 121–126
Ludke, K. 36
Luguetti, C. 104

Macmillan, K. K. 97–98
Marsh, K. 98
Maslow, A. 10
mathematics see numeracy
Mengesha, Z. B. 87
Miller, J. 118, 121
Minkov, M. 135
Mirra, N. 135
Moje, E. 121
Moreno, S. 37
Morris, B. J. 85–86
Motsenboker, C. 114
Myanmar 3, 6–7, 10–11, 133

natural disasters 3, 6
neoliberalism 43, 65, 131–132, 136
Nepal 133
Netherlands 85
Nogueira de Lima, R. 68
non-verbal communication 51–54

numeracy 12, 34–35, 42, 64–75, 97, 123; algebraic thinking 64, 67–71; ethnomathematics 64–65, 68, 101; Hindu-Arabic system 64–65, 97, 101; in learning to play 100–103; as social practice 64–67; supporting mathematical thinking 71–75
Nussbaum, M. C. 136

Pakistan 3, 56, 133, 140
Palmer, C. 104
Pearson, P. D. 121
PERMA model 25
personal development 79–93; collaborative learning 89–92; decision-making 79–84; sex education 84–89
physical education *see* exercise and sport
physical punishment 12–13, 48
play, learning to 97–103; literacy and numeracy in 100–103
polygamy 5, 10
positivity 24–28; positive relationships 54–58
post-traumatic stress disorder 17–19
poverty 7, 9–10
Pranowo, P. 51
prejudice 33, 36, 143
Pugh, K. 132

racism 7
Ramadan 88, 107–108
Ranta, R. 47
rape 6–7
Ratcliffe, M. 135–136
refugee camps 3, 5, 7, 11–12, 38
refugee crisis 1, 3–8, 15; implications for education 1, 8–13
relationship building 54–58
religion *see individual religions*
Resat, F. A. 51
Resnick, L. B. 132
Revised Bloom's Taxonomy 32
Robinson, D. B. 105
Russia 3
Rwanda 6, 133

salutogenesis 140
Sanjakdar, F. 87
scaffolding 66–67, 71, 75, 119
SCARF model 54–56, 58, 140
science and technology 42, 113–126

Sellars, M. 36
Sense of Coherence 140–141
sex education 84–89
sexual assault 52, *see also* rape
Sierra Leone 6
Şimesk, U. 139
SMART goals 40–41
Smit, N. 37
Smith, L. 114
social studies 130–143
Somalia 133
South Sudan 3, 6, 10, 107, 116
sport *see* exercise and sport
Steinberg, S. 132
stress 4, 13, 56; PTSD 17–19
Sudan 6
swimming 107–108
Syria 3–5, 7, 10, 34, 41, 56, 133, 137, 140

Taliban 4, 9–10, 123–124
Tall, D. 68
Tate, W. 132
Technology *see* science and technology
testing 70–71, 114, 125
Thombs, M. M. 139
torture 2, 5–7, 17
trauma 1–2, 4, 10–11, 13, 17–21, 25–28, 47–48, 52–53, 57–58, 74, 97–98, 109, 119, 140; intergenerational 13, 17; PTSD 17–19
triggers 20, 27–28, 50, 103
Tunisia 5
Turkey 3, 36, 139

Uganda 3, 6
Ukraine 3
United Nations: Refugee Agency 8; Sustainable Development Goals 8

Venezuela 3, 7, 9–10, 12
virginity testing 106

Westerman, W. 132
women and girls 4, 6, 8–10, 48–49, 79, 82–83, 85–87, 124; exercise and sport 98, 104–106, 109; female genital mutilation 86–87, 106
World Health Organization 84, 86

Yemen 4–6, 133

For Product Safety Concerns and Information please contact our EU representative GPSR@taylorandfrancis.com
Taylor & Francis Verlag GmbH, Kaufingerstraße 24, 80331 München, Germany

www.ingramcontent.com/pod-product-compliance
Lightning Source LLC
Chambersburg PA
CBHW071412300426
44114CB00016B/2272